# A BIOLOGIST'S GUIDE
# TO THE RAT RACE

# A BIOLOGIST'S GUIDE TO THE RAT RACE

JOANNA MASEL

To my father

# CONTENTS

# PREFACE

Why did I, an evolutionary biologist, write a book about economics and investing? It seems quite a jump, and many people are understandably surprised and skeptical. But interestingly, none of those skeptics are economists or evolutionary biologists. These two are actually sister disciplines, closer than people think. Both study competition, and both study how individuals hedge their bets in an uncertain world. Both study the flow of information, and how individuals try to manipulate those flows. Both study what happens in the past, while struggling to perform experiments in the present. Because many important questions cannot be addressed directly by experiments, both often rely on mathematical models instead. But don't worry; you don't need to know any math to read this book.

I was busy doing biology research, starting on a new project, when parallels between that project and economics jumped out at me. The implications of these parallels were too important to ignore. With a sabbatical coming up, I postponed my biology research, made a big career leap, and started writing this book.

That biology project was and is about the difference between relative and absolute competitions in evolution. To see the difference, think about a running race. An absolute competition pits each runner against the clock. Anyone who finishes the race in less than a certain time is allowed to have children. Those with stumpy legs and flat feet eventually die out, and are replaced by the children of the fast runners. So in the next generation, the average person runs faster.

In a relative competition, competitors race in pairs against one another instead of against the clock. In this cutthroat contest, there are no rules. One competitor is super fast. Unfortunately, he gets tackled from behind. In the ensuing brawl, he receives a solid blow to the head and passes out. The slower guy then wins. In each generation, the competition gets tougher, but not necessarily because the new generation runs faster. Strictly speaking, this relative competition does not favor being fast. What it favors is crossing the finish line before your competitor. Running fast is one way of crossing the finish line first. But evolution is a creative process, and there are many different ways of achieving the same goal. It is hard to predict which of the many solutions will triumph, and not all of the solutions are ones that we like.

There's an old joke about this. Two men are hiking in the woods, and come across a bear, which lunges after them. One man takes out a pair of running shoes. "What are you doing?" says the other, "Don't you know that bears can run thirty miles per hour? There is no way you can outrun it!" "I don't need to outrun the bear," replies the man, slipping on his second shoe, "I only need to outrun you."

Many people want to "get ahead" in life. The question is, what sort of race are they running? In particular, is saving for retirement like running an orderly race against a clock, where everybody can improve their time? Or is the single most important thing about retirement saving simply to do better than the competition?

Most biological competitions are relative. Imagine a mutation that makes a tree produce twice as many seeds. There are already far more seeds than there are places for them to grow into trees. Finding a good spot to grow is like winning the lottery. More seeds means more lottery tickets, and so mutant trees win the lottery more often, become more common, and take over the forest. Now there are twice as many seeds, but each seed is only half as likely to win the lottery and grow into a new tree. The forest as a whole is no better off; it has no more trees than it did before. Nor is the average mutant tree in the mutant forest any better off than the average non-mutant tree in the pre-mutation forest. But in either forest, any individual tree is always better off having the mutation and producing more seeds.

"The mutation is good" is a true statement at the level of the individual, because producing twice as many seeds makes a tree into an effective competitor. But "the mutation is good" is not true at the level of the group. If a mutation were to let trees colonize toxic soil where nothing could formerly grow, then evolution by natural selection would make the group better off as a whole. But in the more usual case of a relative competition for fixed real estate, nothing improves for the group.

Relative competitions can even make things worse for the group. Producing twice as many seeds probably doesn't come for free. Let's assume instead that the extra seeds cost energy, and so a typical mutant tree needs a slightly bigger patch of soil and sunlight to survive. Producing twice as many seeds helps the plant a lot, while needing slightly more space hurts it a bit. Putting the two together, the mutant does better than the original, and will take over. But after it wins, there will be fewer trees than there were before.

My research project studies how "arms race" competitions that occur on a relative scale can interfere with competitions that play out on an absolute scale. In the process of doing it, I became attuned to thinking carefully about whether statements were true at the level of individuals or at the level of groups. Once attuned, I heard discordant statements everywhere. In particular, policy makers are keen to encourage people to save more money for retirement. This is great advice for individuals; the more money an individual saves, the more comfortable their retirement. But is it also a good idea for society as a whole? What happens when everybody tries to save money at the same time? After all, you can't eat money. Is all the extra money being invested in things that will make people's retirements more comfortable? Or are all the savers in a relative competition, an arms race to stake a claim to a larger share of society's relatively inflexible amount of wealth?

Each tree also "saves" its energy and "invests" those savings in seeds to provide for its genetic future. The more a tree saves and invests, the better its future. But the more the forest saves and invests, the worse its future. Biology may have something to teach us here.

These distinctions between relative and absolute competitions, and between the good of each individual and the good of the group, apply to both biology and economics. Absolute competitions bring us absolute increases in prosperity in economics, while in biology they bring an absolute increase in the total amount of living things on the planet. Over the course of both biological and economic history, we began with very little and have a lot more now. In contrast, relative competitions, in both fields, bring us ornaments and arms races rather than true advances.

During my training in biology, I learned to use a standard mathematical model in which competition was relative. In contrast, economists learn standard mathematical models that are based on absolute competitions. These default assumptions, built into the curriculum, can shape the way someone approaches a problem for the rest of their career. As a result, economists are biased towards assuming that competitions increase prosperity. Evolutionary biologists are trained to have the opposite bias, instead assuming that competitions are arms races, where the population grows no larger. In both cases, the truth is probably somewhere in between, but how we are trained affects which situations we see as "normal" and which as "special".

My training in biology gives me a fresh perspective on economics, one that helps correct for the prevailing bias towards assuming that competitions are absolute and always improve prosperity. That's a good reason for a biologist to write a book about economics, and for you to read it. What is more, unlike most people who may give you advice about economics and investing, I have no vested interests. Not only do I have no personal conflict of interest, I do not even move in economics or finance circles where I could pick up attitudes influenced by the conflicts of interests of my peers. I approach these questions as a concerned scientist trying to figure out what is going on.

I'm not the first person ever to propose most of the ideas in this book. To avoid a footnote-packed academic style, I will not detail exactly who has said what before, although I will provide a few references for key facts. Nonetheless, I do want to acknowledge my intellectual debt to two previous books that stand out above the others I have read and learned from. First, while *The General Theory of Employment, Interest and Money* (1936) by John Maynard Keynes is arguably the most influential book in economics, it is still, I believe, underrated. It is mostly remembered for its analysis of the business cycle of boom and bust, but it also contains a wealth of other insights, many of which inform my argument here. The second economics book that I want to single out is the *Social Limits to Growth* (1976) by Fred Hirsch. This underread book details the importance of relative competitions in economics.

Both of these books are rather scholarly, and not easy for a general audience to read. What is more, they focus on understanding how economies work and how policy makers can manipulate them, and offer little or no advice for individual readers to use in their own lives. Like Keynes and Hirsch, I also want to shed light on how economies work. But in addition to this, I will also give practical advice to individuals, explaining what these grand ideas mean for individual investors concerned about a comfortable retirement.

When faced with a relative competition, the path to a comfortable retirement is straightforward. It doesn't matter how much money you save; what matters is that you save until you have more money than other people do. You can achieve financial success by gambling with your savings, but if you are more concerned with the worst-case scenario than the best-case scenario, then you should invest those savings sensibly and conservatively. Save as much as possible and preserve the value of those savings. By saving more and so accumulating a bigger nest egg than others, you can "get ahead" in any relative arms race.

This may be a recipe for a comfortable retirement, but I don't think it is good enough. While I want a comfortable retirement, I don't want my comfort to come at somebody else's expense. In the kind of capitalist system I believe in, if everybody works hard, and if everybody saves a good proportion of their income, then everybody should be well-off, not just those who save even more than the others. I hope that you, my reader, feel the same way.

For this reason, this book does not simply observe that competitions are often relative. Instead, it asks *which* investment choices succeed in creating new wealth in an absolute sense, and which choices simply contribute to an arms race. How can we invest in such a way as to make the pie bigger, rather than compete to own a larger share of a pie of fixed size?

I'll assume that most readers either have money to invest or are at least planning to have money to invest one day. Individual circumstances do make a difference, and so I'll consider a range of investment scenarios at various points in the book, in order to give practical suggestions. That said, I will mostly focus on one, embodied by a character I'll call Jen, who is designed to make some general points.

Jen is 49 years old, earns $80,000 per year, owes $100,000 on the mortgage on her home worth $350,000, and has $250,000 in her retirement account. All this makes Jen a fairly typical middle-class American. To keep things simple, Jen has no living partner, children, or parents. Jen's retirement account gives her a limited range of investment options. As we'll see later, these restrictions are a problem, and the book will go on to give advice to policy makers (to lift the restrictions) as well as individual investors (to take advantage of unconventional options). Meantime, to give Jen a freer hand to make investment choices, we'll give her more money. She inherits another $550,000 from her parents' estate. With this inheritance, symbolizing the transfer of wealth from one generation to another, we give Jen what she needs to enter the world of investing. It turns out that Jen will need this extra money in order to be confident of a comfortable retirement.

Now let's begin the book in earnest, led by Jen's "problem" of figuring out what to do with her newly inherited wealth.

# CHAPTER 1

# JEN INHERITS MONEY

Jen suddenly has money, in the form of a $550,000 inheritance. She could splurge if she chose to. But until this inheritance came along, Jen was comfortable with her lifestyle, and had no trouble supporting it on her $80,000 salary. It is more prudent for Jen to keep the same lifestyle as before, and to put the money away for her retirement. It is a lot of money, perhaps more than she will need, but there are many things that could go wrong, and it is good to have a buffer. For example, what if she ended up sick for many years, and needed a lot of care?

So where should Jen invest this money? In this book, we will follow Jen and try to help her as she thinks about what to do next. This quest is going to take us to some unexpected places. In this chapter, we'll start with some ideas about money, investment, and economics that may be familiar to you. They seem obvious, and are accepted by most people. But don't tune out. We will probe these ideas carefully, until by the end of this book, what once seemed obvious will seem absurd instead. Hold on for the ride, we're going on a grand tour.

Let's begin by considering the familiar, conventional options. Right now, the $550,000 is in the bank. Leaving the money there is a bad deal. Checking accounts pay no interest, and money market accounts are not much better. The best interest rates come from certificates of deposit (CDs), which pay more, but make it hard for Jen to get her money back early. To get the best CD interest rate, Jen needs to lock a large sum away for five years. But even this CD will only pay 2% interest.

Inflation means that over time, things cost more than they used to. Recently, things have become more expensive at an average inflation rate of about 2% a year. If inflation stays at this historically low rate, the interest on her CD will exactly cancel out the damage caused by inflation.[1] Inflation is like a negative interest rate; to calculate the "real" interest rate on Jen's CD, she takes the advertised nominal interest rate of 2% and subtracts the inflation rate. If the rate of inflation goes up higher than 2%, then when Jen gets her CD money back in five years' time, that money, including the interest, will be worth less than it is now.

Another option is for Jen to use some of her inheritance money to pay off her mortgage. Jen has tried hard over the years to pay down her mortgage, and now has only about $100,000 left to go, on a house that is worth around $350,000. She could pay that off tomorrow, and never have to make another mortgage payment. How does paying off her mortgage compare to other investments? Jen pays 3% interest on her mortgage. Jen has such a great deal on her mortgage because with her secure job, and excellent credit rating, lending to Jen is low risk. When she pays off this mortgage, she won't need to pay that 3% interest on the $100,000 balance anymore.

---

1   Jen will actually come out a little behind, because she pays tax on the interest. Tax is paid on nominal interest rates, not real interest.

This is equivalent to putting $100,000 in the bank, where the bank pays her the 3% she needs to make her mortgage interest payments.[2] So paying down a 3% mortgage beats getting 2% on a bank deposit. Three percent is not a great interest rate, but it comes with no risk at all. Three percent is better than other near-zero-risk interest-paying investments such as Treasury bonds or government-insured bank deposits. So Jen makes the leap and takes $100,000 out of her checking account and uses it to pay off her mortgage.

Big financial decisions don't come around often for most of us. At the time, buying a house seemed as much a lifestyle decision as a financial one for Jen. But in retrospect, all those mortgage payments were good discipline to make Jen save. Now, with only a little extra help, the house is all hers. No debt, and no more mortgage payments or rent ever again! She has something concrete to show for her savings: a house to live in, both now and after she retires.

But Jen still needs to decide how to invest the remaining $450,000. She understands the basic ideas behind the usual choices of stocks and bonds and mutual funds, but is certainly no expert. Her job comes with a retirement savings account, and Jen recalls with a shudder the bewilderment

---

2  The US tax system makes this slightly more complicated. If Jen pays $3,000 per year in mortgage interest, this exempts her from paying income tax on $3,000 of her income, an exemption she would lose if she pays off her mortgage. If Jen instead earns $3,000 in bank interest, she also needs to pay income tax on $3,000 more income. So her two options, paying off a 3% mortgage or getting 3% interest from the bank, are tax-equivalent (unless Jen's income is right near the boundary between two tax brackets). If it were not for the mortgage interest tax deduction, then paying off a mortgage would be the tax-preferred option; what the tax deduction does is remove the tax incentive for paying off a mortgage, rather than create an incentive for having a mortgage. The main tax-preferred options in the US today are municipal bonds, so if Jen's main goal was to avoid tax, she could invest entirely in them rather than, for example, pay off her mortgage. The tax advantage may or may not be large enough to override other considerations affecting Jen's choices, such as a lower interest rate or higher risk for the tax-preferred option. This book won't spend a lot of time discussing details of the tax code, because our focus is on how to create new wealth, not on how to avoid paying taxes on that wealth within one particular tax system, a tax system that might of course change. The focus will instead be on the fundamentals of the investment decision, prior to any distortions created by the tax system.

she felt, many years ago, when she picked out funds for that. Checking her retirement account balance, Jen finds that her compulsory payments into that are now worth around $250,000. That's more than she expected. She should probably go over those retirement fund decisions again too, from scratch. Now she has inherited money, her financial position has changed completely, and she needs to rethink things.

Jen's first instinct is to keep the money safe, rather than gamble in the hope of making even more money. The traditional "safe" investment is US Treasury bonds; no matter how much trouble the government gets into, it can always print money, so lending to the Federal government is almost uniquely safe. But US Treasury bonds now pay even less than a fixed-term deposit at her bank! There must be something out there better than that.

At first, it seems like there is a vast and baffling smorgasbord of options. But each of them falls into one of only a handful of broad categories, such as cash, stock, and bonds. First Jen needs to allocate her money between the categories, then she can pick out specific investments within each category.

If she buys stock, she will own part of a company. If she buys bonds, she is lending money to a company or government or pool of mortgage-holders, at an interest rate that is hopefully higher than at the bank. There is no guarantee that interest on either bank deposits or bonds will keep up with inflation, but a higher interest rate obviously helps. As another option, she can buy real estate, although she already owns a house, so maybe she has enough real estate already. Browsing online advice columns, most discuss how much she should invest in stocks versus bonds, as a function of her age and risk tolerance. Unless she wants to become a landlady, buying a second home and renting it out, these seem to be the only two categories of investments she needs to think about. So how much should she allocate to stocks vs. bonds?

Bonds promise that on certain days, they will pay Jen back a particular number of dollars, including interest. If inflation goes up, that number of dollars will effectively be worth less. Everybody knows how stock prices sometimes fall suddenly and dramatically, but luckily they generally recover again eventually. In contrast, inflation can cause the value of bonds to fall, much more gradually but unfortunately also more steadily, without the same opportunities to recover what was lost. In theory, bond losses when inflation rises could be cancelled out by gains when inflation falls. But historically, unexpected inflation has been the pattern (so far). Bonds are more stable in the short term, but over the long term, bonds have historically paid back less money than stocks. This is why most experts recommend more stocks than bonds for retirement accounts.

To get the benefit of stocks, Jen needs to be willing to hold on through what could be a crazy sequence of large rises and falls in stock prices over many years. If she can manage this, then stocks are perhaps less risky than you would think by looking at their wild fluctuations, at least in the long term. Owning a stock means owning something real, namely some fraction of a company. In contrast, a bond is just a claim on a particular number of paper dollars. The fact that a company is a real thing and not just a piece of paper provides protection against inflation. As inflation drives prices up, that includes the price of whatever the company sells, and the price of the company itself. Stocks look risky because of the wild swings in stock prices, but after stock prices go down they tend to come back up again, and the swings eventually cancel out. There is no force that tends to cancel out inflation losses, making bonds riskier than you would think from their seemingly steady prices. The slow-motion and irreversible risk of inflation, both present and future, means that in the long term, bonds can in fact be riskier than stocks.

As Jen reads many advice columns, it seems that only people with shorter time horizons should buy a lot of bonds. This includes people who are close to retirement, or who don't trust their self-control and think they might sell in a panic if stock prices crash. Jen loves her job and doesn't want to retire before 65 at the earliest: that is still 16 years away. Even though Jen isn't fond of risk, she still falls into the category of "everybody else", and is advised to buy mostly stocks, with a moderate amount of bonds to hedge her bets and a bit of money in the bank too. Jen even finds neat online calculators that suggest what percentage of her money she should put in each category. The calculators vary a little in their recommendations but not too much. Based on the consensus, Jen decides on two-thirds stocks, with most of the rest in bonds.

Jen is now well on her way to investing her inheritance sensibly, following the conventional wisdom. We will track Jen as she ponders that conventional advice more deeply and carefully, and finds things that worry her. By the end of the book, she will abandon this conventional advice altogether, reject much of the modern financial system, and find her own, alternative ways to invest for retirement.

# CHAPTER 2

# PICKING STOCKS

Jen wants to split up her money, both her inheritance and her retirement account, between different investments. Two-thirds of the money will go to stocks, and most of the rest to bonds, with a little bit left as cash. That's the broad outline of her investment plan. But which stocks, and which bonds? How many different ones, and how much money in each?

The stock of any one company is very risky, and so investing too much in a bad pick can be disastrous. No investor could have known how dangerous asbestos was, but when it started killing people, the lawsuits followed. Many companies that sold or used asbestos then owed more money than they could pay, and declared bankruptcy. If Jen were unlucky enough to choose stocks like that, then she would have little or no money left for her retirement.

An asbestos-type disaster doesn't usually affect every company in the whole stock market. If Jen spreads her money out across many companies, some of them may be unlucky and go bankrupt, while others may do unexpectedly well and grow huge. Hopefully it will all balance out on average. The worst-case scenario is a big stock market crash that lowers the price of all companies just when Jen retires and needs to sell. But even at times like that, some stocks will be affected more than others. So Jen should split her money up between many different stocks and bonds, hoping that they will rise and fall in value at different times.

Unfortunately, this seems to make Jen's original question even harder: which stocks and bonds should she buy? Now, instead of finding just a couple of investments she likes, she has to find many. Jen can choose each stock and bond herself, or she can buy into a fund that chooses them for her. Outsourcing the decision-making to a fund would certainly be less work for Jen, especially if she needs to pick a lot of different investments. Figuring out whether a stock is a good buy is no easy task.

This gets to the basic question of what it means for a stock to be a good buy. Professional investors try to buy stocks whenever they think a company's "real" value is higher than its current market price. What is a company really worth? The bottom line is that companies are valuable because they make profits. Owning part of a company means owning part of its future profits, which can be returned to stockholders in the form of future dividends. Like all savings instruments, buying stock means handing over money today in exchange for money back later.

So Jen should look out for companies that make good profits and have rosy futures. Indeed, one of Jen's friends made a lot of money through a policy of investing in companies that make products he likes to buy, especially Apple and North Face. He figures that if he likes their products, other people will too, and the companies will do well. Jen also likes these companies' products, the companies seem to be managed well, and they probably have a great future making lots of profit from these great products. But surely she shouldn't buy a fashionable stock at any price; there has to be a ceiling! So what is the right price for a stock? Jen shouldn't buy into the best company at any price; she should buy the best value that she can find.

To understand what price Jen should be willing to pay for a stock, imagine that we have a crystal ball that magically tells us the future of a company, Widgets Inc. This company is going to make $1 million profit per year for the foreseeable future, in a world with no inflation. These profits will all get paid out as dividends to the stockholders. When you add up all the shares in Widgets Inc., they add up to $20 million at their current price. One million dollars divided by $20 million is 5%. This means that each year, stockholders get back 5% of their investment in the form of cash dividends. Buying this stock would then be a good idea, beating the 3% Jen will get from paying down her mortgage. But if the share price were higher, pricing the exact same company at $100 million, then Jen would only get 1% of her investment back each year in dividend payments. It's not a question of whether the company is good or bad, but how its likely future profits compare to its current stock price.

Of course, things are much messier in real life. Jen has no magical knowledge about the future profits and dividends of any company. Predicting a company's profits over the long term is hard. Nonetheless, this is what the stock market is supposed to do. To be listed on the stock market, a company needs to disclose lots of financial information. This information is supposed to help people work out what the company, and hence each share, is really worth.

So before Jen buys stock in a particular company, she should learn a lot about it. How much profit did it make in the past? What happened to those profits; were they paid out in dividends, or invested in expansion plans that will create even greater dividends in the future? What other conditions exist that might make the company earn more or less profit, and pay more or less dividends, in the future? Jen cannot possibly make sense of all that financial information for so many companies.

There is a class of professionals, financial analysts, whose job it is to give advice about which stocks to buy, which to sell, and which to hold on to, depending on how the current stock price compares to predicted future dividends. But who are these analysts really working for? Horrified, Jen reads about analysts who praised a stock in public, while dismissing that same stock in private. Clearly, Jen needs to treat anything a financial analyst says with some suspicion.

Surely there are also some good and honest analysts out there, but why would they let Jen read their work for free? And if they charge a fair price for their advice, how could a small-fry investor like Jen afford it? A serious player in the market, who pays good money to obtain an honest analysis, will be possessive about the report he paid for. He would keep the analyst's recommendations private, and wouldn't put the reports out there for every competitor to see.

Since Jen can't afford to pay her own private financial analyst, perhaps it is best to choose a mutual fund, and let them employ their own in-house financial analysts to make the decisions as to what to buy and sell and when. Otherwise, choosing which analyst to believe seems as hard as choosing which stocks to buy in the first place.

Unfortunately, even honest analysts can get things terribly wrong. A good sign of this is the success of many "contrarian" investors. Contrarians read lots of analyst reports, look for clear consensus across them, and then do the opposite. One of the most famously successful investors, Warren Buffett, is in part a contrarian. It's worked spectacularly well for him. Contrarians count on the fact that mobs overreact. When everybody wants to buy stocks in a fashionable company or sector, and there are only so many shares to go around, then prices go up. When the share price is rising, whoever buys early makes a lot of money; not because profits have risen, but simply because they can sell for a much higher price than what they paid to buy the stock. The enthusiasm of the early winners is contagious, and their success persuades others to copy them. Instead of analyzing prices relative to dividends, people copy whatever the winners did. More people try to buy the same shares, and prices go higher still. Which of course generates even more enthusiasm that this stock is a "winner", prompting even more people to try to buy it.

But in the end, a company only makes so much profit, and cannot pay enough dividends to justify crazily high stock prices. Eventually, reality sets in and prices fall back down. A contrarian investor looks for signs of widespread hype and hysteria that indicate the psychology of the mob. Then the contrarian might place a bet that the stock will lose value. Alternatively, contrarians can look for parts of the market that it is fashionable to dismiss, and buy those stocks up cheap. Betting against the irrational overreactions of a mob can be a great strategy.

Overreactions happen in the housing market too. In the crazy days of the housing bubble, you didn't need a down payment or even to prove that you had a steady income in order to buy a house. This defies common sense; you should not lend money to somebody unless you have good reason to believe that they can pay it back with interest. But even supposedly coolheaded officials like Alan Greenspan praised this subprime mortgage industry as a good thing. For a contrarian investor who was listening carefully to analysts' discussions for signs of hype, the market had clearly become hysterical. For a contrarian, this meant it was a great time to sell.

In 2007, Jen could have sold her house for $500,000. House prices were sky-high then, but rents hadn't increased in the same way. She could have taken the money from selling her house and parked it in the bank, while she rented a home for a few years and tried to be patient. Then in 2011, when the housing market seemed more stable again, she could have bought a similar house for only $350,000. That would have been a great contrarian strategy. Jen likes her house and doesn't like moving, but $150,000 is nevertheless a lot of money. Having watched what happened in the housing market, the contrarian strategy seems logical enough to Jen.

So maybe the contrarians are right about the stock market too. This makes Jen nervous about believing financial analysts' advice, including the recommendations of analysts who work for mutual funds. Some analysts clearly can't be trusted because you don't know who is paying them. But even honest analysts, like any other group of people, are vulnerable to groupthink. Maybe following analysts' advice isn't such a great idea, no matter how honest they are, or who is paying them.

Jen becomes exasperated trying to sort out these different opinions. Some say she needs a mutual fund and its analysts to pick stocks for her, since it is clearly too hard to do the research herself. Contrarians say this is a bad idea, that analysts are vulnerable to passing fashions and group-think in the stock market and they get things wrong. Both camps make good points. Jen doesn't know how to pick stocks herself, but doesn't trust analysts to do it for her. In the next chapter, Jen will learn about a simple solution to this dilemma.

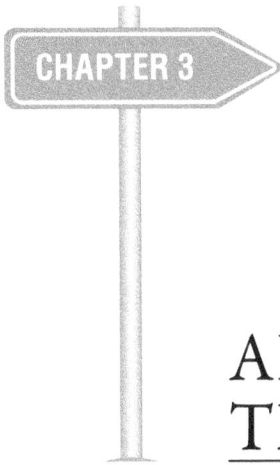

# CHAPTER 3

# ARE INDEX FUNDS THE ANSWER?

In the last chapter, we learned how the future profits of a company determine its fundamental value, and hence what price Jen should be willing to pay for its stock. Unfortunately, it is too difficult for Jen to use those principles of fundamental analysis to pick stocks herself; that's a job for professionals. Jen would love to pay somebody else to research companies and pick stocks for her, but she doesn't trust financial analysts to do a good job. The very fact that almost every analyst enthusiastically agrees that a stock is great may itself be a bad sign. It seems impossibly difficult to figure out which stocks will do well.

Exasperated, Jen wonders whether she might as well roll dice to decide which stocks to buy. Which, it turns out, is the standard economic wisdom. The "efficient markets hypothesis" suggests that the market works so well, with so many clever people doing their research and following good strategies, that all public information about a stock is already reflected in its price. If this hypothesis is true, then whatever Jen figures out about a company is already well known to others. Those other people have already used that knowledge to buy low or sell high until the stock price adjusts to match what it should be. Any information that Jen might read about is already accounted for in the price. She can't beat the market. She might as well pick randomly.

Jen doesn't want to pick just one or two stocks at random. She still wants to spread her bets across many different companies, hoping that they won't all be unlucky at the same time. So should she try to buy shares in every possible company? How many shares of each? There are some practical limits. For example, every time Jen buys or sells a stock, she pays a fee.

Luckily, the financial industry has a solution for her: an "index fund" that buys a huge variety of shares, and tracks the overall performance of a stock market index such as the S&P 500. These funds pool the money of many investors like Jen. Jen can own a small slice of the pool of shares held by the index fund, and hence a small slice of the stock market as a whole. Perfect.

The more Jen reads about this option, the more sensible it seems. "Actively managed" funds hire financial analysts to do research and pick stocks carefully, but that costs money. Every year, the fund would deduct a percentage of Jen's investment to pay for that. An actively managed fund needs not only to outperform the market and prove the efficient markets hypothesis wrong, but also to beat the market by a big enough margin to cover its fees. In contrast, index funds are "passively managed". They follow rules for automatically buying and selling shares so that whatever happens to the market as a whole, the same thing happens to the fund. Passively managed index funds charge much lower fees.

Index funds, by definition, provide average returns. Actively managed funds try to beat the market. But for every fund or speculator that succeeds in beating the average, somebody else out there must be doing worse than average. There are people out there who are systematically beating the market, either because they have really clever strategies at the cutting edge, or because they are illegally making use of insider information. That means there must also be suckers who systematically do worse than average. Those suckers include many actively managed funds of the sort that are available to nobodies like Jen. Indeed, index funds have historically outperformed most actively managed funds. Jen has no confidence that the fund she picks will be one of the minority to beat the market average, let alone to do so by a big enough margin to cover the extra fees.

So based on the online asset allocation calculators that Jen found in Chapter 1, she puts two-thirds of her money, both her $450,000 inheritance and her $250,000 retirement account, into a passively managed stock market index fund. She splits most of the remainder between several index funds for bonds. She keeps the rest of the money as cash in a money market account at her bank. And she owns a house worth around $350,000. Done.

It looks like Jen has made the right decision. Now she can finally stop thinking about investments and get on with other, more interesting things in her life. But she remains curious about some of the stranger things she came across in her reading. Stocks and bonds weren't the only choices. Jen doesn't want to buy any of the other, more exotic possibilities. After all, didn't some of these weird inventions cause a global economic catastrophe?

Intrigued, Jen reads some more about what happened during the financial crisis of 2007-2008. Part of the reason that the world financial system came close to total collapse was that the most sophisticated financial engineers in the world invented financial instruments so complicated that even their inventors didn't fully understand them. Those instruments were sold to people who understood them even less. The investment industry made huge profits creating extraordinarily complicated dud products and selling them to suckers.

Jen doesn't want to be a sucker. Her parents would surely disapprove if she bungled her inheritance. Worried about letting her parents' money be pulled into some financial fiasco, Jen decides on one clear principle that she will use to guide her investment decisions from now on. *Don't invest in anything you don't understand.* Warren Buffett is supposedly one of the most successful investors out there. One of his investment principles is to restrict himself to his "circle of competence". Thoroughly spooked by her reading, Jen decides to do the same. This seems like the best way to protect herself in a cutthroat world where an atmosphere of mob psychology provides a false sense of security, luring suckers in to be exploited.

Jen's decision will be fateful for her. Jen has taken her money out of her bank account and put it into index funds, but only for the time being. As she thinks about it, she realizes that this decision does not satisfy her new principle of investment. So Jen is not done yet. She wants to understand more about the workings of all of those stocks and bonds that she now owns. They seem like very abstract objects. She has handed over money today, trusting that she will be able to get it back later. But how exactly does this exchange of purchasing power today for purchasing power later work? In other words, how will these certificates of ownership that she now holds pay for the things she will need in her retirement? Where will the money to pay her retirement bills come from? What will happen to that money during the intervening years?

Jen is stubborn, and when she makes a decision, she sticks to it. She has the courage to follow her decisions, and her moral principles, to wherever they might lead. Her decision only to invest in things she understands, and her stubbornness in trying to understand them, is going to take her, and this book, to some unexpected places.

# CHAPTER 4

# JEN THE CAPITALIST

Jen could go on a spending spree today, and blow her inheritance. But she would rather save the money for a long and comfortable retirement. She wants to be able to pay for nursing if she becomes disabled in her old age. Jen has no children to take care of her. She doesn't trust the government to look after her either. Some people think that Social Security and Medicare will be broke by the time Jen retires. This may be an exaggeration, but still, benefits are bound to get smaller. Medicare may not cover everything Jen will need, leaving her with high out of pocket medical costs. And even today, Social Security retirement benefits are not large.

Even if the social safety net holds, Jen doesn't want to rely on it. She wants to grow old and die with grace and dignity. Grace and dignity sometimes cost a lot of money. Jen's money might eventually be spent on private hospital rooms, luxurious facilities for convalescence or assisted living, or adequate home nursing. Jen doesn't want to cut corners, and doesn't want her final weeks, months or years to be marked by the indignities that can come with poverty. That peace of mind is much more important to Jen than the fun she could have spending the money today. So Jen saves her money for the future.

If the most important thing were to "get her money back" later, then she could take a big stack of banknotes and put them in a guarded safe in a bank vault: the modern equivalent of stashing them under her mattress. But what she really wants to store up for later is not money itself, but her ability to buy things like food, heating, and medical care. Inflation means that these things cost more each year. By investing her money in stocks and bonds, she expects to get back not just the money she put in, but also interest. At a bare minimum, if the interest only just kept up with inflation, then she could buy the same amount later as she would be able to buy now.

Most people expect their investments to do better than that. A "capitalist" economy means that Jen's $700,000 should earn more interest than just inflation. Jen's $450,000 inheritance and her $250,000 retirement account are her capital. Imagine that the value of Jen's index fund increases at 7% per year. As I write this book, inflation is 2% in the US; let's assume it stays at that level for a while. So 2% of Jen's 7% is eaten up by inflation, leaving Jen with a "real return" on her capital of 7% - 2% = 5%.[3] Every year, Jen could spend 5% of what her capital is worth. Even after doing that for many years, her capital would still be just as valuable as it is now.

Five percent of $700,000 comes to $35,000 per year, increasing with inflation. Jen could retire early, quitting her job now, and live on that

---

3   Tax on interest makes the true number lower. How much lower depends on Jen's tax bracket. We ignore tax in this discussion, in order to focus more clearly on the fundamentals of investment rather than distortions created by particular tax systems. While tax changes the numbers and shifts incentives, it does not change the principles.

$35,000 per year income,[4] without even worrying about eating into the value of her capital. Jen's position would actually be better than that, because she doesn't need to make mortgage payments anymore. Now that her mortgage is gone, she has another $8,000 in her pocket each year.[5] So after quitting her job, Jen would have what feels to her like a $43,000 income: the $35,000 average withdrawal from her index funds, plus another $8,000 per year in free rent. But Jen doesn't want to quit her job and live off her capital; she currently earns $80,000 a year, and she doesn't want to scale back her expenses. Anyway, she likes working.

The word "capitalist" became popular through the writings of Karl Marx, even among people who disagreed with much of what Marx said. A capitalist society can be divided into "labor" and "capital" classes. Jen's option to quit her job and retire early illustrates the distinction between these two classes. Capitalists live by spending money that comes from their capital investments. This money can come in the form of interest payments on loans, dividends paid out by companies to stockholders out of corporate profits, rents paid by tenants to landlords, or by selling a portion

---

4   A $35,000 real income assumes that Jen gets a real return of exactly 5% each year. If Jen counts on an income of $35,000, rather than on 5% of whatever her portfolio is worth at the time, then she will sell a higher percentage of her portfolio when asset prices are low, reducing her long-term return. The $35,000 income is an average based on 5% withdrawal, and is subject to large fluctuations.

5   It would cost $15,000 per year to rent Jen's house. But living there is not free for Jen even after her mortgage is paid off; she still pays around $7,000 per year in property taxes, maintenance, and other owner expenses. So owning her house makes Jen $8,000 per year better off than somebody renting the same house. Plus she owns the house, which might increase in value again. Perhaps by coincidence, $8,000 is the same amount that Jen was making every year in mortgage payments. So whether you look at the extra cash appearing in Jen's pocket each month, or whether you compare Jen's position to that of a renter, the capital value of Jen's house provides Jen with a real return of $8,000 per year. If we assume that housing prices track inflation, this is a real return rate of 2.3% on the current $350,000 market value of the house. This percentage rate will fluctuate together with the estimated sale value of Jen's house, even if the value of the housing to Jen does not change. Unless Jen plans to sell her house, what matters to her is the actual value (currently worth $8,000 per year), not the percentage rate.

of the investments themselves, as their prices increase. Laborers live by spending their wages. Jen's nice job, with a comfortable income, puts her in the "labor" economic class. If she could find an investment that paid 7% interest on her $700,000 capital, and if she were willing to scale back her cost of living, then her inheritance would allow her to quit that job and become a member of the capitalist class instead.

Jen could also keep one foot in each of these economic classes. Her capital, invested partly in stock and bond markets with a 7% rate of return, and partly in owning her own house, is effectively a massive $43,000 pay raise on top of her $80,000 salary. If she spends this extra money, then once she retires and loses her salary, she would have a choice between living on only $43,000 per year, or of gradually spending the $700,000 capital not tied up in her house. That should last her a while, but not necessarily long enough. What if she lives to be 100? Seven hundred thousand dollars doesn't go very far over 35 years of retirement, especially if she needs a lot of expensive nursing and medical care.

If Jen refrains from spending all this extra money, then it isn't hard to prepare properly for retirement. If she saves instead of spends her $43,000 pay raise, then that money gets added to her capital. Even ignoring compound interest, 16 years of $43,000 per year still adds up to $688,000, more or less doubling Jen's capital before she retires. This is on top of continuing her "normal" retirement savings, which are deducted directly from each paycheck, matched by her employer, and deposited directly into her retirement account. Jen plays around with some online retirement calculators. If she doesn't increase her expenses and just keeps saving, she can live to be 100 and not worry about paying for nursing. By age 100, Jen is happy to run out of money. With no children, she's doesn't feel the need to leave an inheritance for others.

There is, unfortunately, a catch. Jen can't be confident that her investments will earn 7% interest. Money in the bank, or bonds, pay much less than that. Paying down her mortgage only gave Jen a 3% return, barely more than the 2% inflation rate. To get anything like 7% interest, Jen is counting on the stock market living up to its past reputation for providing high long-term returns. This in turn depends on how much wealth corporations will create over the next 16 years. Whatever wealth they create, Jen will own a part of it, through her index fund.

Like many people with retirement savings, Jen is now a capitalist. If interest rates and other rates of return on capital are high, after correcting for inflation, then Jen will do well financially. In other words, if capitalism does well as a whole, then Jen is likely to do well too. Most of Jen's capital is now invested in the stock market. Next we will look more closely at the stock market to ask how that investment might succeed in providing Jen the capitalist with the money she will need in retirement.

# CHAPTER 5

# HISTORICAL STOCK MARKET RETURNS

Jen has decided to invest only in things she understands. This means understanding how, by handing over her money today, she will get that money back with interest when she retires. Two-thirds of Jen's money is in stocks, via a mutual fund that passively tracks the S&P 500 index. If she wants to keep her money there, Jen should try to understand this mutual fund better. Stocks make up the majority of her portfolio, and over the long term, Jen also expects her highest percentage returns to come from stocks. On both counts, the fund tracking the S&P 500 stock market index is the number one priority for Jen to understand.

Jen doesn't care about what her stock holdings are worth now, but about what they will be worth during her retirement. She is 49, and so a typical retirement at age 65 is still 16 years away. At that point, she will start taking out money from her nest egg, and using it to pay for daily expenses. She will keep withdrawing money until she dies, i.e. for the next 20-30 years or more.

Jen can afford to take stock price risk now, while retirement is still a long way off. Stock prices might go down this year, but if she just hangs on to stocks for long enough, their price will probably come back up again by the time she retires. But as Jen gets older, it gets harder to use this logic. When Jen has actually retired and needs to sell off her stocks to pay for living expenses, or even as that time gets close, she will need to take fewer risks. Without enough time to "catch up" any losses, stocks are just too volatile over the medium term.

For this reason, Jen should sell a good fraction of her shares in about 15 years' time, and reinvest in more stable bonds and bank deposits then. So she wants to know what kind of stock market returns to expect over this 15 year timespan. To understand what the S&P 500 stock market index might do in the future, let's look to its past. If Jen had invested in that index during some other historical 15-year period, how much interest would she have earned? Figure 1 shows annualized 15-year stock market returns, adjusted for inflation, assuming that dividends are reinvested back into the stock market. In other words, Figure 1 shows what happened to other people in Jen's situation, who retired in different years.

Along the bottom, we see different years of retirement. Those lucky enough to retire and cash out of the stock market at the height of the last boom would have enjoyed an inflation-adjusted return of more than 14% per year on money invested 15 years earlier. Over 15 years, Jen's $700,000 could turn into $5 million or more, even after adjusting for inflation! If Jen is lucky, she might get rich.

But those retiring in 1921-1922 or 1980-1983 would have actually lost purchasing power. Their 15-year stock market investment didn't even keep up with inflation. Even 1% annual losses add up year after year, and

mean getting less than the inflation-adjusted equivalent of $600,000 back
at the end of the 15 years.

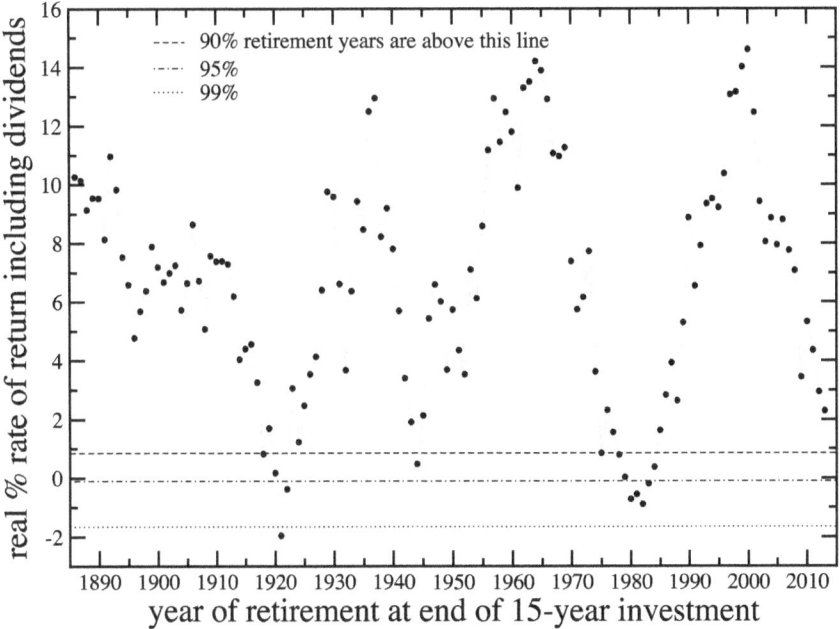

Figure 1: Total real stock market return, based on the S&P 500 index, adjusted for inflation,
compounded over the previous 15 years with dividends reinvested, and converted into an
annual rate. Data from http://www.econ.yale.edu/~shiller/data.htm, based on stock sale at
the beginning of the year indicated.

Which year Jen is born determines which year she will reach retirement age. Jen only has one shot, and she doesn't get to choose which year
she was born. Based on past history, her inheritance might lose value over
the next 15 years. If her retirement year is a repeat of 1982, she'll still have
enough to get by, but things won't be so comfortable. She might have to
work for longer, and she would certainly have to cut back and live in a
more modest way than she does now. Otherwise she would effectively be

betting that she will die before her money runs out. What's more, as we have all read in many a brochure, past performance does not guarantee future results. So there is even more uncertainty about future returns than the already worryingly high level of uncertainty that we see in Figure 1.

Many discussions of stock market investments focus on "average long-term returns". For example, the data in Figure 1 show a long-term average real return of 6%. People, including professional financial advisors, often use average returns like these in their planning. But having a comfortable retirement "on average" is not enough. Jen doesn't have a time horizon of 100 years, but instead plans to sell shares after "only" 15 years. This is not long enough to be confident of getting an average return. Figure 1 shows us that if past experience is a good guide, annualized real returns could be anywhere from -2% to +15%.

The longer Jen can hold on to shares, the more the ups and downs cancel out, and the closer the returns will typically be to the average. For example, somebody hanging on to shares for 30 years rather than 15 would have got returns between +3% and +10%, depending on when they retired, rather than between -2% and +15%.

Jen doesn't have to sell all her stocks after 15 years. She will start needing the money in 16 years' time, and she won't need it all at once. The conventional advice is to shift rather gradually as she gets older to fewer stocks and more bonds; to make a plan for doing this, and stick to it, come what may. Within that plan, Jen could hold on to a substantial portion of her stocks for 30 years or more, reducing the eventual volatility in their return. This is clearly the sensible thing to do, to reduce her total risk. But could she handle this emotionally? Imagine terrible returns for 15 years and a shrinking portfolio just as retirement is looming. Will Jen really have the grit to keep her investments in stocks and risk losing even more of her already-diminished portfolio, right at the time when she is actually retiring? It seems more likely that she would cut her losses before they become too catastrophic, figure out how much money she will have left once it is moved to less volatile investments, and learn to live on that by delaying retirement and scaling back on expenses. It's much easier to risk the stock market either when a final reckoning is distant, or when she has money that she can afford to lose. The scenario where Jen needs to stay in the stock market for more than 15 years is exactly the scenario in which she is least likely to be able to do so. This is why Jen should plan on returns of "only" 15 years.

Planning for an "average" retirement is nowhere near good enough to provide peace of mind. As a bare minimum, Jen wants to be 90% sure that she will be OK. Judging from Figure 1, this means planning on a real return of no more than 1% being enough to support a retirement with typical expenses. If she wants to be 95% sure, she should count on a zero real return, simply keeping up with inflation. Even this doesn't mean Jen can be 100% secure. Even with Jen's inheritance, her retirement could still go wrong. Not disastrously wrong, but nothing remotely like what "average returns" would lead her to expect.

We can now see just how lucky Jen is to have inherited this money. Jen's employer takes 7% out of each paycheck, and pays it directly into her retirement account. Because Jen has worked there a long time, her employer puts in another 7% in matching contributions. Fourteen percent of her income seemed like plenty of money to Jen, and so like many of us, without really thinking things through, she had assumed that her retirement would therefore be fine. But without her inheritance, these payments, now worth $250,000 in her retirement account, clearly weren't nearly enough to be confident of a comfortable retirement.

The online tools had reassured Jen that she was on track for a comfortable retirement even if she lived to be 100. Indeed, they suggested that Jen had more than enough, inviting her to enjoy a more extravagant lifestyle today. But those tools were based on "typical" long-term returns on her capital. Many experts seem sure that investing in stocks via an index fund is the way to go, producing high returns in the long run. Unfortunately, the "long run" needed to get typical returns is longer than 15 years, and so of no use to Jen. Her position is nothing like as secure as the online calculators led her to believe.

Even with a repeat of 1982, Jen would suffer but nevertheless get by, because her inheritance provides a strong buffer. From her strong starting position, the historical risk alone is not enough to stop her investing in the stock market. But it does make her nervous, and so she turns back, again, to the one central decision she made: *"Don't invest in anything you don't understand"*.

If the past is a good guide to the future, then based on Figure 1, she might get rich, she will probably be fine, and there is some chance that it will be a squeeze. But the past might not be a good guide to the future. And Jen doesn't even understand the past; why were some retirement years good and others bad? Was there any way that 15-year real returns for a given retirement year could have been predicted in advance?

Jen is stubborn. She made a decision to be guided by one single piece of investment advice. That advice is completely uncontroversial. Nobody disagrees with it. In fact, it is almost self-evidently true. Unfortunately, "don't invest in anything you don't understand" seems to rule out the stock market, at least for now. Jen is too stubborn to abandon her one principle. This leaves her two choices. One is not to invest in the stock market, because it completely baffles her. The second is to keep trying to understand it.

Jen doesn't have a great plan B for what else to do with her capital, so before giving up on the stock market, she will try harder to understand it. In the following chapters we ask why the stock market might have been a good buy for some 15 year periods, but not for others. Most importantly, can we use that knowledge to figure out whether right now is a good time or a bad time to invest in the stock market? And if it is a bad time, are there any better options out there?

# CHAPTER 6

# FUTURE RETURNS

Jen wants to know whether now is a good time to place her retirement savings in a stock market index fund. What return can she expect, and how does this compare to her retirement needs? If returns are likely to be good, Jen can add some luxury to her life now. She might as well enjoy her money while she is still alive, because it will be no use to her after her death. But if returns are likely to be bad, Jen should cut back and save more to make sure she has enough. Knowing whether returns are likely to be good in an absolute sense tells Jen whether she should save more or spend more.

Jen also wants to know whether, at the price she paid for her index fund, stocks were a good buy compared to other options. It is possible that stocks offer a good return right now but other options are even better. It is also possible that stocks offer a bad return right now but other options are even worse. Knowing whether stocks give better returns relative to other options tells Jen what she should do with whatever money she does save. If stocks are better than other options, then buying them was a good decision. If they are worse, then Jen made a mistake, but luckily one that she can easily fix. Since prices haven't changed much since then, indeed stock prices have even risen a little, Jen can simply change her mind and sell at a profit, even after accounting for transaction fees. Then she can move her money somewhere else better.

To answer both questions – how much money Jen needs to set aside for her retirement in the form of stocks, as well as whether stocks are the best choice for that money – Jen needs to assess what her stocks are worth to her. There are two ways to assess the value of stocks, depending on the time horizon. In the short term, the value of Jen's stocks is straightforward. It depends on how much she can sell them for later, where "later" could be a matter of weeks, months or even years.

If, however, Jen holds onto the stocks for many decades rather than years, then the final share price is less important. This is because in the meantime, Jen will receive many dividends, paid out of company profits. Let's go back to Widgets Inc., the fictional company we introduced in Chapter 2. The stock market values Widgets Inc. at $20 million, and the company pays exactly $1 million per year in dividends. Twenty years of dividend payments add up to $20 million, as much as the final value of the company itself. Indeed, $20 million of incoming dividends over 20 years are worth more to Jen than a $20 million final sale price at the end of the 20 years, because Jen gets the money earlier. Early money is worth more than later money, because Jen can reinvest the early payments elsewhere with an opportunity to earn additional interest before the 20 years is over. On the time scale of decades, dividends are more important than final stock prices.

Some companies, such as Apple, seem to contradict this logic; investors have done well across decades, despite receiving few dividends. This is because the stock price has gone up so dramatically that it compensates for the lack of dividends. Instead of paying out its profits as dividends, Apple has reinvested them, and those investments have helped the company grow rapidly. This doesn't prove that dividends aren't important. Eventually, Apple's growth will slow down, whether its rapid growth phase lasts for two decades or five. Over the ultra long term, the value of Apple, like the value of any company, depends on how much it will eventually pay out in dividends.

To calculate how much Jen is willing to pay for a stock that she wants to hold for the ultra long term, she needs to compare the expected stream of dividends to whatever alternative use she might find for the money. The stream of dividends will determine the long-term stock market return.[6] The main competitors for her investment money are bonds and bank deposits; the long-term returns on these depend on interest rates relative to inflation. So the key to deciding if stocks are a good buy relative to bonds is to try to predict dividends and compare them to real interest rates.

So we now have two strategies for valuing a stock: its market price, or some fundamental value based on the company's expected future dividends. These two valuations apply to the short term and the long term, respectively. These two approaches can be applied not just to individual stocks, but also to the stock market as a whole, and so to Jen's index fund. Since Jen is investing for a distant retirement, what matters to her, both in absolute terms as a savings target, and for relative comparisons among investment options for what she does save, is the long-term value, not the short-term fluctuations in price.

---

6   Final stock sale prices also count to some extent, but fluctuations in those are impossible to guess decades ahead of time. Jen's best possible guess is that the final prices at which she sells stocks in her retirement will be based on expected dividends projected even further into the future.

Many economists claim that "efficient markets" set the stock price of each company exactly equal to the company's fundamental value, or at least to the best estimate of that value that can be inferred from current information about that company. In other words, the magic of the market means that the short-term and long-term valuations should come out the same. The return demanded by the stock market should depend on how bond interest rates compare to inflation, since bonds are the main competition for the investment dollars. The market should set stock prices so that likely future dividends reflect the return that is demanded.

But does the stock market really work like that? During the 2010 "flash crash", the market suddenly lost about 9% of its nominal value in dollars, only to recover minutes later. How could this possibly be caused by genuine changes in the dividend prospects of the companies, or to information about them? No new information emerged during those few minutes about likely future interest rates and inflation. Clearly the long-term and short-term stock valuation methods were not moving in sync.

Maybe the flash crash was a weird aberration. But some economists don't think so. "Animal spirits" can drive the buying and selling of stocks. Optimism and pessimism are contagious, driving the stock market much higher or lower than its fundamental value. As we discussed in Chapter 2, contrarian investors like Warren Buffett, who are driven by fundamentals, exploit this mob psychology to make money. When others want to buy, even though prices are higher than fundamental analyses of companies' future profits suggest are reasonable, a contrarian sells. When others want to sell despite good fundamentals, a contrarian buys. This calms markets and brings stock prices closer back towards their fundamental values. In the short term, or even over the course of a few years, mob behavior can certainly distort stock prices away from the true values of companies. But 15 years should surely be long enough for cooler heads to prevail, and for the market to correct itself. What matters to Jen is the fundamental, dividend-based value of the companies, rather than the sometimes irrational market forces that set their prices in the short term. She's a long-term investor. Over the short term, there may be ways to exploit psychology, time the market, and game the system. That's a game for professional traders to play, but not for Jen. Over the long term, fundamentals are what count.

What Jen wants to do is pretty audacious. Everybody on earth would like to know what the true value of a stock is, and hence what its price should be. This would be a license to print money, by buying when stocks are undervalued and selling when they are overvalued. How can Jen possibly succeed where so many others have tried and failed?

Jen isn't, of course, about to crack the secret of making unlimited money. Her more modest aims have two big advantages, and it is these advantages that make them achievable. Jen's first advantage is her long-term perspective of fifteen-plus years; she will not be buying or selling often. Ideally, she will make one big purchase now, plus lots of small purchases over the years as she continues to receive and reinvest dividend payments and save part of her salary. Then when she retires, if she is lucky she could live off the dividend payments, perhaps supplemented by selling a small fixed percentage of her assets each year. Or if she needs a more stable source of retirement income, she could sell shares around the time she retires and put the money into bonds or bank deposits. No matter how good Jen's buying and selling decisions are, she will make too few of them to make large amounts of money.

Jen's second advantage is that she isn't interested in the details of individual companies, but only in the behavior of the stock market as a whole. She doesn't plan to buy individual stocks, so she doesn't need to know if any individual company is priced correctly. Instead, she will buy an index fund, and so she wants to know if the price of that fund is attractive. This means comparing the dividends she will get from all the companies in the fund to the interest payments she could get if she put her money elsewhere.

So let's look, with Jen, at the long-term fundamentals. To keep things simple, we'll start in the traditional way, looking at one company at a time. We know that a piece of paper certifying stock ownership is valuable because whoever owns the company gets to keep its profits. Paying out money today to buy part of the company means getting money back later when profits come in and dividends get paid. Jen can buy everything she needs today from her salary; she doesn't need her inheritance now. But she will need it later, when she retires. Buying stocks is a way to exchange purchasing power today for purchasing power later.

Let's have a closer look at the relationship between the stock price of a company (cost today) and its profits (the payback later). Widgets Inc. makes and sells widgets, generating a profit of $1 million per year. That money is distributed to the stockholders by paying them dividends.[7] Let's

---

7    Today, many companies that want to return profits to stockholders do not issue all the money as dividends, but instead use some of the money to buy back their own stocks on the open market. With fewer stocks in circulation, each stock certificate then entitles its owner to a larger share of the company's future dividends. The overall effect is similar to what would happen if stockholders all received dividends, and then most of them reinvested their dividends by buying more of the same company's stock, while a few of them sold their stock to balance out those purchases. One difference, when it is companies rather than dividend recipients that use profits to buy more stock, is that stockholders receive more of their return in the form of capital gains rather than dividend income. This helps some stockholders because while both dividends and capital gains are generally taxed at the same rate, long-term capital gains taxes can be deferred. For our purposes in this chapter, the practice of stock buybacks, a quirk of the current tax code and likely also of the way stock options and other incentives are included in executive compensation packages, is merely a distraction. Wherever possible, we will discuss the simpler case where profits are returned to stockholders in the form of dividends.

make this example slightly more realistic by adding in 2% inflation. Now the price of the widgets, the expenses of making those widgets, and the profits based on the difference between the two, all rise steadily at 2% per year, matching inflation in the rest of the economy. The stock price is $20 and there are 1 million shares; at this price, the company is valued at $20 million. If Jen buys stocks in Widgets Inc., her share of the profits represents a return of 5% on the money that she paid for the stocks. Since profits go up with inflation, the stock price should logically rise the same way, making the company worth $20.4 million in one year's time. So there is also a capital gain of 2% that cancels out inflation, making the total nominal return on Jen's capital 7%, and the inflation adjusted return 5%.

If another similar company, Gizmos Inc., also steadily makes $1 million per year profit, but its market price is only $18 million, then something is out of balance. Either stocks in Gizmos Inc. are too cheap, or stocks in Widgets Inc. are too expensive, or both. Intelligent investors might quickly sell $1 million of Widget stocks and use the money to buy Gizmo stocks instead. Then both companies will be valued at $19 million, and both will offer real returns of 5.3% of their current stock market values. If all companies made boringly predictable, steady profits, then markets could quickly adjust stock prices in this way. Then no matter which stock Jen buys at those adjusted prices, she will get the same rate of return on her capital.

The market can also adjust prices without massive buying and selling of stocks and other assets. Imagine that investors have only just learned the relevant facts about Widgets Inc. and Gizmos Inc., and that investors expect a 5% real return from this kind of company, given what they can get from other stocks and bonds. In that case an investor who was willing yesterday to pay $18 for Gizmo stock will, in the light of new information, be willing to pay $20 today. The current owners of the stock, also in the light of new information, will no longer sell for less than that. Because both buyers and sellers have changed their minds about how they value Gizmos Inc., its stock price changes. Now both companies are worth $20 million. $2 million was created out of thin air, because investors changed their minds about what price they were willing to pay for the stock. Similarly, during the flash crash, $1 trillion simply disappeared, and then reappeared again only minutes later. Only governments can create the paper dollar banknotes we carry in our wallets, but this is not the only way to "print money" or to destroy it. Ordinary investors, when they think alike, can create or destroy the dollar value of non-cash financial assets simply by changing their minds about how much current cash they think the assets are worth.

Similarly, imagine that investors who used to expect a 5% real return figure out that economic conditions have become so bad that they now only expect a 2% real return, no matter where they put their money. Let's assume that those investors are correct. While this would be terrible news for our capitalist economic system, the effect on the stock market is more mixed. In the short term, stock prices will soar, with Widgets' stock going up from $20 to $50 per share. Over the long term, however, future returns will be permanently lower.

We now understand the basic theory behind valuing a stock; it all depends on how the returns implied by expected future profits and hence dividends compare to returns that Jen can get elsewhere. Using this knowledge to value real companies is harder. Widgets Inc. and Gizmos Inc. are simple, fictional examples. No real company is so predictable as to make exactly the same amount of profit every year. If they claim to, beware, they are probably fudging their numbers! Jen would rather have a guaranteed return of 4% than a return that, while it would amount to 5% if averaged across all possible worlds, could as easily be -10% as 20% in the one particular world that Jen will live in. Other investors feel the same way, and so efficient markets make unpredictable stocks cheaper. That means that investors should, on average, get a higher return when they buy unpredictable stocks. This compensates them for the extra risk they are taking, namely the risk that their actual return may be much lower than the average return they expect. For example, Jen cares more about being 95% sure that her retirement will be OK than she cares about being "on average" richer during her retirement. Jen is most concerned about risk over a 15-50-year period, but some older or more cautious investors are put off even by short-term fluctuations.

Profits can fluctuate from one year to the next, and there can also be predictable trends over time. To take an extreme example, imagine a pharmaceutical company that gets all its profits from selling a single blockbuster drug. In 5 years' time, the drug will lose its patent, and more efficient generic manufacturers will sell the same drug for less money. The company has no new drugs in the pipeline, and so is doomed; it will make large profits for 5 years, and then go bust. Perhaps the company owns some buildings and lab equipment that could be sold after the company dies, but it has no future as a self-sustaining company. Meantime, it is making $100 million profit per year from its one blockbuster product, and it has no debts. The stock market will price this company at around $500 million, reflecting the amount of money that can be extracted out of it during its remaining 5 years of profit, minus a "discounting" term to compensate for the fact that investors will get this money later rather than now, plus the extra money that can be made selling off the company's assets after the patent ends and the company is liquidated. In contrast, if the $100 million yearly profit were expected to continue indefinitely, rising with inflation, then a market demanding a 5% real return would price the company at $2 billion, four times as much.

This drug company example is still highly simplified, and the long-term future of real companies is of course much harder to predict. The point is that what investors think about future dividends matters a lot. If investors believe that a company will make much higher profits in the future, then its stock will be priced much higher than its current profits would suggest is reasonable. Indeed, popular technology companies can have sky-high market prices, even if they make no profit at all. This doesn't mean that profits and dividends aren't important. It means that the market is betting that these technology companies will eventually make very large profits and use them to pay very high dividends.

All these uncertainties make it difficult to figure out a fair price for a stock, even for trained financial analysts who do nothing else all day. Analysts need to make not just a single crystal ball prediction about future profits, but to consider a range of plausible futures, in order to estimate the riskiness of a stock. They need to make assumptions about what rate of return they could get from alternative investments. And they need to take other things into account too, like whether a stock price is likely to go down at the same time as everything else in their portfolio, or whether the fate of that company is more idiosyncratic, going up and down in its own rhythm rather than following that of the stock market, or the economy, as a whole.

Pricing stocks is a job for professionals, not something that Jen could possibly do herself. But remember, Jen doesn't need to figure out fair prices for any individual stocks. She just wants to know whether the stock market as a whole is a good buy, i.e. whether, based on current stock market prices, she expects an attractive future return on a stock market index fund. If the stock market as a whole is too expensive, she wants to stay away, perhaps buying bonds instead if their returns are more reasonable. In the extreme case of a negative return, negative even in dollar terms without adjusting for inflation, Jen would do better hoarding cash in a bank vault.

No matter whether Jen chooses stocks, bonds, or cash, she wants to know how high a return she should expect. Can she afford to live it up a bit, because her inheritance virtually guarantees a comfortable retirement? Or is a comfortable retirement at risk, hostage to the fate of the stock market or inflation, suggesting she should play it safe and cut back on her spending, starting now?

As a tool in estimating future returns, financial analysts routinely calculate the "price-earnings ratio" for individual stocks. This price-earnings ratio is the basic building block of a fundamental stock analysis. To see why, let's start with the simple case of Widgets Inc., where all earnings get paid out as dividends. Its price-earnings ratio is 20, meaning that each owner of a $20 share gets $1/year in dividends. When Jen turns that upside down and calculates the earnings-price ratio instead, she finds out how large a real return, in this case 5%, she can expect from a simple company like Widgets Inc. This is a real, inflation-adjusted return, because after any number of years of dividends, Jen will still own the same share of the company, which is a real asset whose price will have risen with inflation.

Companies that are expected to grow will have a higher price-earnings ratio, because the ratio is calculated using the current earnings, while what matters to future returns and thus to Jen is expected future earnings. Similarly, companies that are expected to shrink will have a low ratio; our fictional, doomed pharmaceutical company had a price-earnings ratio of only five.

Taking a historical view, stock markets seem to have a "natural", medium-term average price-earnings ratio of about 15. For example, when profits go down, stock prices also go down, preventing the ratio from going far out of balance. When irrational exuberance or panic hits the stock market, stock prices can stray out of line with earnings for a while, but eventually prices go back towards this natural ratio.

If something were to make the long-term price-earnings ratio permanently rise, it would cause a one-time rise in stock prices. After that, the return on capital would permanently fall. A stable price-earnings ratio of 15 means that if all earnings were paid out as dividends, and earnings tracked inflation, those dividends would represent a real return of 6.7%. A similarly stable price-earnings ratio of 20 means that those same dividends yield a real return of 5%.

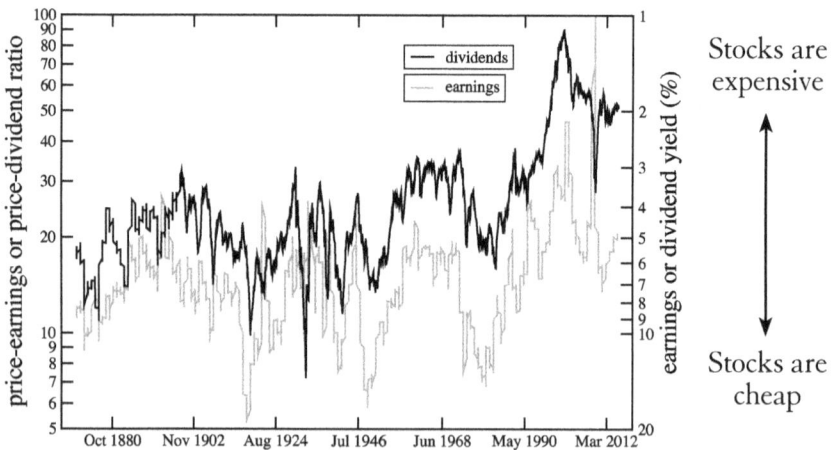

Figure 2: Dividend yield and price-earnings ratio data for the S&P 500 are taken from http://www.multpl.com and shown on a log scale in order to fairly represent compound returns. The financial crisis of 2007/8 shows up as a short-lived spike on the graph.

The logic of using price-earnings ratios to estimate returns is usually used for individual stocks, but the same logic applies to the stock market as a whole. In Figure 2 above, the lower, grey line shows the historical behavior of the price-earnings ratio for the stock market as a whole.

Real companies, unlike Widgets Inc., don't pay out all their earnings as dividends. They may, for example, keep the money and invest it in new stores, factories, research and development, or other expansion plans designed to create even more profit (and dividends) in the future. In practice, almost all companies retain some of their earnings. This can be a great thing when companies invest retained earnings in making a bigger and better company that will earn more in the future. Unfortunately, sometimes the company's managers may waste the money in grandiose expansion plans that eventually underperform. And it is easier to play accounting games with earnings than it is to fake the story told by the hard cash of dividends. For this reason, Figure 2 also shows price-dividend ratios (the upper line, in black) as well as price-earnings ratios (lower, in grey); you can read both by looking at the numbers on the left. If you look instead at the numbers on the right, you see how that translates into the expected real percentage return due to earnings or dividends.

Looking at the stock market as a whole one day in May 2015, Jen learns that the price-earnings ratio is 20.75. This makes today's stocks cheaper than they were during the dot-com bubble when, leaving aside a brief crazy peak, price-earnings ratios were quite often in the 30s. At the other extreme, showing how low things can in principle go, there have been three stock market slumps during which this ratio has fallen lower than 7. A ratio of ~21 is a little higher than historically normal values of around 15, suggesting that the stock market is slightly overvalued. That's not good news for somebody looking to buy stocks. Over a 15-year time horizon, prices would need to fall at an average rate of 2.1% per year in order to restore a historical price-earnings ratio of 15. While other things could cancel this out and still give a healthy overall return, this is certainly not good news for Jen. Either stock prices have a long way to fall, or we have reached a "new normal" in which high prices correspond to permanently lower future returns.

The argument that price-earnings ratios matter is backed up by evidence. On average, people who buy stocks when the price-earnings ratio is high get a lower return; variation in the price-earnings ratio explains about 40% of variation in subsequent real returns.[8] Since the price-earnings ratio is so high right now, maybe Jen should sit on the sidelines and wait for a few years, and buy stock later in some other year when the price-earnings ratio is lower.

Data on earnings can be murky. Since Jen doesn't understand these companies, and doesn't trust their managers, she decides to assume that most earnings that are not paid back to stockholders are either accounting fictions, or will be wasted in some way. While this isn't completely true, she suspects that it is more accurate than assuming the other extreme: that all retained earnings will be wisely reinvested to generate ever-higher dividends in the future. In order to stick to things Jen understands and believes, she looks at the story told by cash, and so she next focuses just on dividend yields, rather than the price-earnings ratio.

The picture painted by dividends in Figure 2 is no more cheerful than that seen from earnings. Recently, stocks have yielded returns of 2% in the

---

8    Joseph H. Davis, Roger Aliaga-Díaz, and Charles J. Thomas. "Forecasting stock returns: What signals matter, and what do they say now?" Valley Forge, PA.: The Vanguard Group (2012). https://personal.vanguard.com/pdf/s338.pdf

form of dividends. Because stocks are a "real" asset, they provide protection from inflation, making this 2% a real return; Jen should compare it to returns of ~4% in dollar terms. So the good news is that a 2% real return is higher, although less predictable, than the return that Jen could get from bonds. This historically low dividend is either a "new normal" return from stocks, or else stock prices are likely to fall by an average of ~2.1% per year for the next 15 years, cancelling out the 2% dividend return and leaving Jen with a real return of approximately zero. The answer might also lie somewhere between these two extremes of a 0-2% real return.

Unless the extreme case of a "new normal" is correct, the price-earnings ratio suggests that stock prices will eventually fall, so perhaps Jen should hold off and wait for them to get cheaper before she buys. But what would she do with her money while she waits, perhaps for years? Inflation will decrease the value of her cash at a rate of about -2% a year. Few bonds today pay as much as 4%, and those that do might have a significant risk of default, making them just as risky as the stock market. Jen may have to settle for a 2% certificate of deposit at her bank, only just keeping up with inflation.

Jen can't see any way out of this mess. Maybe markets are efficient after all; there is no magic bullet that will do better than the other options. The bottom line is that in today's financial markets, Jen should, on average, expect a 2% real return if she is willing to take major risks, and less if she is not. That is only on average. There is no guarantee that she will get the average. And the more risk she takes, the worse an outcome she must be prepared to stomach. This is a problem, because for Jen, getting the maximum possible average return is not the most important thing. More important is a high probability that her retirement will be comfortable. If Jen had more than enough money already, she could afford to take more risk. But the closer to the line she is, the more this means that she may have to settle for an even lower average return in exchange for less risk over a fifteen-plus year time horizon.

Scared, Jen goes back to an online retirement calculator. When she used this calculator before, it came "preloaded" with an 8% expected return. Jen had changed this number to 7% pre-retirement and 3% after, thinking at the time that these were normal returns. Now her sums tell her that 4% is the "normal" result she should expect from the stock market. Frighteningly, there is never any guarantee of normal returns, and so they could be much worse than that.

Jen earns $80,000 per year, and she will keep saving 7% of that income into her retirement account, to be doubled by her employer, plus she also plans to save the $8,000 that used to go towards her mortgage. She assumes that her salary, savings amount and expenses will all go up with inflation at 2%. She plans to retire at 65, and she has $700,000 to invest now.

The next question on the online calculator asks how much she expects her living expenses to go down – it is a normal assumption that expenses decline. And it's true that after Jen retires, she will have more time to cook lunch rather than buy it near work. She might also, as she gets older, become less likely to take expensive long-distance vacations. But in the years immediately after retirement, she would rather take more such vacations, if she can. And once she gets old and frail enough to really spend less, medical expenses and other forms of care could start eating into her budget. Jen can hedge against the risk of catastrophic long-term care expenses of hundreds of thousands of dollars by buying long-term care insurance – insurance that could easily cost $5,000 per year when she retires at 65, and more as she keeps getting older.

So Jen decides to count on maintaining the same effective income as she has now. The only difference is that when she stops earning, she will stop saving 17% of her income: this means she will only need 83% of her current income to continue living in her current style. She ticks the "include Social Security" box and hopes the government will come through on its promises. And crucially, she now assumes that she will earn a long run return of only 4% before retirement, and 3% after retirement when she shifts to less risky assets.

Jen puts those numbers into the online calculator, and is relieved when she sees that she will still be OK. She has enough money to live until she is 101. Phew.

But what if returns are lower? It's not enough just to prepare for an average scenario, Jen wants security. If returns are just 1 percentage point below Jen's expectations, she will get a 3% return before retirement and 2% afterwards. Then the calculator tells her that she will have enough money to make it to 91. If returns are 2 percentage points below, she will make it to 85, with negative returns after retirement, as inflation erodes the value of her assets. If she doesn't invest at all, but keeps her money in cash and counts on inflation staying at 2%, she will make it to 80. Of course, even this decision would not be risk-free, because inflation may rise higher than 2%.

Does Jen really need to plan on living to 100? Jen finds an online life expectancy calculator and fills in their questionnaire. The median lifetime for somebody like her is 91 years, with a 50% chance that she will die between the ages of 83 and 98. That means she has a 25% chance of living longer than 98. Living to be 100 is not some remote possibility, but a plausible scenario that she should plan for. When Jen retires, she can convert some of her retirement savings into an "annuity" that pays a fixed sum each year until she dies. This is a kind of insurance policy against the risk of living longer than planned. Social Security, which pays out each year until you die, is also a kind of insurance against the risk of living longer than planned, but Social Security was already programmed into the calculator. Neither of these insurance programs changes the statistical fact that Jen is likely to live a long time; with or without the annuity option, public or private, Jen should plan for a long life.

Jen is much better prepared for retirement than most people, but even so she is much worse prepared than she would like to be. What Jen wants seems quite modest. All she wants is a low-risk investment that pays a little bit more than inflation. If only there were some kind of inflation guarantee that she could buy.

The US government offers something that should give her exactly this: inflation-protected bonds, called TIPS. These seem perfect, but there is, unfortunately, a catch. People are willing to pay a hefty premium for this protection. Jen can count herself lucky; between late 2011 until mid-2013, 10-year TIPS were literally guaranteed to lose purchasing power; investors were willing to accept a small loss in exchange for a guarantee that losses would be no larger.

Now, 10-year TIPS offer a real return of +0.18%, 20-year TIPS offer +0.54%, and 30-year TIPS offer +0.78%.[9] Those returns may be low, but they are also very low risk. If Jen puts all her money into long-term TIPS, she won't get rich, but her retirement will be secure.

Jen develops a plan for what to do next. She will certainly move more of her money into long-term TIPS. She can afford the extraordinarily low

9    US Department of the Treasury, Daily Treasury Real Yield Curve Rates http://www.treasury. gov/resource-center/data-chart-center/interest-rates

real returns in exchange for peace of mind, protection against both the wild animal spirits of the stock market and the steady and at times more than steady erosive power of inflation. She will buy TIPS by selling some of her "normal" bonds, and maybe by holding a bit less cash. Should Jen also sell some stocks and use that money to buy more TIPS? The more TIPS she holds, the safer she feels that while she will never be rich, she will be OK. But with this big inheritance, it would be nice to at least stand a chance of being rich. By holding some of her money in stocks, she can protect herself against inflation AND expect higher yields on average. The down side is more risk, but with money in TIPS, she feels like she can take a little risk.

So Jen still wants to understand the stock market better. Dividends indicate a 2% real return on current capitalization, but earnings are much higher than dividends. With such a lot of retained earnings, hopefully businesses will use those retained earnings to grow over the years, leading to a long-term rise in real stock prices and a corresponding rise in the real value of dividend payments. It's possible that some or even most of reported retained earnings are overstated and/or wasted, but Jen should nevertheless factor in some reasonable amount of long-term dividend growth. Another thing to take into account is the current state of animal spirits. Would Jen be overpaying or getting a bargain by buying now rather than some other time?

There are a number of ways of trying to estimate this. One method[10] tells Jen that stocks are "significantly overvalued" to the point where

---

10    From http://www.gurufocus.com/stock-market-valuations.php accessed on May 16, 2015. The calculation starts with dividend yield, and then assumes that business growth (and hence dividend growth) will track GDP growth, and that GDP growth will continue at the same nominal rate as it did for the last 10 years. To work out whether current prices are fair, it compares the total market capitalization to GDP, which Warren Buffett described in Fortune magazine in 2001 as "probably the best single measure of where valuations stand at any given moment." It assumes that in the long term, stock prices will adjust to return this ratio to historical norms.

she should expect returns of around 0% over the next 8 years. And that doesn't even correct for inflation. This factors in Jen's 2% dividend return, but then expects stock prices to fall at a rate of 2%, even before correcting for inflation, in order to cancel out their current overvaluation. In other words, this fundamentals-based method predicts that the very volatile stock market will have a lower return on average than the very secure TIPS.

Some of the assumptions used by this method might be wrong. The method assumes that the growth in business and dividends tracks growth in the economy as a whole, tracked by GDP; what if business and dividends instead shrink as a proportion of the economy instead? And it assumes that GDP growth will continue at a similar rate to the past; what if it slows down instead? In either of those cases, Jen's return would be even worse.

Here I suggest a slightly different way of figuring out the likely total return from a stock market index fund. I also take current dividend yield as a starting point. The key missing piece in calculating long-term returns is to estimate the size of future dividends, compared to dividends today. This seems like an impossible question to answer, but it can be broken up into just three smaller and somewhat easier questions:

1. How much larger will the economy grow?
2. What percentage of that economy will go into corporate profits?
3. Will Jen's share of corporate profits grow or shrink?

In the next two chapters, we will discuss economic growth, and then in Chapter 9 we will tackle the last two questions. Putting the answers to all three questions together, this will provide an alternative way of estimating what kind of return Jen should expect on her stock market index fund. Then it's time for Jen to decide whether she wants her high-risk investments to be in stocks. Or perhaps, if she is going to take some risks with part of her money, there are better investments than stocks out there that are more likely to yield a moderately high return.

# CHAPTER 7

# ECONOMIC GROWTH

The economy produces a certain amount of goods and services. Jen can use her money to bid for these things. One way for Jen to get more of the things she needs and wants is for her power to purchase these things to go up, while somebody else's purchasing power goes down to compensate. A better option is economic growth, so that the economy produces more things overall. A bigger economic pie makes it possible for everybody to be more prosperous, including Jen in her retirement.

Some fraction of the growing economic pie goes to labor, and some to capital. This affects Jen, because some fraction of capital's share will go to corporate profits, and some fraction of that will go to Jen's dividends. As a step towards helping Jen figure out how large her share of the economic pie will be, we ask in this chapter how big the total pie will grow.

Jen the capitalist hopes that her money will buy more in the future than it does now. With her mortgage paid off, Jen currently saves $13,600 of her annual $80,000 income, with another $5,600 in matching savings from her employer. Some of Jen's remaining $66,400 income pays her taxes, and she spends the rest. This means that if Jen could freeze the current purchasing power of her money, and if she retired tomorrow at exactly the same standard of living, her $700,000 would finance her nearly $70,000 annual expenses for a bit over 10 years. If she works and saves for 16 more years first, then she has enough purchasing power for 15 years of retirement. Jen expects to be retired for longer than that. She is therefore hoping (and expecting) that the purchasing power of her money will not just be frozen, but grow. This will allow her to keep up the same standard of living for more than 15 years of retirement.

Jen doesn't want her purchasing power to go up just because somebody else's goes down. She doesn't want her comfort to come at somebody else's expense. For her to get richer without making anybody else poorer, we need economic growth.

There are two ways for an economy to get larger. First, as the population gets bigger, the economy may simply keep up with the number of people. In other words, more people produce, and more people consume. The average person is no richer, but the economy is bigger because there are more people.

If the population were growing really fast, this alone could be enough to boost the value of Jen's shares. This is because Jen isn't just any random person in the economy, she is the owner of capital. Through her stocks, Jen owns a share of the economy. This becomes a share of a larger economy when new workers are added to the economy, workers who were not owners when they were born or migrated to the US, but who nevertheless produce things. In this scenario, when companies retain most of their earnings instead of paying them out to Jen in dividends, that money is invested so that companies grow to keep up with the growing population.

As a capitalist reinvesting her earnings, including using her dividends to buy even more stocks, Jen's wealth would grow as the overall pool of capital grows. Jen the capitalist's increased wealth, in a society that is no richer on average, is balanced out by a smaller average share going to poorer migrants and babies. Population growth could help make Jen rich.

Unfortunately for Jen, US population growth is likely to be quite slow over her time horizon. Indeed, without immigration, the population might even shrink. Population growth certainly won't be fast enough, on its own, to create the kind of economic growth needed to add significantly to Jen's wealth.

We are really interested in the second driver of economic growth, the one that allows the same number of people to produce more and better goods and services. Economists call this an increase in "labor productivity". Growth that is fueled by labor productivity rather than by population growth can help everybody, including both capitalists like Jen, and also workers selling their labor in order to make it from paycheck to paycheck.

Higher labor productivity is not enough, on its own, to make economic growth happen. With higher labor productivity, the economy could keep making or doing the same things, while using fewer workers to make those things happen. If no more goods or services are produced than before, there is no economic growth. But the fact that fewer workers are needed to get things done could let the others retire in comfort.

Unfortunately, many of the no-longer-needed workers are likely to already be the poorest members of society, the ones that employers value the least and are least interested in keeping. They are unlikely to own a lot of capital like Jen, and they won't all be above retirement age. Aside from a small minority on the left, society does not seem inclined to increase tax rates in order to take the benefits of higher productivity away from those doing the producing, and redistribute those benefits so that the unemployed, including retired people with little capital, are just as well off as they would be if they were working.

In this scenario, Jen's capital might let her retire and keep spending, but many others will be forced into "retirement", irrespective of their age or savings. When those people can't afford to buy things anymore, the businesses who used to sell to them will suffer. Producers will not produce more unless someone is buying. Stagnant or falling sales could hit Jen's dividends and so hurt Jen too. Despite the increased labor productivity, the economy may actually contract. This is because poor people spend more of their paychecks than rich people do. When rich people gain purchasing power at the expense of the poor, they buy fewer things. When fewer things are bought, the economy gets smaller. Greater economic equality therefore stimulates the economy, while increasing inequality depresses it. Improvements in labor productivity can cause economic inequality to increase, depressing the economy and making Jen's dividends smaller.

In a more commonly evoked and optimistic vision, increased labor productivity creates economic growth. The hope is that when fewer workers are needed to do the old work, some will switch to new jobs, producing new kinds of goods and services, or simply more of the same. Adding more and/or new goods and services while keeping all the old ones then drives economic growth. This economic growth provides job opportunities for everybody to earn a share of the increased wealth. In this buoyant economy, Jen's dividends do well and she has money to spend in her retirement.

So what will we produce with our increased productivity? Do we want more of the same things, or do we need to invent new things?

Sometimes, more of something can be a huge economic boon. For example, building more high-quality roads to create the national highway system led to massive economic growth by enabling people and goods to move around more freely, spurring consequential changes in the whole economy. But this only works when there is a shortage of roads. When there are enough roads already, building more of them is a waste of money and land. Similarly, producing more food than people need to eat will generally lead to waste and/or obesity. Producing more of the same is generally necessary when the population is growing, but it is not always useful at other times.

In developing countries, there are some clear shortages, and economic growth can clearly meet them. Many of the companies in Jen's stock market index fund are multinationals, and so their future dividend growth could come from emerging markets. While this could be a great source of dividend growth, it does make Jen uneasy. Remember, she wants to invest only in things she understands. Jen is already struggling to understand likely stock market returns at home. While she is making progress towards this goal, she is less optimistic about understanding economic conditions all across the globe.

Of course even in the US, many people do want more than they have, and one would think there would be opportunities for dividend growth when companies find ways to fulfill these desires. We will discuss this issue a lot more in the next chapter, when we will see that sometimes these desires are, unfortunately, unfulfillable. This is because if you give everybody the latest fashion, it stops being the latest fashion; it becomes the boring standard, and people will want something even newer. In the meantime, let's think only about those economic advances that have obviously been good things, unambiguously improving everybody's welfare.

In the last 150 years, we have got used to the idea that new technological and economic changes improve our lives dramatically. Dramatic change requires true innovation. Many of the most important innovations that have transformed our lives in this way are one-off events, not trajectories that we can simply keep following. Instead of being at the mercy of the elements, we live in a bubble of comfortable, constant temperature through the miracles of heating and air-conditioning. Today we have electricity; its production and distribution could be made more efficient, but the big change is having it at all. We have gone from transport at a walking pace to airplanes, both for ourselves and for goods we buy, but there is no sign that air travel is continuing to get faster or that a new transportation technology is coming. We have gone from slowly transported letters to essentially instant email and phone calls. Communication can't get any faster than it already is. We have indoor plumbing today; even the most innovative Japanese toilet technology can only add so much to this basic innovation. Education has been transformed as high school became standard, college stopped being rare, and more educated workers found more productive jobs. It is not clear how useful it is to keep adding ever-more years of school for everybody; indeed, education may now become in large part an arms race in pursuit of a better job. All these incredibly important and beneficial economic transformations were, in their essence, one-offs. We cannot simply produce more of the same, but must continue to find new innovations.

To avoid "more of the same", we need to find things of true value that people might not even know that they want, and then deliver them. What made the greatest technological breakthroughs in history so transformative is that they prompted a flurry of other innovations. For example, people prefer to use an electric washer rather than wash their clothes by hand. But until electricity was available, it never occurred to them that such a thing was possible. Luckily, improved power and transport infrastructure also created large increases in productivity and hence production. Innovations like electricity both created new things that people wanted, and increased our ability to produce such things. With the two coming together at the same historical moment, we got massive economic growth.

Electricity grids, railways, and the modern network of roads were all invented a long time ago. The most recent big technology breakthrough of this kind was the information revolution. This gave us a variety of new products, from computers to the internet to cellphones and smartphones, which allow us to access a bewildering variety of new services. Some of the advantages, while wonderful, do not lead to economic growth. For example, Jen loves being able to quickly find the answer to almost any question over the internet, much of it through free services such as Wikipedia. She believes that when everybody gets access to information, everybody's life gets better. But because most of these services are not sold at a profit, nobody is receiving stock market dividends from them.

For information technology to drive economic growth, it is not enough to make our lives better, although that is certainly nice. In order to fund more than 15 years of Jen's retirement, some of these improvements must create new products that people buy. The first iPhone was clearly this kind of innovative product. Jen can count such a product as a genuine advance contributing to her retirement wealth. She can then decide to spend her extra retirement wealth either buying an iPhone herself, or she can forgo the new invention and instead use the wealth to fund more years of retirement.

Replacing a third-generation smartphone with a fourth-generation smartphone is not the same kind of advance. Jen hopes, but can't be sure that there will continue to be a steady stream of new products as intrinsically desirable as the first smartphone.

As well as creating new products, information technologies also make it possible to automate once repetitive jobs, and find new efficiencies both in services and in manufacturing. We are still pretty bad at finding these efficiencies; most large information technology projects end up as failures, after going massively over budget. Maybe there is a lot of room for economic growth here, by using information technology to improve labor productivity, e.g. via large numbers of smaller, more incremental changes. Let's hope so. Apart from information technology, no other technologies with that sort of transformational potential can be spotted today.

Information technology is the good news. It's not hard to come up with much gloomier scenarios for future economic growth. What if we run out of oil? Or if climate change creates environmental catastrophe? Or if both combine to cause shortages of water, and hence of food? Water shortages could easily trigger catastrophic wars over natural resources.

Now that we have experienced rapid economic growth for a couple of hundred years, it has begun to feel inevitable. It is not. When the Roman Empire collapsed, parts of Europe suffered economic collapse, and were reduced to barter. So far, economic growth, whether or not it has improved overall welfare, has meant using more and more of the earth's resources: fossil fuels, minerals, and fresh water supplies including aquifers. There are limits to all of these things. Some prehistoric civilizations are thought to have collapsed because of shortages of fresh water and the exhaustion of overcultivated soils. We may one day share this fate. Today we use canals to bring fresh water from the Rocky Mountains to the Southwestern deserts, but this may simply postpone the problem. Once-huge rivers, vital to our agriculture, no longer reach the sea. All the water is used up first.

Many doomsayers have pointed these problems out before, and predicted disaster. So far, they have all been wrong. That doesn't mean they will always be wrong. If something is finite, we cannot keep using more and more of it forever. This is an inevitable mathematical truth. There may be more of the resource than we first thought, delaying the day when it runs out. But it will run out eventually, even if we don't know exactly when.

For example, nobody doubts that there is only so much copper on our planet. Many of our current technologies use copper wires. Maybe we can make the same devices with less copper per device. Maybe we can waste less copper, and extract the remainder from landfill to reuse it. But somewhere there is a limit at which there is no more copper. Maybe we can then invent alternative technologies that don't need so much copper. But some things cannot be substituted so easily. We will always need fresh water, food, and a source of energy.

We keep finding more oil, and so it has not run out when the first doomsayer predicted that it would. But no matter how much more we find, oil is, in the end, finite. We will run out sometime, whether in five years or in a thousand. Maybe we will stop burning fossil fuels before the oil runs out, for example because of the catastrophic effects on the climate. But if we do continue for long enough, perhaps sometime after Jen has died of old age, the oil will run out.

The rate of return on stocks depends on what you think the future looks like. The last 150 years experienced the fastest economic growth ever. This is unlikely to continue. Information technology is the only big new revolution going on right now, and its final effects are unclear. So far it looks good, but not quite as transformational as electricity or railroads. What is more, free services such as Wikipedia illustrate how less of that transformation may be monetized and captured by the stock market than for previous technological revolutions. And it is easy to come up with more pessimistic scenarios of economic catastrophe. We don't know whether these catastrophes will happen in the next 15 or 50 years. They might, or they might not. But even if they don't, there are still plenty of reasons to be skeptical about whether the next 15-50 years, the time that Jen cares about, will see economic growth anything like as rapid as in the last hundred years.

# CHAPTER 8

# POSITIONAL GOODS AND THE COST OF LIVING

Increased labor productivity seems achievable, and makes it possible to produce more goods and services. Many people want more than they have. This suggests that we can grow the economy by producing more, and giving people what they want. The economy grows, the benefits of this growth are shared, and everybody can have more of what they want and be better off.

Unfortunately, things are not that simple. Sometimes what people want is not to have more of certain things as defined in absolute terms, but rather to have the newest and best out of whatever choices are currently available. The difference can be subtle, especially since the two sometimes go together; some new products are better than the old ones in a meaningful sense. Computers today really are better than computers twenty years ago. They can do all of the old things faster and better, and they can do new things too.

But sometimes the "best" is strictly relative and cannot be justified on an absolute scale. This year's fashion in clothes is almost certainly no "better" than last year's fashion. People want this year's items to show that they are ahead and not behind. Unfortunately, when the "best" is a relative concept, there will always be a shortage of it. If you gave everybody the best, then it wouldn't be the best anymore; it would now be the boring standard. If everybody has this year's fashion, then some people will want this month's fashion, or this week's, to stay ahead of the curve. New fashions may get produced and thrown away faster than ever before, and this may even show up as economic growth, but it won't make us better off.

Biologists call this the "Red Queen effect". The term comes from Lewis Carroll's "Through the Looking-Glass". Alice and the Red Queen run as fast as they can, but after all that effort, find themselves in exactly the same place.

> *"Well, in our country," said Alice, still panting a little, "you'd generally get to somewhere else — if you run very fast for a long time, as we've been doing."*
>
> *"A slow sort of country!" said the Queen. "Now, here, you see, it takes all the running you can do, to keep in the same place. If you want to get somewhere else, you must run at least twice as fast as that!"*

It's impossible for everybody to have the newest, most fashionable items. The whole point of such items is to be ahead of somebody else (or, as the case may be, to keep up with them, or at least not fall too far behind). Economists call such things "positional goods" or "status goods".

Competing to buy newer, bigger, or simply more goods leads to a Red Queen effect, and not to true improvements in quality of life. Positional goods are inherently scarce, and so it is impossible to satisfy demand for them. In other words, if more people were able to obtain a Ferrari, this would satisfy the new owners, but then current Ferrari owners would want something else.

Positional goods are an arms race, where only relative position matters. Because of this bottomless demand, positional goods can absorb the fruits of economic growth, with ever-increasing resources wasted in their production. Economic growth involving positional goods has competitors running like Alice just to maintain (on average) their relative position, without getting anywhere on an absolute scale. The faster they run, the higher the economic growth, but this growth does not make anyone better off.

Not all positional goods are, like Ferraris, accessible only to the richest. Young people with modest disposable incomes aspire to the latest fashion items, driven by the same motives as Ferrari owners, but with a different standard for what is desirable – relative to their peers. People who struggle to set aside a prudent cash buffer for emergencies or pay for health insurance do not let these genuine, absolute needs prevent them from buying the largest car, largest flat screen TV, or most powerful video game console they can – largest and most powerful not on any absolute scale, but relative to what their peers have. The American middle class persistently buys larger houses than they need to live comfortably, taking as their reference point what other people own.

If these positional arms races lead to more economic activity, they can boost profits and hence Jen's dividend income. Unfortunately, there is a catch. Those same arms races can also increase Jen's expenses.

For example, owning a car (any car, not just a Ferrari) was once a luxury enjoyed only by the affluent. Eventually, cars became so common that car ownership was more or less taken for granted. Today, even the poor are sometimes forced by circumstances to work longer hours or forgo other purchases in order to scrape together the money to buy and run a car. This is because you need a car in order to live and/or work in many US neighborhoods. The distances between homes and jobs, or homes and shops, are just too far away to reach by foot or bicycle, and public transport is inadequate. Owning a car started out as a luxury positional good, but eventually became a necessity after society organized itself around cars.

To see this, imagine a city with trains, buses, and streetcars, but no cars. You are the only person with a car. With no other car traffic, you move around the city quickly and conveniently. This makes car ownership a valuable luxury. Now imagine that economic growth provides every person in the city with a car. Fewer people use the trains now, and so services are cut. The cars are stuck in traffic. The buses are stuck in the same traffic as the cars, and so go slower than before (and even slower than the already slow cars). And the city itself changes, with people spreading out into the more car-friendly suburbs. Getting around the new sprawled city by car is now no more convenient than getting around the old, more compact city without one. But now, doing without the car has become practically impossible. However expensive cars are, people need to keep buying them. Living carless, as one used to in the past, is just not an option.

Each car provides private benefits for its owner, but congestion and other public costs for everybody else. The cost that any one car imposes on any one bystander is small. But the public costs of many cars on many bystanders can be large enough to cancel out, either partly or completely, the private benefits to each of the car owners.

Another way to look at this is to note that Jen spends 15% of her time and income on transport. Eighty years ago, people also spent around 15% of their time and income on transport. Economic growth in the last eighty years has made people richer, but it has also increased how rich people need to be in order to get around effectively. All that economic growth in the transport sector was supposed to make people better off, but didn't.

Imagine some new invention in the future, something disruptive like car ownership, that comes along during Jen's retirement. Will she buy one? As the sort of person used to earning $80,000 a year, she doesn't expect to be the very first person to get one, but she probably will eventually. She won't be the first among her friends, but she probably won't be the last, either. And she will get one much sooner than a really poor person would.

The retirement calculators that Jen uses make no reckoning for this kind of extra expense. They assume that Jen will continue to buy the same kinds of goods and services as she does now. They make no allowance for Jen suddenly wanting to buy new stuff that didn't used to exist, on top of the old stuff that she has always bought.

Typical retirement calculators assume that continued economic growth fuels a healthy return on capital, and that when Jen reinvests these returns, the growth in her assets will be compounded. Some economic growth comes from innovations that create "new necessities" to fuel economic growth. The continued appearance of such innovations is built in to assumptions about Jen's future dividends. So these items are counted on the income side of Jen's projections. Unfortunately, they are generally not counted under expenses.

When Jen receives financial returns on these innovations via dividends and stock price increases, she can only spend these returns once. She can either use her steady percentage share of a growing economy to keep up with living standards that grow in line with the economy, or she can compound her return, buying a larger percentage share to fund more years of retirement at her old standard of living. She can't double count on her gains to do both.

If Jen really wants this new kind of item on top of all the things she normally buys, then her expenses will grow faster than the inflation rate suggests. If she wants her expenses to rise no faster than inflation, and she wants or needs this new item, then she will need to cut back on something else. When Jen prefers the new item to the old, then this exchange increases her well-being. But from the transport example, we see that sometimes all the new item does is provide her with what she used to have before, which has now been taken away. Like Alice and the Red Queen, Jen needs to run as fast as she can just to stay in the same place.

What is more, if everybody cuts back on other expenses in order to buy the new must-have item, then even if they were all better off through the choice, this still doesn't give us economic growth. We simply have a transfer of economic activity; less of one thing and more of another. Dividend growth in some places is then cancelled out by decline elsewhere. Jen shouldn't be counting on such transfers to be both good for her satisfaction with her spending and good for her financial return on capital.

Many new inventions like cars, which seem useful when you think about owning one yourself, don't look quite so amazing when you compare a world where everyone has them to a world where nobody does. Based on this thought experiment, cars are perhaps about 70% positional and only 30% a real advance. Many other inventions score no better. This means that society is better off if everybody gets a car, but the advantage is much smaller than you would think from calculating GDP growth minus inflation.

The example of cars shows how the transition of objects from luxuries to essentials can, like inflation, act to increase the cost of living. Inflation measures how much paper money it takes to buy "the same" basket of goods and services over time. This basket is generally designed to resemble those bought by a "typical" consumer. To see how much richer we have become, we measure how much money we earn after correcting for inflation. Measuring inflation isn't too difficult from one year to the next, because the things we buy don't change that fast. But changes in spending patterns accumulate over time, until, over several decades, typical consumer spending patterns become almost unrecognizably different, making it difficult to decide which products we should be comparing.

There are still some goods and services that stay much the same. For example, we still buy bread and eggs, and we can compare their prices now to their prices one hundred years ago. But even with such a simple example, there are complications; should we compare the eggs of the past to today's battery-farmed eggs bought at the supermarket, or to locally-raised, free-range, pasture-fed, organic eggs at five times the price, since these most closely resemble the eggs of 100 years ago?

The cost of eggs is one of the simplest possible examples; comparing most other goods and services is much harder. For example, how do we compare transport costs? Do we compare the price of gasoline per gallon? In other words, should gasoline be treated as something consumers intrinsically want? No, gasoline is just a mildly annoying intermediate step towards what we consumers actually want to buy, which is convenient transport. For example, Jen needs to commute 4 miles to work. Should we therefore calculate the cost of transport per mile, and compare this across time? Or should we calculate the average cost of transport from home to work, or home to the grocery store, independently of how many miles it is in whichever society we currently live in?

This gets to the core question: what are consumers really trying to purchase? We all want food, entertainment, and physical comforts provided by such things as heating, cooling, and a soft bed. When GDP goes up, is this because these needs are being met better now that we are richer? Or are we purchasing more, newer, bigger and/or finer things mainly to keep up with the Joneses, in an arms race for social position? Does economic growth supply old needs better, or does it supply new ones created through these arms races? Have we reordered society so that we now need to consume more intermediate things, like gasoline, in order to get the important things that we really want, and which we used to be able to get for less?

One of the thorniest issues in measuring inflation is to account for changes in the "quality" of goods and services. The quality of a positional good can be estimated in two fundamentally different ways. On an absolute scale, the first cell phone was clumsy and expensive. This didn't stop people wanting it when it first came to market, because it was new and different and its high price conferred social status to the owner. Later, cell phones fell dramatically in price even while their quality improved as measured on any sensible absolute scale. But when we take into account the fact that part of the point of having one was to show off in a relative competition for status, we see that the "quality" of the experience that a consumer gets from a prestigious purchase depends on how many other consumers have made similar purchases. This means that cell phone quality goes down in terms of the pleasure it gives the buyer. Having the smallest possible flip-phone once conferred status and was high quality; now, phones with larger screens are considered desirable. Inflation measurements try to capture changes in absolute quality, but does nothing to capture this kind of positional quality.

Positional goods do not tell the complete story of economics. As we saw last chapter, past economic growth really has improved our lives in many ways. There were extraordinary revolutions in transport, including a national highway system for cars and trucks, and the development of airplanes. Goods could be delivered and sold to ever larger markets. They could thus be manufactured according to increasing efficiencies of scale. This was accompanied by equally extraordinary revolutions in manufacturing methods, taking advantage, for example, of electric power. Distribution networks for electricity and telephones were rolled out. Electric power and new manufacturing methods facilitated the birth and spread of a tremendous range of innovative products, from indoor plumbing to washing machines to hospital intensive care facilities to televisions. High school education became standard, college was no longer rare, and more educated workers found more productive jobs. Past economic growth has made us better off. We live longer, we are less often hot or cold or wet, and we have access to more education and other forms of knowledge.

But economic growth has also produced things which, despite being nonexistent or luxurious in the past, are simply essential today. This invention of new necessities may happen again in the future. Jen needs to prepare for this, and consider the fact that inflation does not capture the full extent to which her cost of living will rise.

Some great new invention may start as a luxury, become a necessity, and in the process drive economic growth, and also contribute dividends to Jen's bank balance. But Jen will eventually need that extra dividend money to buy this good herself. This is true no matter where she lies on the curve: an early adopter buying when it is still a luxury, an average consumer buying when it has become normal and expected, or a holdout buying only when it has effectively become essential. Whichever category she normally falls into, there may be new things to buy in her retirement. Groups like the Amish can perhaps hold out against this process, at least in part, but trying to do the same as an individual is a hopeless task. Making cars created economic growth, jobs, and dividends for capital owners like Jen, but now she and others need higher incomes just to be able to move around in their society and reach the same quality of life as before.

Positional goods are those whose value comes entirely from what they imply about your social position relative to others. This is true whether Jen's motivation is to be ahead of others, to keep up with others, or to at least not fall too far behind what her peers consider "normal". Innovation in purely positional goods fuels zero-sum arms races, producing no overall improvement in welfare. To the extent that positional goods dominate future economic growth, Jen can't expect her welfare to improve either.

But even non-positional inventions that do improve Jen's welfare, such as a wonderful new medical treatment, can still drive up Jen's cost of living. This increased cost is not really optional when it is administered to her in the hospital as the standard of care while she is barely conscious, and she is billed for it later. Even if not all new necessities are purely positional, Jen's retirement planning still needs to account for the possibility that the cost of living might rise more than the official inflation figures indicate.

The real problem for Jen's retirement planning is that economic innovations, positional or otherwise, get counted under expected future income, but are excluded under expected future expenses. If enough of them get sold to provide dividend growth, then Jen will be buying them them too, subjecting her to and subject to higher expenses. Because this expense is not included in inflation, the retirement calculators are telling Jen the wrong thing.

How great an increase in the cost of living should Jen plan for? A good first estimate might be that most per capita GDP growth (and with it, dividend growth) corresponds to products that Jen will also want to buy. When the time comes, Jen also wants to be able to afford not only that fancy new status symbol, but also that wonderful new medical treatment and that genuinely useful new device, neither of which have been invented yet. So Jen can't count on GDP growth coming to the rescue by increasing the return on her capital.

Jen should therefore expect a real return equal to her dividend yield (around 2%) after correcting for all increases in the cost of living, not just inflation. This is the day-to-day share of the economy that routinely goes to the owners of capital; in the long run, capital gains will simply track GDP growth. For Jen to do better than that via big returns from the stock market, her gain as a capitalist must come at somebody else's expense. This is a depressing way to get by, and obviously not everybody can do it at the same time.

If society does become better off, Jen's gains above 2% will go to purchasing these benefits. Jen's desire to consume will increase in line with per capita GDP. Even when everybody's lives are improving in an absolute sense, not everyone can "get ahead" of the others at the same time. The money that Jen spends keeping up will not be available for her retirement.

# CHAPTER 9

# JEN'S SHARE
# OF THE PIE

To predict how the stock market will perform in the future, people look to the past. Different people make different assumptions about what stays roughly constant during business as usual, and what changes. Many assume that real stock market returns in the future will resemble real returns in the past. The problem is that stock market returns have fluctuated wildly over the past 100 years, even when averaged over long-term time horizons like Jen's.

A better approach is to find some fundamentals that fluctuate less over time, such as the ratio of stock price to company earnings or dividends, or the ratio of the total value of the stock market to the total size of the economy. These fundamentals-based approaches are the source of the dismal predictions of low future stock market returns that Jen found in Chapter 6. Depressingly, current values of stock prices, dividends, and GDP growth predicted real returns of 0% over the next 8 years, after correcting for inflation, but not the other increases in the cost of living discussed last chapter. What is worse, such a dismal outcome is not a worst-case scenario; it is simply what she should expect on average. If Jen is even moderately unlucky, she will get even less than that. Unfortunately, alternative investments don't look much better.

Over the long term, Jen will receive most of her stock market return via dividends paid out of future company profits. To ask about future company profits, we therefore used the following three questions to break things down in Chapter 6:

1. How much larger will the economy grow?
2. What percentage of that economy will go into corporate profits?
3. Will Jen's share of corporate profits grow or shrink?

A first guess is that the economy will keep growing at a "typical" rate, and that corporate profits will track the economy and so stay at or return to a "typical" percentage. We ask in this chapter how much of her stock market wealth Jen can spend while still maintaining ownership of a constant share of the corporate profits pie. Extra savings by Jen will buy her a bigger share of the pie, extra spending will diminish it.

Our first two preliminary answers assume that the future will resemble the past. But in Chapter 7, we looked more closely at the first question, and reached the depressing conclusion that the kind of economic growth we have seen over the last 150 years is rather miraculous and highly unusual in the bigger picture. There is a risk of serious stagnation in the future. At worst, environmental or other catastrophes could cause major economic disruption and the economy could shrink.

What is more, the correction for inflation going in to GDP growth numbers does not include the other increases in the cost of living we described in Chapter 8, where goods and services that were once non-existent, and which begin as luxuries, become so standard, with society organized around their consumption, that it becomes practically impossible to go without them. These kinds of consumption arms races can drive GDP growth, but they also drive up the cost of living. Some things, like better health care, improve the conditions of Jen's retirement, albeit at a cost. Others are just needed to keep up with the Joneses and leave Jen no better off than she was before the new goods and services were invented. In all cases, the return on Jen's investment due to economic growth driven by the invention of such goods and services can either pay for more years of retirement, indexed to inflation alone, or it can keep up with additional increases in the cost of living driven by relative competition and new necessities. It can't be double-counted to do both.

In this chapter, we look at the remaining two questions, to see how they change the so far rather depressing picture. Given that economic growth creates an economic pie of a certain size, how much of it will Jen own, through her share of corporate dividends?

Let's start by asking how much of the total economy goes to corporate profits. Again, while nobody knows the future, we can look to the past as a guide. In Figure 3, we see corporate profits as a percent of all forms of income within America.[11]

---

11    We use gross national income as a measure of the total size of the economy, rather than the more familiar gross domestic product, in order to account more appropriately for corporate profits earned in one country, but paid out to stockholders in another.

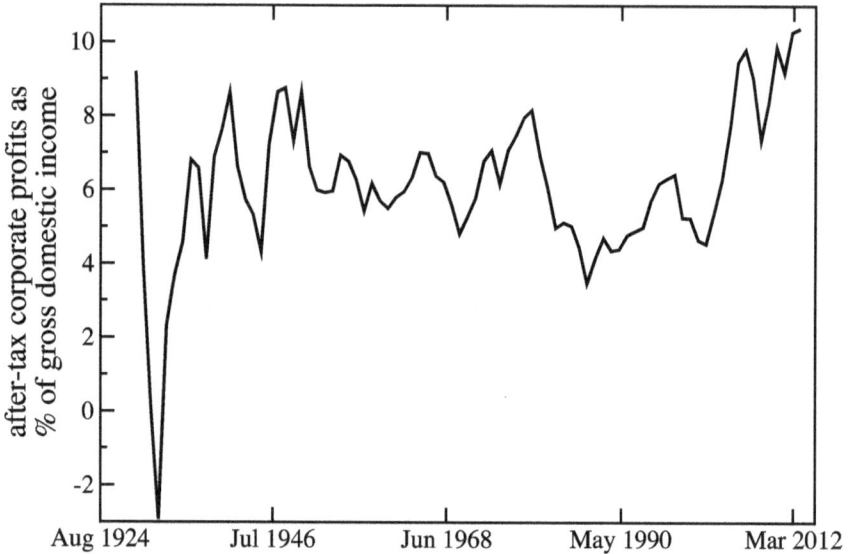

Figure 3: Data retrieved from US Bureau of Economic Analysis, FRED, Federal Reserve Bank of St. Louis https://research.stlouisfed.org/fred2/graph/, May 10, 2015.

Across the time period shown in Figure 3, an average of 6.6% of US income has gone into corporate profits. In 2013, profits made up 10.4% of all US income, a situation even more extreme than the previous record high of 9.2%, which was seen just before the great stock market crash of 1929. While this could be a "new normal", or indeed profits might take up an even higher share of income in the future, you should be suspicious of any arguments that invoke a new normal. It is more likely that eventually, things will go back to the old, historical normal, with more of the fruits of economic activity going to wages and less money going to profits. In other words, our best guess is that after-tax corporate profits will fall from 10.4% to more like 6.6% of gross national income. Taken by itself, this means a sizable fall in the total value of the stock market.

Such a loss, spread over Jen's 15-year time horizon, is equivalent to a fall in stock prices of -3% per year.[12]

So far, the news is not good for Jen. Profits are unusually high as a fraction of the economy; profits may come down, bringing long-term dividends and stock prices with them. Stock prices are higher than usual relative to profits; either stock prices are currently irrationally high and will fall, or this represents a "new normal" of low future returns. Neither situation is good news for Jen. Even if the economy continues to grow at the unusually fast rate we have come to expect from the last 150 years, Jen will nevertheless get a rate of return well below historical averages. And in yet more bad news, this kind of growth is far from guaranteed.

Turning to the last of our questions, when Jen owns a set of stock certificates, do they represent a constant share of the corporate pie? Or does she need to keep buying stock in order to keep up? Right now, adding up all the stocks in the stock market comes to about $22 trillion. Two-thirds of Jen's $700,000 is invested in stocks, meaning that Jen owns 0.000002% of the stock market. Will those mutual fund shares still add up to 0.000002% of the stock market when she retires?

This assumption is fairly reasonable as a first approximation. Companies grow, but the most common way they finance that growth is by not paying all their profits out as dividends, but instead spending their profits on investments in the company's future. The supposed reason why dividends

---

12    These numbers are for after-tax corporate profits. Pre-tax, the situation is similar but slightly less extreme. It would take 15 annual -2% falls to bring the pre-tax ratio from its 2014 value of 11.5% to its historical average of 8.5%. In both cases, these negative returns only take into account final stock prices and not dividends, so the effect on Jen's total return may not be quite as bad as that. Even if more of the future economy goes to wages rather than corporate profits, profits are unlikely to disappear overnight, and in the meantime Jen the capitalist will receive her share of them. If dividend yields stay at 2%, then as corporate profits drop, both dividends and stock prices will drop with them, but Jen will already have received some dividends first.

are so much less than earnings is for companies to finance their growth. When a company successfully invests retained earnings in growth, all existing stockholders share in the growth. This practice does not dilute or concentrate the percent share represented by any given stock certificate.

More rarely, the total value of the stock market goes up when new companies "go public" in an IPO and issue new shares. Old companies also issue fresh shares from time to time when they need extra capital to grow, or when workers who are paid in stock options exercise those options. Each time new stocks are issued, Jen's percent share of the stock market will go down a little. On the other hand, when companies use retained earnings to buy back stock, whoever sells that stock sees their percentage share go down, while Jen's percentage share goes up. There probably won't be a huge imbalance between these opposing forces over time. This means that if Jen neither buys nor sells stock Jen will still own about 0.000002% of the stock market when she retires. In the meantime, she can spend her dividends without diluting how much of the corporate pie she owns.

Jen takes stock of her situation and options. The online calculator suggested a real return of 0% over the next 8 years. Jen is therefore looking at a real return of 0% in the medium term while share prices adjust from their current overvaluation, and then 2% dividends after that. Alternatively, she can wait out the stock market and invest in bonds to get a barely positive real return until the next stock market crash, and then 2% dividends after that. Either way, at these low levels, Jen certainly cannot afford to live just on her return on capital. In other words, Jen will mostly have to sell stocks to pay for things after she retires, rather than just use dividend payments. To have enough stocks to sell, Jen needs to build up a large nest egg. Given that the capitalist pie is not growing fast enough, this means that Jen needs to save money in order to buy a bigger share of it.

Jen was already planning to keep buying stocks and bonds over the next 16 pre-retirement years. Jen also buys new assets when she reinvests her dividends, rather than spending that cash on living expenses. Jen intends to save more money than that, by continuing payments into her tax-deferred retirement account, and by setting aside the money that she once used to pay her mortgage. If Jen's calculations turn out too depressing, she will also try to cut back her expenses, in order to save even more money for a comfortable retirement. Much of those savings will be used to buy more stocks. Every time Jen buys more stocks, her percent share of the stock market goes up a little.

Jen may have a comfortable retirement, but if she does so, it will be because she saves at more than the usual rate, increasing her percentage of society's wealth. This takes care of Jen's retirement, but what about everybody else? It is logically impossible for everybody to save more than average. In the next chapter, we will explore what happens when lots of people try.

# CHAPTER 10

# SUPPLY AND DEMAND FOR CAPITAL

So far, we have encountered a mystery. Why are stock prices so high? At their current prices, future returns on stocks look abysmal. Surely these prices are not driven by analysis of the fundamentals. When stock prices rise so much higher than fundamentals suggest are reasonable, this is normally described by terms such as "irrational exuberance". But how can stock prices be driven too high by animal spirits at a time when so many people are pessimistic about the future economy? The media are full of stories of economic doom and gloom. Apparently we only narrowly escaped a second 1930s-style Great Depression. Meantime, many college students that Jen teaches count themselves lucky to find work as waiters after they graduate. Economic news varies from abysmal to "things are improving a little", but nobody seriously seems to expect that a new age of prosperity is just around the corner. This is not an era of irrational exuberance anymore.

The big puzzle is why more people don't realize how ridiculously overpriced stocks are, and sell them while prices are high. The answer is surprisingly simple. Stockholders don't know what else to do with their money. Ask analysts to justify buying stocks today, and many point out how low bond yields are. In other words, they don't deny that stock prices are high, with low rates of return likely. Instead they argue that no matter how expensive stocks are compared to future corporate profits, stocks still look good relative to bonds. Inflation can destroy the value of money kept in cash, in a bank account, or in bonds that pay a fixed rate of interest. In contrast, stocks provide some protection from inflation. Stocks represent a percentage of a company: as inflation goes up, the monetary value of that company should go up too.

People have their money invested in shares not because it is a good deal, but because they can't find anything better. The alternatives look even worse.

Capital markets, like all markets, obey the law of supply and demand: the supply of profitable companies with shares (real capital in the form of equity/ownership of future profits) for sale, and demand in terms of the amount of money (financial capital, e.g. from their savings) that investors are willing and able to spend buying stocks. Or, saying the same thing another way, there is a large demand for places to invest money productively, and not enough supply of such investments.

This logic can be broadened to include all capital assets, not just stocks. The forces of supply and demand set the price for how much money an investor needs to pay now in order to acquire an asset that will give them back an expected amount of money later. In other words, the balance of supply and demand controls the rate of return. Right now there is a large supply of financial capital, and not enough demand. The more that people like Jen want to buy the same few real assets, the more expensive they become, and so returns on capital drop.

Until recently, Jen was on the other side of this market too, through her mortgage. When Jen took out that mortgage, her bank owned a piece of paper saying that Jen would pay the money back, with interest, or else forfeit her house. Jen's house is a real asset that provides her with a place to live in the future, and saves her from paying rent. Jen's steady job is also one of her assets. When Jen promised to make mortgage payments, she effectively sold part of her future-earnings asset to her bank, in order to pay for a second big asset, her house.

Jen was paying only 3% in interest, which is only a 1% real return on capital when adjusted for inflation. Lenders are willing to settle for such a low return because Jen, with her steady job and her excellent credit history, is likely to pay the money back. Even if Jen can't or won't pay, there is a backup option: foreclosing on Jen's house and selling it to get money back that way. On top of that, there are government agencies who help guarantee Jen's mortgage. In today's market, investors will accept extremely low returns on such safe investments. Indeed, even on riskier investments, they accept returns that are not much higher.

When returns on capital fall low enough, we expect new borrowers to appear. Maybe a chain of stores has a new model that was successful in their home town, and now they want to expand to new locations. Setting up a new branch costs a lot of money, and the chain may not have enough cash sitting in its corporate bank account. Instead, it could borrow the money for a new building now, and make a profit from the new store later. Sales in that new store need to be big enough to cover not just the running costs, but also the interest and principal payments on the loan. Otherwise it doesn't make sense to open the new store. A plan that didn't make sense last year might, if interest rates have fallen lower, make sense today.

The same logic applies to a manufacturer buying more modern, efficient equipment, to a family building a new house to live in, or to a developer building a new house that he thinks he can sell to a family. All of these are capital investments. Low returns on capital for lenders mean great deals for any borrower who can come up with a good idea for turning money now into something that will pay off later. While most of what goes on in capital markets is the buying and selling of existing assets in the form of bonds and stocks, occasionally new assets are created. Low interest rates in well-functioning capital markets make the creation of new assets more attractive.

Here is how the conventional economic reasoning goes. Returns on capital won't keep dropping lower and lower forever. At some point, now that borrowing money is so cheap, new borrowers will appear. This creates new return-generating assets, increasing demand for financial capital and bringing it back into balance with supply. These borrowers have plans that only work if they can get financial capital cheaply enough.

But how cheap does financial capital need to be before enough new people venture into the market, borrowing the money in order to spend it on real capital assets that create something of value for the future? What if the borrower paid the inflation rate, and nothing more? Would Jen still lend her money on those terms, or would she keep her money instead? Well, this borrower would at least keep Jen's money safe from inflation; the value of her savings will still be there for her to spend during retirement. Jen doesn't want the money now, she wants it when she retires, so she would still lend the money if this was the highest return she could find for the amount of risk. She doesn't like getting such a low return, but she doesn't have much choice.

Even though inflation is low today, some interest rates are even lower. Economists call this a negative real return. In real, inflation-adjusted terms, lenders are actually paying borrowers to keep their money safe. If, indeed, it is safe. For example, short-term US Treasury bonds now pay a lower interest rate than the current inflation rate. As we saw in Chapter 6, from late 2011 to mid-2013, 10-year inflation-protected TIPS were guaranteed to pay below inflation. Despite the huge budget problems of the US government, and a political system that seems too gridlocked to solve them, some savers were nevertheless willing to pay the US government to keep their money "safe". Other savers may prefer to keep their money in cash, foregoing the low bond interest rates currently on offer. These savers may hope that interest rates will rise; by holding on to cash, they will be ready to buy bonds on more favorable terms then. In the meantime, these savers pay for this hope, as inflation slowly erodes the value of their cash.

If there is no inflation, then there is nothing to lose by holding on to cash. Jen could either keep her money in government-insured bank accounts paying little or no interest, or, if she is really paranoid, she could withdraw her savings in cash, and put the stacks of $100 bills in a secure vault. With such low real interest rates, why risk lending it to somebody who might not pay it back?

A still more extreme reason to hoard cash is the possibility of deflation, when things get cheaper every year. This happened in America during the Great Depression, and more recently in Japan. When prices keep dropping, it makes sense to wait as long as possible before buying something, making hoarding cash a sensible thing for individuals to do.

But hoarded cash is bad for economies; we need to save wealth, not just to save money, as we will discuss in much more detail next chapter.

Individuals may benefit from hoarding cash, but society only benefits if savings get directed towards wealth-creating investment.

So what has gone wrong? Why is the capital market so far outside its "normal" balance, even to the point where some people withdraw from the market and hoard cash or cash-like deposits instead? The price of capital (i.e., the interest or other return that must be paid later in exchange for the money needed to create new capital now) is incredibly low. For safe investments, it may be barely above zero, sometimes even negative in inflation-adjusted terms. The price of capital, like other prices, is set by the balance between supply and demand. Even at such a low price, there is not enough demand. In the absence of demand for it, some savings are hoarded as cash, rather than spent on real investment.

When people start hoarding cash because of near-zero nominal interest rates and/or deflation, economists call this a "liquidity trap". The price of capital is supposed to keep dropping until enough new borrowers appear, borrowers who have ideas about how to invest the money in a way that is only worthwhile at low enough interest rates. But nominal interest rates will never drop below zero, because a sensible saver will simply hoard banknotes rather than agree to that.[13]

One "solution" to the cash hoarding problem is higher inflation. Then nominal interest rates can be above zero, attracting savings away from cash and towards investment, while real interest rates can go as low as they need to in order to attract new borrowers. This makes it possible to find a balance between supply and demand. Real interest rates may need to fall

---

13   An exception to this occurs when demand deposits are more convenient than cash, and depositors are willing to pay a fee for this convenience. This exception is less relevant to long-term savings instruments.

all the way into negative territory before enough new borrowers appear. With negative real interest rates, a chain of stores can open a new branch even if the deal is a net loss. As an investor, Jen would be willing to buy into that loss. Jen won't be able to work forever, so she needs to preserve some of the current purchasing power of her wages for the future. She would prefer to have a net gain of purchasing power through her thrift, but failing that, she will settle for the smallest possible loss. In other words, Jen will take the best return she can get for her retirement, even if that means accepting 1% interest in a time of 3% inflation, and watching the value of her money erode away.

Liquidity traps are usually discussed in the context of Keynesian business cycles of boom and bust. Negative real interest rates obviously go against the idea of ever-increasing wealth in a capitalist economy. If real interest rates are negative in the long term, then the capitalist model is broken. Few people are so gloomy, so liquidity traps are usually seen as a short-term problem, in particular as an obstacle to getting the economy out of a deep recession. Governments try to lower interest rates during a recession to get the economy going, and they raise interest rates during a boom, to cool things off. In a liquidity trap, they can't lower interest rates any further. Liquidity traps can be used to argue in favor of inflation, or to argue for stimulating the economy in a different way, through direct government spending rather than via changes in the interest rate.

In this book, we will analyze our current liquidity trap in a different way, as a structural issue rather than as a temporary matter of the business cycle. This means looking into the forces that determine long-term supply and demand. Why is there so much supply of financial capital willing to settle for very low returns? And why is there so little demand for financial capital even at low interest rates? Too little demand means that there are too few good ideas around about how to forgo something of value today in order to get back something of even more value in the future. In much of the rest of this book, we'll talk about where some of the best opportunities are today, and why the savings of people like Jen are not reaching them. First, let's consider the issue of supply.

Too much supply means that too many people are desperate to forgo something of value today in order get back something in the future. For the market to do a good job matching supply with demand, people should buy more of something when it is cheap, and less when it is expensive. Negative real returns mean that saving for the future is expensive; this should make Jen less inclined to save. Logically, the only alternative to saving is to spend the money now on something she can enjoy immediately. But Jen wants the money in her retirement, not now, despite the fact that the money will buy less later. Indeed, low returns make Jen more concerned about her retirement, and so more motivated to save. Instead of saving less because the expensiveness of saving makes it unattractive, Jen wants to save more to compensate for how little each dollar of savings will return. Jen wants to maintain the same quality of living in retirement as in the present. She prefers the option of cutting back modestly throughout her life to the option of living it up now and then having to downgrade her lifestyle later. So poor returns encourage Jen to cut back her spending now, lowering her current standard of living to match what she might achieve in her retirement. Jen's reasoning means that as the price of real assets goes up, demand from Jen goes up. This is the opposite of what is "supposed" to happen in a normal market that balances supply and demand.

Could part of the reasons for today's low returns be that there is too much demand from people like Jen who are desperate to save money for their retirement? Perhaps. People born between 1946 and 1964 are classed as "baby boomers". During those post-war years, there were a lot of babies born. Later, there were fewer babies. One important economic number is the "dependency ratio". This means how many people are too old or too young to work, relative to the number of people of working age. People of working age need to support all the dependents. The boom of babies in the post-war years had a big effect on the dependency ratio. When the baby boomers were children, somebody, mostly their parents and schoolteachers, needed to look after them. Now that they are adults, they are working, paying taxes, and looking after others. When they retire, which is just beginning to happen, somebody will have to look after them. Looking after a frail old person with a lot of health problems can be even more expensive than looking after a baby. Looking after so many baby boomers will be a big challenge, and raises questions about who will pay.

Some baby boomers hope that the US government's Social Security and Medicare programs will support their retirement. After the baby boomers retire, payments into these programs will be much smaller than payments coming out of them. Social Security has been preparing for this by running a surplus and saving this money in a Trust Fund. The Trust Fund took the money and invested it somewhere safe. One of the safest investments around is US government bonds. And so the Social Security Trust Fund (i.e. the government) has been lending these savings to the rest of the government. In other words, the government has written itself a big IOU.

Cutting through the weirdness of the government lending money to itself, what really matters is that Social Security is a tax on current workers and a payment to current retirees. In the past, Social Security has collected more in payroll taxes than it has paid out to retirees, and so the difference has been available for general government spending. This can be a good thing, especially if the government uses this money to invest in the future, as we will discuss in Chapter 13. As the baby boomers retire, fewer taxes come in and more distributions are paid out, reversing the flow of cash. At first this transfer will occur automatically, as the government continues to pay principal and interest on Treasury bonds as part of its normal budget. These payments will transfer money to cancel out the IOUs held by the Social Security program. Taxes may need to rise in order for the government to afford these payments, but this would be true no matter who owned those government bonds.

At some point, perhaps around 2033, Social Security will own no more IOUs and will "go broke", meaning that incoming cash will only pay for about three-quarters of promised benefits. But this precise date won't necessarily matter in practice. The missing quarter of Social Security distributions could then be paid out of general taxation money, rather than out of the special Social Security payroll tax. It doesn't really matter whether these general taxes are used to pay back the IOUs of government bonds, or whether they are transferred more directly to retirees. One branch or another of the government has promised to pay money to retirees, and the US government will either make good on this promise or it won't. Taxes will need to go up in order for the government to keep making payments to retirees, whether those taxes are Social Security payroll taxes or whether they are regular income taxes. Tomorrow's workers may or may not rebel, and vote to cut the baby boomers' Social Security and Medicare payments, rather than see one or other of their taxes go up sharply. In the meantime, the Social Security program has been buying a lot of Treasury bonds, and so contributing to the demand for financial assets, regardless of their high price and low returns.

Jen was born in 1966, so she is a little younger than the baby boomers. When she retires in 2031 at the age of 65, the boomers will be between 67 and 85 years old. Most baby boomers will still be alive, but almost none of them will still be working. Many of them will be sick in their old age and costing Medicare a lot of money. With so many people receiving benefits, it seems inevitable that the size of Social Security and Medicare payments will be cut back by then.

Jen doesn't want to count on Social Security and Medicare. Social Security payments aren't large today, even before the cuts that are bound to come. Plenty of baby boomers agree with Jen; they don't expect government programs to pay enough to fund their retirements, and have saved money themselves. Some of them saved throughout most of their working lives, while others started seriously saving towards the end. Or, like Jen, some baby boomers inherited money from their thrifty parents, and then put that money aside rather than spending it. The baby boomers' money is mostly invested in their houses, in the stock market, and in bonds.

If you read the news, you will see a lot of doom and gloom that people haven't saved enough. Some baby boomers calculated that they were going to be fine with what they had, but were caught out when the stock market crashed, or when the price of their home, which they had intended to sell, collapsed. Others didn't even like to think about their retirement while they struggled to pay their bills month to month. Some, like Jen, have an employer-provided defined contributions plan, but their contributions to that don't add up to nearly enough. But even if the baby boomers haven't saved enough money to pay for their retirements, they have saved some. The money they did save has contributed to the supply of financial capital and the demand for assets.

On top of Social Security and their private savings, some baby boomers are also entitled to a defined benefit pension from their employer. These employers include companies as well as state and local governments. Just like the government runs the Social Security program, these employers run pension plans, deducting money from paychecks today, and using the money to buy assets (although generally not buying their own corporate bonds, and hence an IOU from themselves!). These defined benefit pension plans intend to sell those assets later to pay pensions. But most of these employers haven't set aside nearly enough money either. In part, this is because they were too optimistic, assuming that high historical stock market returns would be repeated, and that the money in the pension funds would grow rapidly if they used it to buy stocks. They weren't and didn't. If and when the stock market falls from its current high valuation, things will look even worse for corporate and state and government pension plans.

When (and it seems to be a case of when, not if) these pension plans fail, it can send the employer bankrupt, whether the employer is a large company, or the city of Detroit. When this happens, the employees of some companies will be covered by a government pension insurance program. This program, the Pension Benefit Guaranty Corporation, also has most of its money invested in stocks and bonds. If financial assets decline in value, this will not only cripple many pension funds, but their insurer will also be crippled at the same time. Already in 2014, the Pension Benefit Guaranty Corporation had only $90 billion in assets to cover $152 billion in liabilities.[14]

Neither individuals nor institutions have put aside enough money. But they did put aside some. And even these inadequate savings by and on behalf of the baby boomers may be enough to drive up the prices of stocks and bonds.

Aging baby boomers may not be the only reason why there is such a large supply of financial capital today. China sells more to other countries than it buys from them. If China let its currency become more valuable, this imbalance might end. But in the meantime, China makes a lot of money selling things overseas, and spends relatively little of that money buying things in exchange. The difference between the two has been accumulating in massive foreign currency reserves of around $3.7 trillion.[15] The large supply of capital coming from China helps keep American interest rates low. China has been letting Americans have cheap goods today, but hopes to get something back later, with a small amount of interest thrown in.

The rapidly increasing wealth of the 0.1% richest members of society might also contribute to the oversupply of capital. Consider Frank, CEO of a large company and a typical example of a very rich person in America today. He works long hours, and is exhausted at the end of the day. He is rich enough to buy whatever he wants. But thinking of things he wants, shopping for them, and enjoying them, all take time. And time is one thing Frank doesn't have a lot of. Maybe his wife doesn't work, and they

---

14   Pension Benefit Guaranty Corporation, Annual Report, Fiscal Year 2014 www.pbgc.gov/documents/2014-annual-report.pdf
15   http://www.tradingeconomics.com/china/foreign-exchange-reserves accessed August 29, 2015

have a division of labor; he earns the money, and she figures out how to spend it. But with a massive amount of money, spending it on the "right" scarce goods, ones that impress their friends, can be hard work. Very rich people today literally have more money than they know how to put to real use, and so they need to get creative in their positional competitions over cars, yachts, or private jets, as we discussed in Chapter 8. Give money to a poor person, and they have no trouble thinking of things they need or want, and then finding the time to go shopping. Poor people tend to have much more urgent needs. Of course rich people spend much more money in dollar terms than poor people do, but it amounts to a smaller fraction of their total income. The rest tends to be saved. In fact, a significant portion of Frank's huge income comes in the form of a generous pension plan, far more generous than the pension plan that his company offers to ordinary workers. This capital, earned and saved by the rich, is chasing the same investment opportunities as the Chinese government and the retirement savings of the baby boomers, their pension providers and the insurers of their pension providers.

Finally, if all these savings in the system weren't already enough to add up to an oversupply and so reduce the rate of return on capital, government policy in recent years has deliberately sought to keep interest rates at extraordinary low levels. It has done this in part through the Federal Reserve Bank's policy of "quantitative easing". This means printing money and using it to buy bonds, expanding demand for financial assets in order to deliberatively drive interest rates down. This is an attempt to stimulate the economy during a recession, when not enough money is being spent. The government wants anybody with a good idea for spending money to be able to get that money cheaply. Cheap money is supposed to stimulate more spending and create jobs at a time of high unemployment and low inflation. Interest rates would have been low anyway, given retirement savings, Asian savings, and increasing inequality. Government policy has driven them even lower.

The oversupply of financial capital is almost a perfect storm. It would be even worse if everybody saved "enough" money for their retirement. We don't need more savings: we need more productive places to invest all the money that is already available. Lots of savings is a great thing when there are lots of good places to invest it. We have lots of savings, but where should they go? In the rest of this book, we will discuss where money could be spent today so that it delivers something at least as valuable in the future.

# CHAPTER 11

# THE DIFFERENCE BETWEEN MONEY AND WEALTH

Baby boomers have been saving money for their retirement. Companies and governments have also been saving money for the baby boomers' retirement, via their pension plans. China has been saving money and lending it to America. And as societies become less equal, more money ends up in the hands of the rich, who are more likely to save it than are the poor. Add all of this up, and a lot of money is being saved.

But if all that people are saving is "money", then we have a problem. Money means pieces of paper, or scores kept in a computer.[16] You can't

---

16   Economists use the words "money" and "money supply" to count cash and bank deposits and a few other types of assets that can instantly be used to buy things, and which are easy to measure. They do not include other liquid but somewhat less stably valued assets like stocks and bonds that people could sell quickly for money, and which they could then use to buy things. They certainly don't include less liquid assets such as what people believe they could sell their house for. The use of the word "money" by economists doesn't entirely agree with what ordinary people mean when they talk about how rich they are or how much money they have. In this book, I sometimes use the word "money" to mean what economists call "financial capital" or "financial assets". I think this is closer to how non-economists use the word "money". In other words, I often use the word money to describe the amount that people believe, perhaps mistakenly but based on current markets, that they could redeem their (potentially real) assets for. As we will see, if they all try to redeem their assets at the same time, their assets will be worth less.

eat money. If what we needed was more money, the government could simply print it (and indeed the US government has been printing more money, in a quantitative easing program designed to keep interest rates extraordinarily low). Money is valuable because you can buy things with it. You can spend money buying useful things like food and shelter, or buying desirable things like a luxury holiday. Useful and desirable things are wealth, whether or not you used money to buy them.

Saving money is not enough; we have to do something with that saved money to get us ready for the baby boomers' retirement. We don't just need to save money, we need to create and save wealth through investing in the future. Later in this book, we will talk about specific activities that might help us do that. First, this chapter discusses what money, wealth, saving and investment mean in general terms.

Saving means that Jen could spend her entire paycheck buying goods and services to consume today, but she decides not to. Jen makes this present-day sacrifice because she is afraid of poverty in her retirement. To be useful not just to Jen as an individual but also to society, this sacrifice needs to be converted into a meaningful investment that will create future wealth.

Money is just a tool that makes spending more convenient. To invest means to spend money, not to squirrel it away. Money can either be spent on pleasures to be enjoyed today, or it can be spent creating something worthwhile to be enjoyed in the future. If we don't spend the money at all, but simply "save" it in a bank vault, then we might as well simply burn the money today, and then print it again in the future.

At any point in time, society has a certain "productive capacity", or ability to get stuff done. How people choose to spend their money determines, via markets, how that productive capacity gets directed, and so what gets done. People have three choices as to what to do with their money. They can spend it on something to be consumed immediately. They can spend it creating something that will generate wealth in the future. Or they can exchange the immediate purchasing power represented by that money for some form of written promise entitling them to future wealth. Written promises can take many forms, including a stock certificate, a bond, a promise from a bank to return the money, or a promise from the government that the cash under their mattress can be used to buy things in the future. The person who buys a written promise is counting on the seller to make sure that the purchasing power they are giving up today is spent to create future wealth.

As Keynes pointed out, *"no one can save without acquiring an asset, whether it be cash or a debt or capital-goods"*.[17] Every time Jen uses her saved dollars to buy stocks, there is somebody else out there selling those stocks in exchange for dollars. Jen the saver is forgoing consumption today in order to buy the stock, while that other person may be "dis-saving" by selling the stock for cash to pay for everyday consumption. If the seller is simply rebalancing their portfolio, and uses the cash to buy a different stock instead, then that second stock also has a seller. Each transaction in the chain passes the money along until eventually someone, somewhere, either spends the money creating new wealth that did not exist before (i.e. invests in the creation of physical capital), or spends it on current consumption.[18]

---

17    John Maynard Keynes (1936), The General Theory of Employment, Interest and Money, p.81.
18    The cash may also be physically destroyed by a central bank, in which case the chain of transactions ends, and dis-saving occurs without spending on current consumption. Similarly, printing money is also an act with no transaction partner. But the creation or destruction of cash makes up only a tiny proportion of net saving.

If you add up all the savings in the world, and subtract the amount of dis-saving, the difference must come out exactly equal to the total amount of true investment. This isn't because Jen's decision to save rather than consume causes someone, somewhere, to decide to invest. Jen doesn't have that kind of magical power. Each person and institution decides how to spend their money, whether on consumption or on investment. If they do not spend all their money, they save. If they consume more than they have, they dis-save.

The reason that net savings and investments balance out is because all asset transactions have two parties, where each saver/buyer must be paired with either a dis-saver or an investor. Without two parties, the transaction can't take place. Jen's decision not to consume makes her eager to buy bonds or stocks or whatever other asset she can find, even at high prices representing low returns. The person who sells Jen an asset may use the money on consumption, adding to dis-saving rather than investment. Jen can't control that.

To see more clearly how things balance out, let's imagine the most extreme case possible, where many people like Jen are desperate to save, but nobody knows how to invest, and so no new assets come forth. The price of each existing asset will rise in a bidding war until some owners get greedy, and sell in order to increase their consumption. Feeling rich, they cash out part of their now large paper wealth, and live it up for a while. For example, during the housing bubble, many homeowners took advantage of high house prices, used their house as an ATM to refinance, and then used the money to consume more. This is a form of dis-saving that they would not have been able to do had house prices been lower. We condemn these dis-savers as morally irresponsible, but somebody had to do it. If they didn't do it when their house was valued at $1 million, somebody else would have done it when house prices reached $2 million.

For every lender, there is a borrower. The lender is purchasing an asset, namely the borrower's promise to make a steady stream of payments in the future. Sometimes the borrower uses the money to buy another asset, for example using a mortgage loan to buy a house to live in. Now there are two transactions: the mortgage loan, and the sale of the house. The lender's saved money now goes not to the borrower, but to the man who sold the borrower a house. Does that man spend the money, or does he use it to buy yet another existing asset? One way or another, either the borrower or some other recipient of the money many steps down the line will use the cash either to invest (e.g., by building a new house), or to consume. If people do not come up with enough good investments at the current interest rate, for example if there is a glut of housing and it is much cheaper to buy an existing house than it is to build a new one, then more saving and lending by some people will fuel borrowing and consumption by others. When there isn't enough investment, saving will be matched by dis-saving. Each saver acquires an asset whose value can be redeemed in the future, and the seller of that asset acquires and uses the current-day purchasing power that the saver chose not to use.

A still darker scenario described by Keynes occurs when saving, i.e., unwillingness to consume, is eventually matched down the line not by greedy dis-saving following windfall asset prices, but by involuntary investment, when a company makes things it cannot sell and ends up stockpiling inventory. This company will then cut output and employment. Whoever loses their job as a result will then stop saving and start dis-saving. In this dark scenario, savings and investment stay in balance in the short term through inventory build-up, and in the long term through a shrinking economy that makes people less eager to save.

If we want to build an economy where there is more investment in the future, the best way to do that is simply to invest more, not to save more and hope that investment will follow. It's not enough for people to save money for their retirement. Saved money is lent out at interest, directly in the case of a bond, or more implicitly in the case of stock ownership, where the buyer hopes to get their money back with interest in the form of dividends and capital gains. Every saver is in essence a lender, and for every lender, there is also a borrower. The borrower is the one doing the actual investing, by spending the money in such a way as to create wealth. All the advice about how people need to save more is misguided. There are plenty of savings in the system already; our problem today is to find good places to invest all that saved money, whether it is our own saved money or somebody else's. Once we solve the hard problem of finding where the good investments are, we can figure out the easier problem how to direct the saved money to those investments.

Our challenge as a society is to find more good investments to match the already abundant savings in our financial system. How do we exploit the current low interest rates, and spend today's money in such a way as to create future wealth? We can't directly save that much food; it would rot in warehouses. We certainly can't save nursing and medical care. So as a society, we need to invest in things that will make food and medical care easier to provide in the future than they are today.

The first step is to stop thinking about "saving money", and start thinking about ways to spend money to create wealth. In some sense, money is an illusion, with no true value. If I waved a magic wand and doubled everybody's money, nobody would be any wealthier. They would have more money, but the price of everything might also double.

Money is certainly a useful illusion. Without money, we would be reduced to barter. It is not practical to pay the plumber or the doctor with a certain amount of bread or eggs or meat, and the items that you have to offer might not match the items that he would like to receive. It is much more convenient to pay him in "points", known as dollars, that he can exchange for whatever he wants. A modern economy is clearly impossible without money.

What money really does well is set prices. How do we compare the value of a plumber's work to the value of his daughter's college education? With money, doing this is so easy that we don't even have to think about it. We put them on the same points scale, in dollars.

Money can even store value over short periods of time. The plumber's income is spread out over the year, while his daughter's college fees are due at particular times. Money can seamlessly fill the gap between the two. In the short term, this works well. One month, Jen might spend less money than she earns, and the extra money accumulates in her bank account. The next month, she splurges on a nice holiday, and her bank balance dips back down. The points system can handle this, helping things average out.

But the longer the delay between earning money and spending, the more problematic money becomes as a store of value. The problem could become catastrophic with the retirement of the baby boomers. The baby boomers are all saving at the same time, and later, they will all want to spend at the same time. This affects prices in the stock market, in the housing market, and in markets for all kinds of assets in which baby boomers think they have "invested" their money. Right now, lots of baby boomers, and the pension funds that are supposed to support them, are making a last-ditch attempt to save. This is increasing demand for financial assets such as stocks, and driving their prices up. When the baby boomers need to pay nursing home fees later, they will sell those assets. When many of them do this at the same time, it will steadily, over the course of several retirement decades, drive the price of assets down.

The baby boomers saved money. But they didn't save food, and they didn't save medical and nursing care. They saved money, and handed it over to the stock market, and asked the companies there to spend more money investing in the future. But do the baby boomer savings, when they are spent buying stocks, cause companies to invest more in the future?

When a privately owned business wants to grow fast, it might decide to "go public" and list itself on the stock exchange. By selling shares, the company raises capital, money that the business can spend trying to grow. This is an example of genuine investment; a company has an idea for creating value in the future, and by selling stock on the open market, it takes people's money today and spends the money to build that future.

But when Jen buys a stock that is already being traded on the market, the company doesn't get Jen's money. Jen's money goes to whoever owned the stock before. Money changes hands, and stock ownership changes hands, but no genuine investment takes place.

Luckily, there are also some more indirect ways in which Jen's stock purchase helps put capital into the company's hands, capital that the company may put to good use. Jen's desire to purchase that stock goes a small way to driving up its price. Stocks are riskier than bonds, so the return on a company's stock should be higher than the return on the same company's bonds. The return on bonds can be calculated easily, and the return on stock can also be estimated from its price-earnings ratio and other facts about the company. As the stock price goes up, some canny financiers may notice that there is no longer a big enough incentive to justify owning risky stock rather than safer bonds. So they will sell the company's stock, and buy the company's bonds instead. Now the company's bond price goes up, as well as its stock price. This means that the company can borrow money more cheaply than it could before, by issuing new bonds that pay a lower rate of interest. The company may also own some of its own shares; in this case raising money by selling those shares is also more inviting at a higher stock price.

So when Jen buys stock on the open market, she helps that company borrow at a lower interest rate. Last chapter, we saw that some investments depend on the interest rate. Some investments are expected to pay for themselves so many times over that they should happen at almost any interest rate. Other investments might be net losses, unable to generate enough wealth to pay for the interest on the loan. Generally speaking, people will invest in the former, and not in that latter. But some investments are right at the margin. A small difference in the interest rate can be enough to make or break the business plan. Jen's purchase allows companies to borrow more cheaply, which helps make those marginal investments happen.

The problem is that a company may not have marginal investment ideas that need the extra money. Many companies today are already sitting on huge sums of cash, profits from their sales, money that they don't know what to do with. Under those circumstances, raising stock prices does not cause real investment to take place. So when baby boomers try to "invest" their savings in the stock market, no money is spent (i.e. truly invested) to create wealth as a consequence. The baby boomers are simply buying existing stocks. This is a finite class of asset whose price is set by supply and demand. Increased demand from baby boomers creates a steady increase in stock prices over decades, a slow-motion boom that will turn to slow-motion bust when they all retire and sell.

This isn't just true for the stock market. It is true any time that many people and their money chase a finite class of assets. There is only so much land in a given city block, or city, or country. Land is something of genuine value. But more people wanting to buy land doesn't normally lead to the creation of more land, except in the extreme case where land is reclaimed from the sea. Instead, it pushes the price of land up, without changing its value to those who use it.

Buying gold is not much better. Yes, more gold can be mined from the ground to meet the demand, but this is like printing more money. The main effect of a fashion for "investing" in gold is to push the price of gold up, without the glittering, beautiful quality of gold becoming any more intrinsically valuable.

The baby boomers all want to buy a financial asset with their last few years of paychecks. Later, they want to exchange this financial asset for the things they need after they retire. All of these financial assets will become more expensive now when baby boomers try to buy them, and less expensive later when the baby boomers sell them. When stock prices rise unreasonably high, savvy investors flee to bonds or commodities. But then those prices also rise, and the same problem appears for all classes of financial assets. When all transactions simply exchange existing assets for money, without prompting real investment, then all the baby boomers are doing is saving "money". And they won't be able to eat money.

This spells bad news for Jen. She is a bit younger than the baby boomers. They will all retire before her, dragging asset prices down. By the time Jen needs to sell her assets to pay for her own retirement, prices will have hit rock bottom. Maybe things are even worse than her worst calculation. Maybe a semi-comfortable retirement is not such a sure thing after all.

All this talk of supply and demand for capital, and market prices for assets, can be quite confusing. It's clear that the demographics of the baby boomers cause asset prices to rise and then fall, in comparison to some other imaginary universe with steadier birth rates. But economists do not agree on how large this effect will be. Maybe it's just a small blip on top of everything else that happens in markets. Inheritances might help smooth out demographic blips. Some people even argue that efficient markets are already taking these long-term factors into account.

Which view of stock prices is correct? The one that says that Jen should save her money, buy financial assets such as stocks, and trust the capital markets to give her money back later when she needs it? Or the one that says that the total price of all financial assets such as stocks is driven by supply and demand, and hence by the demographics of the baby boomers?

It's possible for both views to be right. This would mean that when Jen saves money by deciding not to buy a new car, her sacrifice leads, through efficient capital markets, to the creation of something valuable somewhere else. Something that will be worth two new cars, perhaps, after a number of years. This is what capital markets are supposed to do. They are supposed to take Jen's financial capital, and direct it to somebody who can spend it to create something valuable for the future. Money may change hands many times in complex transactions, but the end result is to direct savings towards investment spending.

We would all love this happy view to be true, with capital markets efficiently directing Jen's savings to productive investments. But does the world show signs that this is true? If it were true, we should see businesses full of great expansion ideas, eagerly seeking to borrow the capital to make them a reality, if only that capital were offered to them at a slightly lower interest rate. Unfortunately, instead we see businesses sitting on piles of cash that they don't know how to spend. Meantime, savers choose between near-zero interest rates on safe investments, and low interest rates on risky ones. The capital markets are broken. Even at rock-bottom interest rates, there are too few people who want to take Jen's capital and spend it in a productive way.

To see economic fundamentals more clearly, imagine you have a pair of magic glasses. Wearing these glasses, you can no longer see money or prices. After all, money is just a convenient illusion, a points system for making transactions more convenient. Your new glasses filter out the illusion, allowing you to see the true wealth of society more clearly. When you wear these glasses, you can no longer see who owns what. But you can still see, indeed more clearly than before, what there is to be owned. You see the total size of the pie, without seeing how it is divided up. And how does that wealth look? Is society's ability to provide things of real value, things that the baby boomers will need, growing fast enough to cope with the massive changes in the dependency ratio?

Try to imagine wearing these glasses. Think about the spectacular transformation of our society in the last hundred years or so that we talked about in Chapter 7. Is wealth really still growing as miraculously fast as that? When I try to free myself of the illusion of dollar signs, ignoring prices for houses and stocks and pension funds, I cannot see that the physical basis of society is transforming itself in a way that prepares us for the dramatic change in dependency ratio that is coming.

With this insight from the magic glasses, Jen is now ready to expand on her guiding principle, "don't invest in anything you don't understand". The key question here is what it means to "understand" something. Jen is now less driven to understand all the financial details of individual companies on the stock market. Instead, she wants to understand, in a more general way, how spending money today will translate into a future stream of revenue. She wants to understand the nature of that future revenue stream, not only in cash, but also in terms of something of real value, something she can still see when she puts on these glasses. For example, money spent building a house gives somebody a place to live. Money spent putting in insulation means not having to spend as much on heating and cooling later. Only things that generate value in the future can truly be seen as "wealth". If Jen's investments pass the "glasses test", this means that they don't merely shift a stream of revenue from somebody else to her. Yes, she wants to be rich, but she also wants to live in a rich society. Her investments should create a stream of benefits that would not otherwise exist.

If Jen keeps her money in cash or something similar, rather than spending it on something tangible like a house, then her money is not a true store of the kind of value that we can see when we wear the magic glasses. Money is better understood as a promise, from society as a whole, that you will be given something in the future, in exchange for your work or sacrifice today. Saving money means loaning your current efforts and income to society. You expect that loan to be paid back. Over the short term, these loans are so reliable that we forget their nature. Money works so well as a store of value over weeks or months that we forget its true nature, and we expect it to work just as well over years or decades. It doesn't.

If Jen wants to store value for her retirement, she can't just hand money over to a mutual fund and ask its managers to harness "the market" to store it for her. She will have to take more responsibility herself. For every lender, there is a borrower. Who will Jen lend her money to? Who will make best use of it, and then pay it back?

In the case of a stock market index fund, the identity of "the borrower" is extraordinarily diffuse. Jen therefore cannot track how her act of buying a stock market index fund will have an impact on the creation of wealth by companies. Without knowing the use to which her money will be put, Jen can't be convinced that placing her money in the stock market will lead to the kind of societal wealth that Jen can still see when she wears her magic glasses.

In case that weren't reason enough to avoid stocks, Jen also believes that stocks offer a bad deal for her personally. Now that Jen has a better feel for valuing the stock market as a whole, she believes that stock prices are too high overall. Stock prices are high relative to earnings, earnings are high relative to GDP, and future GDP growth doesn't look good. If Jen's aim is to protect herself against inflation, she is better off settling for the low returns offered by Treasury Inflation-Protected Bonds (TIPS).

Jen won't invest in stocks anymore, neither individually nor via index funds. She wants to sell, but first she wants to decide what to do with the money instead. Her new choice needs to pass the "glasses test".

After ruling out stocks, what seems to be left is bonds, including but not limited to, TIPS. From a financial perspective, bonds are certainly easier to understand than stocks. When she buys stocks, Jen is implicitly making a very precise valuation of the total worth of a complicated company. For bonds, she doesn't need to evaluate every aspect of the company, she just needs to make a good guess about how likely it is that the company will still be around after a certain number of years, doing well enough to pay its debts rather than declare bankruptcy.

Jen would also like to lend her money directly to companies that pass the glasses test, companies that she believes will put the money to good use creating wealth. Ideally, she would like to do this without going through middlemen and their fees. The best way to avoid middlemen and their fees is to buy bonds when they are issued by companies, and then to hold on to the bonds for their entire term, until the company pays back the money in full. As a long-term investor, Jen is happy to hold on to bonds for decades. She won't retire soon, and so there is no reason to get her money back early by selling before maturity. This strategy would allow her to avoid a lot of fees. What is more, if Jen buys a newly issued bond, she will know that her money is going directly to a company who actively wanted to raise the money, and so presumably had a plan for making good use of it. This suggests that the bond purchase passes the glasses test.

Jen logs on to her retirement account, and searches for upcoming new issues of corporate investment grade bonds. Her search returns only eight, with estimated yields between 1.25% and 3.75%. Every single one of them is a bank or other financial institution, which seems odd. That wasn't what Jen had in mind. Banks are supposed to be in the business of lending money; why are they borrowing it? Presumably to lend to others ... which means that Jen is back with a middleman.

Through some more online reading, Jen learns that buying primary issues of most corporate bonds is largely an insider's game, closed to small-fry investors like her who don't have friends in the financial industry. Jen could still buy existing bonds on the secondary market. If she does this the day after those new bonds are issued, she will pay implicit fees to the middleman who "flipped" the bond, but she can nevertheless still support the market for new bond issues by companies that have a particular use for the money in mind. But this strategy looks complicated. The internet is full of dire warnings that making individual purchases in the bond market is no easy task for amateurs.

For now, Jen is keen to sell her stock market index fund. At this point, she is convinced that buying stocks fails the glasses test version of "don't invest in anything you don't understand". What is more, from what she does understand at a more individual-based, financial level, stock prices seem unreasonably high, even compared to low interest rates available elsewhere. So Jen sells her stock market index fund, and uses some of the proceeds to buy long-term TIPS. TIPS are her low-risk low-return safety net.

Jen would like to take a little more risk in search of a higher interest on the remainder, but she doesn't know how. For the time being, she parks the rest of her money in several low-fee bond-index-tracking mutual funds and exchange-traded funds. She chooses some short-term ones as an alternative to holding cash, hoping that their value will stay pretty stable or rise slightly until she is ready to sell them in favor of some better opportunity. The others are medium-term, not nearly as long as her TIPS. For the time being, she'll pay the management fees and risk losing money if interest rates go up, driving bond prices down. At least bonds shouldn't lose value quite so dramatically as stocks. One of the main things that could drive interest rates up is inflation. Happily, she is partly hedged against this with her TIPS; beyond that, there is not much else she can do about it. She has to do something with her money, after all. Even cash is a choice, and one that is vulnerable to inflation too.

Meantime, she'll think some more about who she would ideally like to lend to via bonds bought on the secondary market. Or she'll give up, and lock her money away for 5 years with a bank certificate of deposit paying 2% interest. Or maybe, if she thinks hard enough, using the glasses test, Jen can come up with some better way to take her money and turn it into wealth.

# CHAPTER 12

# THE MORAL DIMENSION

If you are lucky in your choices of stocks or bonds or properties, then the things we normally call your "investments" will pay you back with interest. But maybe your gain was somebody else's loss. You bought a stock for less than its "true" value, and then sold it for more than its value. Unfortunately, that means you bought it from somebody who lost money on the deal, and sold it to somebody who also lost money on the deal. Not everybody can make good picks at the same time. These stocks were a good "investment" for you, but that simply transferred to you an advantage that would have in any case gone to somebody. For this reason, as we discussed last chapter, it is a misnomer to talk about Jen "investing" in existing stocks, bonds, or real estate. When she buys one of these existing assets from somebody else, all that happens is that various pieces of paper change hands. Depending on what happens to asset prices next, one person may win on the deal and the other lose.

If Jen picks good things to buy with her savings, then Jen's present sacrifice helps Jen's future retirement, but because it is at somebody else's expense, it does no good for society as a whole. So where did the improvements we see in society come from? Capital owners like Jen and workers without savings are both spectacularly wealthier now than they were 200 years ago. But who is responsible for this dramatic improvement in the material conditions of our lives? Was it savers like Jen, buying stocks and bonds?

At first, the historical promise of compound interest to create wealth seems nothing short of miraculous. If your grandfather had the equivalent of just $10,000 in today's dollars, and had invested it 80 years ago at a real interest rate of 5%, never spending any of it, then you would have $500,000 today. But who did he lend money to? Did the borrowers spend the money on immediate consumption, dis-saving at first when they received the money, and saving later to pay your grandfather back with interest? Or did the borrowers invest in real assets that made society wealthier? If so, who deserved the most benefit from that wealth and who received it: the borrowers or your grandfather?

One way or another, society has become wealthier over the last 80 years, and perhaps your grandfather's savings contributed to that. But if everybody had done the same thing as your grandfather, saving money and lending it out at interest, who would have borrowed it? For every lender, there must be a borrower. It is the borrower, and not your grandfather, who did the investment spending to create more wealth. Your grandfather simply lent the money.

If your grandfather had frittered away the money on daily pleasures instead, would the same wealth still have been created, but perhaps belong to somebody else? Would the same borrower simply have found a different lender to fund his investments, perhaps at a slightly higher interest rate? In other words, did your grandfather's savings cause the creation of wealth, or did he in his foresight succeed in extracting a share of that wealth from others?

The way Jen saves is quite common today. A portion of each paycheck is diverted into her retirement account, with dividends reinvested and the money locked away until she retires. After buying a house, Jen made regular mortgage payments, including some extra ones to pay down the principal faster; the regular principal payments are common forms of saving, and plenty of people make extra prepayments too. Perhaps Jen saves a little more than the average for her generation, or for the baby boomers, although she, unlike some, does not have a defined benefit pension, and so no employer is saving on her behalf.

But if Jen and others are doing so much saving, who is doing the borrowing? Is Jen's saving balanced out by spending on investment? Or is Jen simply in an arms race to save more than the next retiree, bidding up asset prices? Real wealth is the pie; it means something in absolute terms. Saved money is a points system for buying a share of the pie. The more money you save, the bigger a share you can afford to buy. There is no set price for shares of this pie. It's a bidding war, an arms race to save and buy more than others. Unless this arms race causes extra investment and so creates a bigger pie, then the comfortable retirements of the winners come at the expense of the losers.

The arms race aspect of saving worries Jen. She may not get as high a return on her capital as past generations did, and so her retirement may end up less comfortable than she first thought. But after playing with numbers for a while, she now believes that she will get by OK, especially if she is willing to cut back a little. At least, so long as the future doesn't include catastrophic environmental or economic collapse, in which case all bets are off.

From Jen's position of relative comfort, her future is not just about survival and making ends meet. This raises meaning-of-life questions. How should Jen live? What is important? What is Jen's life all about, what is its purpose? We mostly think about these questions in terms of caring for others. But living a moral life isn't just about direct interactions between people. What Jen does with her money is also part of her life. For example, she might give money to charities, or buy certain products rather than others on ethical grounds. Jen's morals should also help guide what she does with her savings. After all, the money Jen gives to charity or directs to more socially responsible alternative products is peanuts compared to her $700,000 nest egg. There are some mutual funds that advertise themselves as "socially responsible", only buying the stocks of companies that meet certain ethical criteria. But Jen has already decided not to invest in the stock market, on the basis that insofar as she understands it, it seems to be overvalued. What other options are there for investing her money in a socially responsible fashion?

Jen likes her comforts, but she never set out to get rich. And she is uncomfortable with the idea of her retirement coming at somebody else's expense. With some room to maneuver in her financial plan, she is not committed to increasing her personal position in any way she can, no matter what it takes. She would rather be a little poorer, or go through a bit of inconvenience, if that means that her savings create new wealth. A smaller win for Jen perhaps, but also a win for the rest of the world. And perhaps this investing strategy will even make Jen financially better off personally too.

Part of morality is being kind and generous to other humans, as a character virtue. In another view, being kind and generous is a means to the end of benefiting others. As an extension of that, morality includes building an economic system that allows as many people as possible to flourish. History suggests that capitalism is better than other economic systems in creating a prosperous society. The capitalist ideal is that spending money (capital) on the future will create more wealth. As real investments pay out compound interest, society's wealth will go up and up and up, and everybody will be better off in the end. This is the heart of what is good about capitalism, and Jen wants to contribute to its success. Investing her inheritance began as just a financial question about paying for her retirement. It can also be an ideological question. Soldiers have fought in the name of defending capitalism. Each of us with money to spare should fight our own small, internal wars to figure out how best to allocate our capital.

Jen originally abandoned the stock market not for moral reasons, but because she doesn't know how to make money trading stocks. Many of the best brains of her generation went into finance, and have been honing their skills throughout their career; Jen can't compete with them. Every gain they make by clever trading, passing around one kind of piece of paper (money) in exchange for another (a financial asset), is a loss for somebody else trading those assets. Often, it is a loss for an amateur like Jen, who isn't as good at playing this game.

But even if Jen knew how to make a lot of money on the stock market, she wouldn't want to do this at somebody else's expense. Instead, she wants to contribute to a world in which everybody can be a winner. At the heart of morality is the Golden Rule to act as you would have others act. So Jen wants to find an approach to savings and investment that, were it shared by everyone, would make society better off as a whole. This, surely, is the true wonder of capitalism, the ideal worth fighting for. If the stock market is a casino, not everybody can win. Making money by picking the right stocks won't satisfy Jen. She wants to know that her decisions lead to investments. Real investment means spending money in a way that actually creates the sort of value that she can still see when she puts on her magic glasses.

If Jen owns stocks that do well, and she makes money, that doesn't guarantee that the increase in her money reflects an increase in society's wealth. How much money Jen has today tells us what percentage of society's total wealth is hers. Jen wants to increase the size of the future pie, not compete over how much of it she owns. Jen wants to understand her investments, both how they help her, and how, when she puts on her magic glasses, they help society as a whole. What sort of investments will meet this test?

# CHAPTER 13

# INVESTING IN THE FUTURE

Jen wants to invest in the future. So what does the future need? What can Jen do, and how can Jen spend money today, in order to store wealth to provide for tomorrow?

Let's start by taking the idea of "storing" wealth literally. Jen has a wonderful apricot tree in her yard; in a good year, there is no way she can eat all the fruit before they go bad. Not wanting to waste, sell, or give away all the fruit, Jen makes a big batch of preserves and then eats the jars one at a time over the course of the next year. She can't eat all the fruit while it is fresh, but if she doesn't use or store the fruit somehow, it will rot on the ground. Storing food is a way to store wealth. If Jen were concerned about hurricanes, earthquakes, or other disasters, she could also store tinned food and bottled water in case the distribution of food is disrupted in her area. Taking advantage of a windfall crop, or setting aside a reserve for disasters, are two good reasons to store food.

But it makes no sense to buy food now when you are working and have money, and store it for decades in the hope of eating it after you retire and are poorer. The food would go bad in the meantime. You will certainly not come back to your fridge or cupboard to find that the food there has multiplied, and that you now have more than you put in. The value of a good wine may increase when cellared, but this is the exception rather than the rule. It is impossible to stockpile, in physical warehouses, all the goods and services we need to take care of retired baby boomers.

Luckily, capitalism offers some better options for creating wealth. The miracle of capitalism occurs when the value of what you store today is multiplied, and you get back more than you originally put in. There are four ways in which effort today can be converted into new "capital" that will pay dividends long into the future. The first, stockpiling, does pass the magic glasses test, but will not take either Jen or society very far. Try to keep seeing the world through the magic glasses as we look at the next three, looking at how things contribute to society's wealth, without the complications of who owns them and how the money flows.

In the second category, there is physical infrastructure, including buildings, roads, electricity grids, factory machinery etc. It takes a lot of work to build these things, and then they can be used for many decades afterwards. Building them is expensive, and using them is valuable. While a few may be "white elephants", most pass the glasses test.

Third, there are less tangible stores of value. For example, a store is worth more than the building and the shelves and the things for sale on those shelves. A lot of work has gone into discovering what people buy, organizing for those things to be delivered to the store, and hiring people to sell those things at regular, predictable hours. The store is worth more than the sum of its parts. The added value was created by all the work it took to start a successful business.

This sort of added value can be measured for profit-making businesses, whether they are small family firms or large publicly listed companies. Added value also exists, although it is harder to measure, for organizations that cannot easily be owned and sold. These include government bodies and charitable and other not-for-profit non-governmental organizations. The same idea can be extended to include less formal "organizations", such as more diffuse social networks. Knowledge, for example a protocol for the most effective way to accomplish a task, is also an intangible store of value. The work put in to create and fine-tune organizations and knowledge can pay dividends long into the future. All of these pass the glasses test, but we need to beware that when we take off the glasses, what we see is dominated by the for-profit sector.

Finally, there is human capital. Imagine Ted, unemployed and sitting at home playing a computer game, putting all his efforts into getting a better score. He probably isn't creating any human capital while he does this. But what if Ted spends his unlooked-for free time learning a useful skill? Maybe he learns to program that computer, or takes a course to become a technician operating complex medical machinery. If he does this, then his efforts today, and those of his teachers, will pay themselves back for many years into the future. This too passes the glasses test.

With the baby boomer retirements looming, so that far fewer workers will soon work to support far more dependents, we as a society need to do everything we can to store more wealth. To prepare for this, we need to store wealth in one or more of the four ways above: stockpiles, tangible physical infrastructure, intangible improvements, and human capital. If we take a narrower view of just one country, a fifth option is to lend money to outside the system, but this only raises the question of what that other society will do with the money. So out of the four, where are the best opportunities today to store more wealth? How can and should Jen contribute to each of the four categories to provide for her own retirement? And what can and should we do collectively as a society to build these four kinds of wealth, and provide for everybody?

The first type of wealth, stockpiles, seems a lost cause. There is little scope to stockpile on the massive scale required. For example, the US government currently stockpiles strategic reserves of oil. These stockpiles add up to as much oil as the country typically burns in 37 days. That isn't long, and storing dramatically more oil is not a trivial matter. However, when oil is naturally found in the ground in a form that is easy to pump out and use, this is a kind of a natural stockpile. Right now we are literally burning through our stockpiles of natural resources, rather than creating new and valuable stockpiles. With artificial stockpiles so hard to make, it seems crazy to destroy natural ones with our current abandon. We should stop doing this, or at least, more realistically, slow down. Creating stockpiles on the scale required is an impossible task, but to prepare for the future, we could at least stop destroying the natural stockpiles that we already have.

Unfortunately, our current economic system depends on the heavy use of natural resources. Suddenly running out of natural stockpiles would be a disaster; it would be better to wean ourselves off them gradually.

Replacing some of our current taxes with a carbon tax and other taxes on natural resource use would be a step in the right direction. These taxes would give people and businesses an incentive to use up our natural resource stockpiles more slowly. Markets are powerful, and respond well to prices. For example, does it help the environment to buy locally-grown food? Growing locally sounds like a good idea, but maybe agriculture near you is less efficient in its use of agricultural land and energy than other places are. So maybe it is better for the environment, as well as cheaper, to produce fruit and vegetables in the most efficient places and then ship them to everywhere else. Or maybe not; perhaps the fuel needed for the transport eats up all the efficiency savings. It's hard to figure out what is the most environmentally sound thing to do. A well-designed natural resource tax could make the price difference between two competing products reflect differences in how much wealth was burned up in their manufacture. Then decision-making would be easy; you could simply buy the cheapest, with a clean conscience. With the right price incentives, markets will find a way to create as much new, manufactured wealth as possible while at the same time destroying the least natural wealth. Right now our economy is quite good at achieving the first goal, but it does so at the expense of the second.

Unfortunately, new taxes on natural resources could have devastating consequences if they meant that the poor could no longer afford to heat their homes or commute to and from work. One simple and fair solution is a "tax and dividend" scheme, where every member of society receives back an equal share of all the natural resource taxes collected. After all, the natural resources being used belong to us all, not just to whoever built mines to extract them. In this scheme, the poor will pay more tax than they do now on essentials like transport and heating, but the dividend they get back will more than make up for this. That dividend will be even more valuable to the poor if they find ways to respond to the incentives and lower their energy use. Then less of their dividend will go to paying their energy taxes and more of it will be available for something else that they couldn't afford before. As people and companies find efficiencies and change their patterns of consumption, the price incentives to conserve natural resources will gradually transform our economy, and make us better off while slowing down the destruction of natural wealth.

Changing our tax system will be hard work. It is politically difficult, and probably needs to be done in stages. We need to measure the amount of natural resources being used, for example taxing fossil fuels according to their carbon content when they come out of the ground or into the country. This measurement system needs to be built. At first the tax should be small, to keep the stakes low while we make sure that the measurement system is working smoothly and fairly. Later, the taxes (and of course the dividends) can be larger, providing bigger and more powerful incentives to conserve natural wealth. The effort we spend now restructuring incentives will pay off in the future as we lose less of our natural wealth. This makes the fruits of these efforts an intangible store of value.

Unfortunately, this is still an unhappy discussion about how to slow down the destruction of wealth. Of course we need to do this, but let's move on to a rather more optimistic discussion about how to create new wealth.

Physical infrastructure looks more promising than stockpiles. For example, if Jen makes her house more energy efficient today, this provides a valuable return in lower energy bills that she can enjoy over the life of the building. Jen took a step in the right direction last year. When her hot water heater broke down, she replaced it with one that takes heat from the sun. Jen could be more proactive about energy efficiency, and retrofit the least energy efficient aspects of her house, rather than waiting until something breaks before replacing it. But ideally, energy efficiency should be integrated into the design of buildings from the beginning. This takes commitment from builders, and informed activism from buyers.

Governments have an important role too, by providing financial incentives and regulatory nudges for energy efficiency in private infrastructure projects. Meantime, there are still a few things Jen can do. An investment of around $10,000 in solar cell panels on Jen's roof is estimated to bring Jen a return of ~8% over the life of the panels. This is an easy investment decision for Jen to make.

We need to think not just about individual buildings, but also about larger scale infrastructure. For example, today's electricity grid has issues. Sometimes it fails catastrophically, plunging areas into darkness. Blackouts are expensive, disrupting businesses as well as people's lives. In the long term, it can be cheaper to make the power grid more reliable so that blackouts are rarer, smaller, and shorter. An improved electric "smart grid" is a good example of a worthwhile investment, where effort today pays off in the future. In addition to avoiding blackouts, a smart grid would be more energy efficient, and would enable future innovation in the power sector, such as giving consumers real-time information that helps them manage their power usage. As more people like Jen install solar cells, demands on a smart grid will rise. Looking through our magic glasses at the costs and benefits for society as a whole, a smart grid is a no-brainer.

Removing the glasses again, it's not clear who will pay for this investment. A private company that spends a lot of money doing this work will have a hard time getting its money back. This is especially true if many companies, whose power production and usage are interconnected, would all need to work together to improve the system. What if one portion of the grid is the most likely to start a problem, but a different section, run by a different company, has most of the customers who will be hurt by any disturbances?

Government intervention is necessary to manage or resolve these problems, and so make sure that important investments in physical infrastructure happen. Each company has a particular set of incentives from its own perspective, leaving the government as the only institution with the motivation to look at what is best for society as a whole. Governments can either pay for infrastructure directly, or they can create a system of incentives or mandates for others to pay; either way, government involvement is needed to make the investment happen.

For Jen's retirement planning, this is a problem. To allocate her $700,000, she needs to know what *she* can do to invest in retirement, not what the government can do. To find good investment opportunities, Jen puts on the magic glasses, and sees lots of infrastructure opportunities. But when she takes the glasses off again to figure out how to allocate her money to those investments, she discovers that many are in the government sector rather than private hands, and so there is nothing she can do about them.

Upgrading the electricity grid is a huge undertaking, but the advantages of government investment in physical infrastructure also play out on smaller scale. For example, last year Jen spent over a thousand dollars fixing the suspension on her car. The roads in Jen's town have a lot of potholes. Each time Jen drives through a pothole, her suspension and tires suffer a little, and come one step closer to needing repair again. Every day, many people drive through each pothole. In the long run, it is cheaper for everyone to pay slightly more tax so that the cash-strapped local government can fix all the potholes. By paying tax now, drivers will be avoiding a bigger bill later. The transportation research group TRIP estimated that the average urban motorist in the US pays $402 per year because of badly maintained roads.[19] Cars need to be repaired and replaced more often, and they also use more gas on bad roads. Drivers, passengers and cyclists also get a non-financial benefit from government spending; driving is more comfortable with fewer potholes. Potholes cause traffic jams and even accidents.

Investment by local governments in road maintenance pays both financial and non-financial dividends in the future, at an excellent rate of return. Indeed, paying even more to do things properly can yield an even better return on investment than doing things on the cheap. One pothole near Jen's house was recently patched so badly, filled in a hurry with cheap material, that the filler started crumbling within days and the pothole was back within the month. Six months later, the repair crew finally came back to repair the same spot again. This is clearly a waste of money; it would have been cheaper and more effective to do a more thorough repair to begin with. Indeed, preventative maintenance before potholes even appear may be the most cost-effective investment strategy of all. Spending more money maintaining physical infrastructure, and spending enough to do things properly, can be a good investment even on quite short time horizons. It's worth paying more tax for, because it saves taxpayers more money than it costs, providing an excellent rate of return.

Some infrastructure projects have long time horizons of many decades. To prepare for the baby boomers' retirement, we should be investing in those infrastructure projects now, while plenty of people are still working. Later, after the baby boomers retire, we can sit back and enjoy the benefits

---

19   TRIP, a national transportation research group, 2010 "Hold the Wheel Steady: America's Roughest Rides and Strategies to Make our Roads Smoother" http://www.tripnet.org/urban_ roads_report_Sep_2010.pdf

of these investments. The relatively few people still working won't need to repair our roads and bridges and dams so often, since this work was done recently. Instead, workers could focus their efforts on shorter-term needs, like the basics of life and elderly care. By the time the baby boomers have long stopped retiring and are instead dying out, our neglected infrastructure would have started to crumble, and be in need of repair. The ratio of workers to dependents will be recovering by then, and it will be time to start investing again. We should invest now, while the dependency ratio is still relatively high. Then we can ease off when the dependency ratio is low, and start investing again when it rises again.

Unfortunately, this is not happening. We are not investing today. Much of America's current infrastructure was built during the Great Depression and after the Second World War, and some of it is even older. Today it is crumbling. Roads, ports, air traffic control, and railways are all in bad shape. Thousands of bridges are structurally deficient and need major repair. Toxic sites wait decades without being cleaned up. Sewage systems leak and many dams are at risk of failure.

Cleaning up failures is typically more expensive than avoiding them. New Orleans knows only too well what can happen when not enough is invested in levees. Failing to prepare for storm surges and hurricanes is horrendously expensive; preparing for them yields an excellent rate of return on investment in comparison. Investing in such infrastructure projects will make us better off than if we do not invest. But government budgets are tight, and public infrastructure is neglected. We are not doing enough work even to maintain the infrastructure we have, let alone investing in new infrastructure for the future. This is true even for "no-brainer" infrastructure, where the money-saving calculations are clear.

We can all do our part, as individuals, to make better investments in physical infrastructure, by choosing to pay extra for durability and energy efficiency, just as Jen paid a little more for her new hot water heater. Companies can do the same, although their time horizon is usually shorter than that of individuals, and they are under more pressure to cut costs now and make a larger short-term profit. But in the end, most of society's scope for improvement in this area lies in the hands of federal, state and local governments. There is of course a lot of privately owned physical infrastructure too, but most of it consists of buildings. We recently had a housing bubble, and built more than we need; we need to put all of that to good use before resuming much private construction. This leaves the biggest potential for building new and valuable infrastructure in government hands. This is especially true for defenses against hurricanes, floods and storm surges, and catastrophic power outages.

Right now, governments don't have the money to pay. This could change overnight if voters were willing to pay more tax. These are the same voters who "should" be saving more for their retirement. Paying taxes that go towards building infrastructure is, in fact, a way of saving for retirement. Paying more tax today means a more prosperous society later, one with resources freed up to give back to the former taxpayers. Paying taxes for flood defenses today is a good investment, much cheaper than losing your home in ten years. A lot of the infrastructure in question must be paid for by governments, because it is either enormously inefficient, or will simply never happen any other way. Voters who refuse to pay more in tax to fund infrastructure projects are voting against long-term investment, investments on the same timescale as their personal savings for retirement.

Remember, investment doesn't mean saving money, but instead means spending money to create wealth. Investment, not saving, is the important thing that needs to happen now. Productive capacity today needs to be directed towards building something of value for the future, even if this means making sacrifices today. This is the core reality we can see when we put on the magic glasses that make the illusion of money disappear.

Once we acknowledge this core reality of what needs to happen, we can address the more technical questions of financial engineering. In other words, how can Jen make sure that the money that she saves ends up benefiting her retirement?

In a market economy, the way we make investments happen is by using money to signal that this investment, rather than something else, is to be done. For many investments, this spending must be done by governments. There are two financial architectures that can match savings with this investment spending. The simplest option is to increase taxes today, taking money away from Jen and other taxpayers, preventing them from using that money to spend on their individual wants and needs, and allocating the money to levees, smart grids, or other investments instead. Paying taxes that go towards these investments is just as much a form of saving as paying into a retirement account. The benefits from these savings are provided by the infrastructure and intangible improvements that previous government spending created. With this financial architecture, Jen has no choice either about saving or about how her savings are invested.

Another option is for governments to issue bonds to pay for the investment, rather than raise taxes today. Now it is the bondholders' savings, rather than the taxpayers' incomes, that are no longer available for current consumption, and that act as the money-signal that this investment should happen rather than something else. Taxpayers sacrifice nothing up front. But as taxpayers receive the eventual benefits of the bridge or sewage system, their future taxes will be used to repay the bonds with interest. In this option, avid savers like Jen choose to save and invest in the government today, and future taxpayers will pay her back.

So building these important kinds of public infrastructure involves a choice between a sacrifice by current taxpayers, or one by future taxpayers. The first option is a kind of compulsory savings program; everyone who is earning money today pays today, and everybody who is still around later enjoys the benefits. The taxpayers are the savers who get to enjoy the return on their investment/taxes. When government bonds are used instead, nobody is forced to save. Whoever is earning money tomorrow will pay through their taxes for a benefit that everybody enjoys tomorrow. The return on the capital goes, in the form of interest payments, to foresighted individuals like Jen who saved money and bought the government bonds. In contrast, if the government had originally paid for the investment out of current tax revenue rather than by issuing bonds, that interest would effectively be earned by all the taxpayers on whom the saving was forced, rather than just to bondholders.

Some people don't think it's the government's job to force saving on people. Those people, if they see the merit in an investment, will prefer to avoid raising taxes now, and instead have the government (on behalf of the taxpayers) go into debt by issuing bonds. Later taxpayers, who enjoy the benefits, are the ones who will eventually pay. Other people prefer to force everybody to save through their taxes, so that everybody shares the returns on those savings, leading to a more equal society. There is no obviously right answer as to how much to use bonds (i.e. future taxes) versus current taxes. Reasonable people can disagree.

What is clear, when we put on the magic glasses, is that there are some great opportunities today to invest in something worthwhile (physical infrastructure), opportunities that will provide an excellent return on capital. Ironically, Jen is desperately looking, so far in vain, for investments that offer attractive rates of return for her savings. Many other savers have the same problem as Jen, and are struggling to find good investments for their retirement. The problem is that our financial system as a whole sends too much of our savings to the private sector. Channeling retirement savings into stock markets will not make these public infrastructure investments happen. Most of the opportunities we have discussed in this chapter can only be paid for by governments, and so must ultimately be paid for by taxes. Governments can raise taxes now, and force people to save for their retirement by spending those taxes on government investments rather than current government consumption. Or governments can borrow money for those investments now, giving a return to those like Jen who choose to save money, at the expense of future taxpayers who will pay the money back with interest. But one way or another, we cannot take advantage of all the great investment opportunities in physical infrastructure projects unless the government pays.

The use of bonds to finance government investments can be extended much further. All kinds of imaginative government bonds can be invented, taking advantage of all kinds of "investments" that spend effort today in exchange for returns later. For example, putting people in prison is expensive. Perhaps by investing a relatively small amount of money today, and spending it on preschool and other programs, we will see fewer at-risk children end up in prison. This would be a great financial investment; effort spent on preschool today will pay off tomorrow through lower prison costs. When there are so many retired people to look after, we won't want full prisons, nor high rates of unemployability among those of working age. Social impact bonds, also known as "pay for success" bonds, let savers invest their money in these kinds of early intervention programs. Savers assume the risk if the program is unsuccessful at saving money, and share the rewards with the government if the program does save money. Of course we could invest in preschool anyway, paid for by our taxes. But if people don't want to be forced to save through taxes, there is an option for private savings, with some individuals investing in government programs voluntarily, via social impact bonds. Jen would certainly be happy to buy social impact bonds; they may be risky and unproven, but at least the money is going to something she believes is important.

Social impact bonds are a great way of moderating the dangers of statist "command" economy, by letting private citizens vote with their bond money about which investments should be made. What's more, in order to calculate how much money to pay back to bondholders, we need to do proper evaluations of programs funded by social impact bonds, something that happens too rarely with taxpayer funded programs. To get accurate results, these evaluations can take the form of "gold standard" evidence of a randomized trial, e.g. by allocating eligible children to the scheme by lottery, and following up carefully to see the extent, if any, to which lottery winners do better than lottery losers. In the process of calculating whether bondholders' bets have worked, we will learn a great deal about what kinds of interventions work best. The involvement of private investors should help create a better market for social interventions of proven effectiveness.

There are lots of ways to invest, as a society, our collective savings in our future well-being. But the stock market will not do it for us. In this chapter, we identified four ways to store wealth that pass the glasses test: stockpiles, physical infrastructure, intangible improvements, and human capital. Stockpiles have only a limited role to play in preparing for the retirement of the baby boomers and others. Later in this book, we'll see how individuals can create wealth through human capital. For the other two forms of investment — physical infrastructure and intangible improvements — we have seen significant potential, but so far not in the private sector. Perhaps the private sector is close to maxed out in how much savings it can usefully absorb. Putting on our magic glasses, ignoring money and the distribution of wealth, we are reminded that the most important thing is the size of the pie, not how it is divided up. Most of the opportunities we have found so far for making the pie bigger, both through physical infrastructure and through intangible improvements, require collective action, via governments. We therefore need to be creative about ways to get government programs to work better.

# CHAPTER 14

# PREPARING HEALTH CARE FOR THE BABY BOOMERS

Last chapter, we discussed four types of investment. In each case, we as a society exert effort today in return for a payoff later. Our first option for investment, to stockpile goods, won't get us far. Indeed, our task is simply to slow down the destruction of existing stockpiles. The second option, investing in physical infrastructure, seems more promising, although so far we found much better opportunities in the public sector than we found for private capitalists. In the last chapter, we also mentioned a few examples of options three (less tangible improvements such as organizations and knowledge), and four (human capital).

Human capital is extremely important. Later in the book, we will return to this subject, and argue that human capital is the most important area of all for investment. But first, in this chapter, we linger a little longer on option 3, intangible improvements. I want to discuss just one area in which I see a lot of room for intangible improvements. Even if human capital is the most important area for investment, we also need to invest in whatever comes second.

To find out where, as a society, we should invest, let's put on the magic glasses to look at the future. Now we can't see, and don't need to worry about, who owns what or who is going to pay. Think about what work will need to be done when the baby boomers are old. A much smaller number of workers will have to do all of it. What kind of systems and knowledge can we create today that would make that job easier?

One set of economic needs stands head and shoulders above the others. As they get older, the baby boomers are going to need a lot of medical care and nursing. In 2013, the US spent 17.4% of its GDP on healthcare.[20] As the population gets older and sicker, this will likely rise even higher. But it may not all be well spent. In the US, we already spend much more than other countries, but this extra spending doesn't make Americans healthier or live longer than people elsewhere. Indeed, in 2011 the head of Medicare and Medicaid estimated that 20-30% of US health spending is "waste" that yields no benefits to patients.[21]

Clearly, there is a lot of room to do better. Any investment we make today acquiring knowledge, learning how to provide more effective care at lower cost, is going to pay off in the future. With so many baby boomers to look after, and so few working age people to look after them, this knowledge will soon be needed even more desperately than it is today. Healthcare costs already bankrupt governments, companies and individuals alike. As the baby boomers age, things will tend to get worse.

---

20　Centers for Medicare & Medicaid Services, National Health Expenditure Data, https://www.cms.gov/Research-Statistics-Data-and-Systems/Statistics-Trends-and-Reports/NationalHealthExpendData/NHE-Fact-Sheet.html
21　New York Times, Dec 4, 2011, "Health Official Takes Parting Shot at 'Waste'" https://www.nytimes.com/2011/12/04/health/policy/parting-shot-at-waste-by-key-obama-health-official.html

Just by cutting out waste, we could make healthcare cheaper without any sacrifice on the part of patients. While some Americans, especially the uninsured, don't get the care they need, many others are getting treatments that they don't need. You might think there is little harm in that. Unfortunately, this is not true. Those tests and treatments are not merely a waste of scarce resources, they can also do substantial harm to the patient receiving them. If we stop doing certain kinds of medical procedures, looking after retired baby boomers will be both cheaper and more humane.

Doctors often talk about balancing the benefits of a treatment against its risks. This makes it sound like the benefits are certain, but, regrettably, there might perhaps be harm as well if you are unlucky. In fact, nothing is certain in medicine, least of all the benefits of a treatment. If anything, it is the harm and side effects that are near-certain. Cutting bodies open is obviously not harmless, and swallowing or injecting strange chemicals may also have unwanted side effects.

We do these violent medical acts because we believe that they have benefits which outweigh the obvious harm. Those benefits may or may not be real. Even "effective" treatments may, on balance, be harmful rather than helpful for certain groups of patients. For example, it is common for a treatment to be studied only on patients with a severe form of an illness, and then used on less sick patients who have less to gain and more to lose, reversing the balance between benefits and harm. Even worse, some treatments come into common use without the proper study that would have shown that they are harmful. Figuring out which treatments these are, and stopping them, will make people healthier. Not treating can improve the quality of health care, in addition to its obvious benefit of reducing the cost. Less really can be more.

Some treatments persist, even after we know that they are useless or harmful. For example, antibiotics don't cure the common cold or other viral infections. But some doctors prescribe them anyway for these conditions. Prescriptions keep both patient and doctor happy. Patients feel satisfied when they leave the doctor's office with a prescription; it reassures them that going to the doctor was worthwhile. Writing a prescription ends the appointment earlier with fewer questions, and so makes a doctor's life easier. It harms patients by killing off natural gut bacteria; this might not be a serious problem, but any harm is too much harm when we are talking about a treatment that has no benefits. Much more seriously, overuse of antibiotics leads to the evolution of resistant strains. This makes us all much worse off in the long run, vulnerable to untreatable and possibly lethal infections in the future.

As a second example, when somebody is having a heart attack, an angioplasty can open the coronary artery, and a stent may be left in to keep it open. This is a fantastic medical advance, a miracle of modern medical care. But today, many patients with chronic but stable heart disease also get angioplasties, even when they are not in the middle of a heart attack. While the procedure can reduce chronic chest pain, it does not make patients less likely to have a heart attack or die.[22] Given the serious dangers from the surgery itself, patients are better off skipping it, and sticking with drugs alone. This is another case where the cheaper choice, of not having surgery, is also the better choice for the patient's health.

---

22  Boden, William E., et al. "Optimal medical therapy with or without PCI for stable coronary disease." New England Journal of Medicine (2007) 356:1503-1516 http://www.nejm.org/doi/full/10.1056/NEJMoa070829

As a third example, older men are routinely screened for prostate cancer, even though according to the evidence, screening does not save lives. Worse, there is a lot of evidence that routine PSA screening finds harmless cancers. Many prostate cancers grow so slowly that they would never cause symptoms. Indeed, if you look hard enough at the prostates of men older than 80, men who have died of something else, most of those old men have tiny cancers. These men died from other causes without ever knowing they had prostate cancer, or suffering symptoms from it. You may think that there is no harm in knowing. But once cancer is found, we don't know which ones are harmless, and so we usually treat them all. Prostate cancer treatment can leave men impotent or incontinent or both. Those are pretty serious side effects.

Think about this from the point of view of a man left impotent and/or incontinent. If he hadn't been screened, maybe he would have died decades later without ever finding out about his tiny, nonaggressive prostate cancer. Or maybe he would have simply found out later, and started treatment later, with no change in his prognosis, whether that prognosis was good or bad. For him, more health care did not mean better health care. The irony is that this man, despite the side effects of his treatment, might feel grateful for the prostate screen, believing that it saved his life. But his life was probably never in danger, and his suffering from the diagnosis and treatment was probably all for nothing. Ignorance would have been harmless bliss.

Partly, overtreatment in our health system is a cultural issue. Patients like to see that doctors are doing something. Doctors prefer to treat patients, rather than stand on the sidelines and watch. The rare patient who prefers less treatment may not know that this is a serious option, so instead he goes along with the treatment that his doctor recommends. The rare doctor who wishes to explore non-treatment options needs to spend a lot of time explaining her unusual attitude to her patients. She may also worry about being sued for failure to treat. The doctor will be paid little for this conversation, and will forgo what might have been substantial payment for the treatment. Doctors' lives are easier, and they are also financially better off, if they shut up and treat.

Most American medicine works according to fee-for-service. This system creates perverse incentives to overtreat, creating a conflict of interest pitting patient care against financial incentives. An alternative system, used by some of the best health clinics in America from Mayo to Kaiser, is to pay doctors a fixed salary. A doctor who is paid a salary won't earn more money for treating more aggressively. Nor will she earn more money for treating less aggressively. Instead, a salaried doctor, especially if she has no reason to fear litigation, has no incentive to focus on anything other than what is best for her patients. Reforming our health system to put more doctors on salary is one way of investing in the future.

The question of whether to treat becomes even more loaded as life approaches its end. This is a big financial issue: about 25 cents out of every Medicare dollar are spent on care during a patient's final year of life.[23] A lot of this care is futile.[24] It takes patients away from sickbeds at home, and puts them in hospital instead. The treatments are exhausting and leave dying patients less time to say goodbye to their loved ones.

---

23  Riley, Gerald F., and James D. Lubitz. "Long-Term Trends in Medicare Payments in the Last Year of Life." Health services research 45, no. 2 (2010): 565-576. http://onlinelibrary.wiley.com/doi/10.1111/j.1475-6773.2010.01082.x/abstract
24  Gawande, Atul. Being Mortal: Medicine and What Matters in the End. Doubleday Canada, 2014.

And ironically, aggressive treatment sometimes shortens rather than extends lives.[25]

Many people are understandably worried about medical rationing. They don't want to see the elderly or disabled denied care simply because it is too expensive. But this isn't just a question of costs.

If you ask Americans whether, when they are old and very sick, they want their pneumonia treated with antibiotics, CPR to resuscitate them if their heart stops, or a feeding tube when they can't eat, many of them say yes. They are horrified that rationing might deny them such care. But if you ask them how they would like to die, they say they want to die peacefully at home, certainly not hooked up to machines in a hospital. There is a disconnect here. These are exactly the same questions, asked in two different ways. People need to think carefully, and decide which one they want.

One of the few certainties in life is that we will all die eventually. But it's hard to talk about death. When the time comes near, some people refuse to believe that they or their loved one will really die. If a family is in denial and tells the doctor to do everything he can to try to save an unconscious patient's life, the doctor is required to do it, unless the patient left clear written instructions to the contrary. If the family isn't there to make the decision, and the patient's wishes are not known, doctors generally still treat aggressively.

Ironically, many doctors who aggressively treat their dying patients are terrified that the same thing will happen to them. They have seen many

---

25    Temel, Jennifer S., et al. "Early palliative care for patients with metastatic non–small-cell lung cancer." New England Journal of Medicine (2010) 363:733-742 http://www.nejm.org/doi/full/10.1056/NEJMoa1000678; Connor, Stephen R., et al. "Comparing hospice and nonhospice patient survival among patients who die within a three-year window." Journal of Pain and Symptom Management (2007) 33:238-246 http://dx.doi.org/10.1016/j.jpainsymman.2006.10.010

patients brought back from the brink of death in order to survive, at huge expense, for just a few more weeks or months, paralyzed and hooked up to machines. Some doctors even get "do not resuscitate" tattoos, just in case whoever is treating them doesn't look up their paperwork and see their instructions there.

As a small step towards fixing these problems, an early version of Obamacare included a provision allowing Medicare to reimburse doctors for having a conversation with a patient to find out how they wish to be treated towards the end. When patients understand that they are talking about the end of life, most don't want aggressive care. It's good to have this conversation calmly, ahead of time. Patients can go home, think about it and talk to their families before signing any forms. And of course patients can change their minds, and their written and verbal directions, at any time. Then perhaps five or ten years later, a doctor who knows that this is an end of life situation can let an already-unconscious patient die in peace, according to their written wishes, without fear of legal retribution.

Unfortunately, this provision prompted a scandal about "death panels". As a tragic result, the provision did not make it into the final bill. American society has a taboo on openly acknowledging that death is inevitable, and discussing how it will happen. And doctors who want to do the right thing by breaking this taboo and discussing end of life care with their patients, before things are on an emergency footing, cannot legally be paid by Medicare for their time. Naturally, few of them do it. This is something we can fix. It is the humane thing to do for dying patients, and it will also save money. Indeed, we could even go further, and provide incentives for patients to make these decisions ahead of time with the help of a specialized, non-directive counselor, who might in certain circumstances also be or work with a minister of the patient's religion. These political fixes to our incentive structures are a kind of investment. They will take work now, and pay off later.

Overtreatment is clearly a deep cultural problem in our society, a collective failure to think things through, a failure that has become embedded into our medical systems. It will take a lot of work to reform our health care system so that not treating is taken more seriously as an option.

But when should the option not to treat be taken? Sometimes, especially at the end of life, there will be a tradeoff; treating may lead to a longer life of lower quality. This should be a question of informed patient choice between quality and quantity of life. At other times, the decision not to treat is even easier, because there is no tradeoff. Some treatments do more harm than good. We have already discussed three known examples of harmful treatments that occur today: antibiotics for viral infections, angioplasties for stable heart disease, and routine prostate screening of asymptomatic men.

There are probably many more damaging treatments out there. Doctors currently use these treatments on patients with the best of intentions, believing, based on the information available to them, that they are helping. Knowing more about which treatments are harmful for which patients would both improve patient care and save money. This is where we could spend money today on good quality medical research that will provide both a financial and a medical payoff in the future.

There are many fancy theories about how diseases work and which treatments should, in principle, help. These theories don't always work out in the real world. When a patient is treated by a doctor and gets better, we assume that the treatment helped. But perhaps the patient would have got better even faster without the treatment.

This is why randomized clinical trials are the "gold standard" of evidence in medicine. The idea of a randomized trial is as simple as it is powerful. Take a group of patients who have the same diagnosis. Divide the patients randomly into two or more groups. Give each group a different treatment, or a placebo. See who does better. If a group treated in a particular way does better, then that is how we should treat the next patient with that same diagnosis. If the placebo group does as well or better, then we should not treat. If the results are mixed, e.g. the treated group lives longer, but the placebo group has a better quality of life, then the decision to treat should be based on the patient's personal preferences.

Every patient is, of course, different. Patients have different preferences and attitudes to treatment, and they may also have physiological differences that affect whether a drug works in the same way for them as it did for the patients in the clinical trial. Differences between patients are potentially endless, and we are never going to understand all of them. The best thing we can do is put patients together in groups that are as similar as possible. These groups are called "diagnoses". As we discover that some specific difference is important, we create more refined diagnostic categories. If we suspect that one type of patient might be different in an important way from other patients with the same diagnosis, and might therefore need a different kind of treatment, then we should do a new randomized trial, enrolling lots of patients of that same special type. That trial will teach us how best to treat patients of that type. It is from these kinds of randomized trials that we know that patients with one diagnosis (having a heart attack) benefit from angioplasty, but patients with a different diagnosis (chronic but stable heart disease) do not, and should be treated with drugs alone.

More high-quality randomized trials means more evidence, both to say when a treatment is on balance useful for patients with one diagnosis and should be used more, and also to say when a treatment is on balance harmful, and should no longer be used for that diagnosis. Right now, doctors simply don't have enough evidence to back up the treatment decisions they need to make. Let's give them the evidence they need to know which treatments are not only wasteful but harmful too, and to cut out that needless and expensive waste.

Wearing our magic glasses, we see that doing lots of these trials is an ideal way to invest in the future. But after taking off the glasses, we are left with the question of who will pay. Different organizations have different reasons for sponsoring trials. This leads to biases in which studies are done, and how. For example, the angioplasty study, supporting drugs alone rather than drugs plus surgery, was paid for by the pharmaceutical industry.

One reason there are too few studies investigating which patients don't benefit from existing treatments and should no longer receive them is that 79% of clinical trials are paid for not by governments or charities, but by industry.[26] And industry has no incentive to do these trials. Instead, the private sector's incentives are to do those clinical trials that lead to sales and profits. In exchange for doing successful clinical trials on new treatments, the government's Food and Drug Administration (FDA) grants companies a monopoly on marketing that drug or device for that condition for a certain number of years. In other words, generic competitors are not

---

26   Mello, Michelle M., Brian R. Clarridge, and David M. Studdert. "Academic medical centers' standards for clinical-trial agreements with industry." New England Journal of Medicine (2005) 352:2202-2210 http://www.nejm.org/doi/full/10.1056/NEJMsa044115

allowed to enter the market and sell the same treatment for less money. If the company owns a patent, their government-granted, profit-generating monopoly can last longer. We grant these monopolies to companies in order to give them an incentive to do research that helps us.

Companies have an incentive to find treatments that they can sell for a lot of money. This is not always the same thing as finding out which treatments help people and which ones harm them. For example, some diseases look like better market opportunities than others. A drug that completely cures a disease may not sell for as much money as a drug that merely manages it, and must be taken every day for the rest of the patient's life. And companies have a huge incentive to research new, patent-protected drugs, rather than find new uses for old, off-patent drugs.

Whenever they can, companies will test their new product against a placebo, rather than against the best alternative treatment that is currently available. That's all the FDA requires of them. Patients and doctors alike tend to assume that the "new" FDA-approved treatment must be better than older (and often cheaper) options. Since this preference for the new ensures that the product will sell well anyway, companies have no incentive to risk these sales by finding out whether their new product is in fact any better than whatever was previously available.

Drug companies want to sell their product to as many people as possible. Ideally, they will handpick the patients in the trials, maximizing the potential gain from the treatment and minimizing the potential harm from side effects and complications. If the drug works in these placebo-controlled randomized clinical trials, the FDA will approve it for all patients with that diagnosis, not merely those who closely resemble the handpicked subset. These other, more typical patients may have a milder case of the disease in question and may also have other unrelated health problems. For them, the benefits of the drug will be smaller, and might not outweigh the potentially larger harms.

A more extreme problem is that once a drug is sold in pharmacies for one condition, doctors are free to prescribe it "off-label" for any other diagnosis, without FDA review of the evidence that the treatment is effective. Until recently, drug companies were not allowed to "market" the drug for these other purposes. A lot of off-label marketing happened anyway. For example, in 1998 the FDA approved the use of thalidomide for treating a rare complication of leprosy. Despite the fact that this condition is essentially nonexistent in the US, sales of thalidomide rose to $300 million by 2004, presumably due to off-label prescribing.[27]

Occasionally, off-label marketing has been prosecuted. Then in December 2012, the 2nd US Circuit Court of Appeals ruled that off-label marketing is protected free speech under the First Amendment. The FDA did not appeal this decision, so it looks like free speech protections have changed the game, opening up the doors. Once a drug has been tested and approved for one purpose, and the government has even granted a monopoly in exchange for doing those tests, the drug can and will be marketed and sold for other purposes, for which it has not been tested, and for which nobody knows whether it does more harm than good.

The last thing a drug company wants to do is conduct a new clinical trial to test their bestselling drug on a different set of patients. They can already sell their drug, both as a placebo-tested, approved treatment to patients with one disease, and as an off-label treatment to patients with

27   Ismail, M. Asif "FDA: A shell of its former self" (2005) The Center for Public Integrity, http://www.publicintegrity.org/2005/07/07/5785/fda-shell-its-former-self

a different disease, or even just a milder case of the same disease. Drug and medical device companies have little or nothing to gain by doing quality research to find out exactly which patients benefit from a treatment. Rigorously performed new trials, if successful, may persuade a few more doctors to prescribe their treatment, but most doctors can already be persuaded by lower quality medical evidence combined with effective marketing techniques. But while they have little to gain, companies have a lot to lose by doing quality research, should the evidence go against their treatment.

As a result, the vast majority of clinical trials today look at new treatments not yet in use, rather than old ones already in common use.[28] And on those rare occasions where somebody does test the current standard of care, a worryingly high proportion of studies conclude that current practice should be changed, with current treatments abandoned.

Companies have a lot to lose by doing this kind of study, but society has a lot to gain. This is one kind of investment that still makes sense when we wear our magic glasses. Our healthcare system will be both cheaper and more effective if we find out that certain patients who currently receive a medical treatment would actually be better off without it. We want to do research that shows us how to pay less for healthcare, while getting as good or better outcomes than we do now. We may also be willing to pay more for a new treatment that is clearly better than the old ones, but this is not the only thing that we want. When new treatments are tested, we may get an expensive improvement in care, or we may get nothing,

---

28    Prasad, Vinay, et al. "A decade of reversal: an analysis of 146 contradicted medical practices." *Mayo Clinic Proceedings*. Vol. 88. No. 8. Elsevier, 2013 http://dx.doi.org/10.1016/j. mayocp.2013.05.012

depending on how the results come out. But when existing treatments are tested on different groups of patients, we may get an improvement in care that actually saves money. Unfortunately, clinical research is done primarily by players whose only incentive is for us to pay more, and so they have no motive for doing such studies.

What is more, our current system for privately funded clinical research only gives incentives for research into drugs and medical devices that are patented or otherwise new and not yet available for sale. This incentive system does little to sponsor research into the best use of our huge arsenal of existing, off-patent drugs and other treatments. Many of us assume that it is a good idea to take common over-the-counter drugs like aspirin or ibuprofen to reduce fever from common infections, or to help a sports injury heal. But we don't know for sure. Nobody has ever done the randomized trials necessary to find out.

Neither does the FDA provide incentives for research on surgical procedures that cannot be patented. Nobody has a monopoly on angioplasties, although they can patent a new kind of stent. No private company has an incentive to do randomized trials on surgical procedures, trials that give us knowledge that saves money and improves patients' lives. As a result, most surgical procedures have never been tested in randomized clinical trials.

For example, vertebroplasty is an invasive treatment for osteoporosis-related spinal fractures, where tiny cracks in the spine are filled with an acrylic cement. The FDA does not regulate such procedures, and so the procedure came into common use based on positive testimonials rather than randomized clinical trials. Eventually, governments funded randomized trials to study it, although belief in the procedure was so strong that it was hard to find patients willing to risk being assigned a placebo. To the surprise of the doctors conducting the trials, vertebroplasty turned out to be no better than a sham procedure.[29]

Occasionally, medical treatments work so dramatically well that randomized trials are not needed. For example, quite a few patients with appendicitis die unless they can get surgery, compared to virtually no deaths otherwise. This huge and immediate effect makes the benefits of the treatment obvious, even without a randomized trial. As appendectomies became common, death rates from appendicitis plunged. This historical evidence is strong, much stronger than in the case of vertebroplasty.

But most medical treatments have slower and less dramatic effects. The only way to really know whether they are worth doing is to do a randomized trial. Even with something as clear-cut as appendicitis, there are still many things we don't know. For example, the evidence about appendectomies came from an era before antibiotics. Many people with uncomplicated appendicitis get better simply with antibiotic treatment, and no surgery. The only way to know which treatment is better is to do a randomized trial.[30] Even when we consider what seems to be an extreme example of a procedure for which trials are widely considered unnecessary, there are still questions for which only randomized trials can tell us the answers. But nobody is going to make a profit from doing those trials.

Clinical trial priorities look different from a public health stand-point than from an industry standpoint. There is no shortage of public

29   Grady, D. "Studies question using cement for spine injuries." New York Times, Aug 6, 2009 http://www.nytimes.com/2009/08/06/health/research/06spine.html
30   Salminen P, Paajanen H, Rautio T, et al. Antibiotic Therapy vs Appendectomy for Treatment of Uncomplicated Acute Appendicitis: The APPAC Randomized Clinical Trial. JAMA. 2015;313(23):2340-2348 http://jama.jamanetwork.com/article.aspx?articleid=2320315

investment opportunities, with a lot of low-hanging fruit waiting to be plucked. Without discovering a single new treatment, we can gain a lot from "comparative effectiveness research", comparing different existing treatments for the same condition. We can invest far more in behavioral research to discover how best to change diet and exercise habits, and how to quit smoking and other drugs of dependence. We can improve checklist and handwashing practices in hospitals; this has the potential to radically lower rates of medical errors and hospital-acquired infections.[31]

Government agencies such as the NIH spend a lot of money on medical research, but most of this goes to basic science. Basic research is also important and I believe taxpayers should continue to fund it, but the largest, most immediate impact on patients comes from randomized trials, in clinics, on real patients. A few clinical trials are initiated by academic medical center hospitals and funded exclusively by the NIH. Others are run by bastions of "socialized medicine", namely the military and Veterans' Affairs. But most clinical trials today are sponsored by pharmaceutical and other for-profit companies. This creates a problem in terms of misaligned incentives between the public good and the decision makers.

You might think that change is difficult, because only the pharmaceutical industry has the expertise to conduct these trials. But while pharmaceutical and medical device companies fund most trials, they don't have direct access to patients, and so don't conduct the clinical trials in-house. Instead, they generally outsource some or all of the work to "contract research organizations", who in turn contract with individual doctors and medical clinics who enroll, treat, and monitor results for the patients

---

31   Gawande, Atul. "The checklist." The New Yorker, Dec 10, 2007 http://www.newyorker. com/reporting/2007/12/10/071210fa_fact_gawande

undergoing each possible treatment within the trial. This makes change easier than you might think. Which clinical trials get done depends on what sponsors are willing to pay for, rather than on the in-house expertise of the sponsors. We, through our taxpayer dollars, could set up a system to choose which trials we want to do, taking into account both current knowledge from the basic and clinical sciences, and also social science analyses of the number of peoples with a condition and the treatments currently available to them. The government could help choose which clinical trials to do without getting into the business of doing clinical trials itself. We can use the same for-profit contract research organizations that are already experts at this work. Nobody would stop pharmaceutical and medical device companies from also sponsoring ethical, properly designed trials of their choice, according to their priorities. We as taxpayers would simply sponsor additional clinical trials according to the somewhat different priorities of society at large. We might also investigate institutional changes that could make high-quality trials cheaper to conduct in cases where risks to patients are no different from those encountered in routine medical care, and which therefore do not require the same safeguards as trials of brand-new treatments.

We already have the knowledge base to identify some examples of useless or harmful medical care. There are doubtless many more cases of harmful care that doctors prescribe in the false belief that it is helpful, with the best of intentions and using all available evidence. A good investment for the future is to spend money today to do the research, find out what works, stop doing things that don't, and make ourselves healthier. Jen would be happy for her retirement savings to pay for this. The aim of this investment spending is to gain new knowledge about how to get better medical outcomes, while paying the same or less. If it can be avoided, we don't want to ration useful care just for the sake of controlling costs. But we do want to ration care that is useless or indeed harmful, or better still, eliminate such care altogether.

# CHAPTER 15

# PUBLIC VERSUS PRIVATE INVESTMENT

Using our magic glasses, we have looked for things that we as a society could do today that would pay us back later with interest. We found some good options. Through our government, we can put in place new incentive structures such as carbon taxes, harnessing market forces to drive the preservation of wealth in the form of natural resources. We can invest more in the maintenance and improvement of public physical infrastructure such as roads, bridges, sewers, levees, etc., paying for these investments either through increased taxes today, or through bonds that savers like Jen can buy, to be paid back through increased taxes later. We can raise this money, whether now or later, by taxing the rich; when all rich people are hit equally, this de-escalates arms races to consume things that are newer, larger, and more fashionable than one's competitors. Because these positional battles for status are relative not absolute, damping their excesses does no damage to people's welfare. We can fund comparative effectiveness research to create knowledge about how to provide better healthcare at lower cost. And I have hinted that the biggest potential gains of all may be in human capital, which could (let's wait and see as this book continues) involve increased public investment in education.

On the basis of this list, you are probably thinking by now that I am a died-in-the-wool leftist. For every problem, I see government intervention as the solution. My investment priorities involve new carbon taxes, more redistribution, and increased government spending on public infrastructure and medical research.

In fact, I am a big fan of competitive markets. When they work, they work spectacularly well. Maybe the problem, in a perverse way, is that markets work too well in such cases. They have worked so well, for so long, that the low-hanging fruit has already been taken. If the private sector really did have good, not yet funded ideas about how to invest in the future, then there is no shortage of savers like Jen out there, keen to lend the money. If you are a large company and have a great idea for creating wealth, you can already borrow money at an extraordinarily low interest rate through bond markets. And Jen can lend you that money through her retirement account. The problem is a shortage of borrowers with access to the bond market and with good ideas about how to put money to good use, even at these low interest rates.

The conventional economics answer is that to find borrowers, interest rates need to go even lower. To get out of our current liquidity trap and increase investment, real interest rates need to be negative, i.e. lower than inflation. The only way to get there is to have higher inflation. This is not a happy scenario. Saving money today so that we can get less purchasing power back later is a terrible way to prepare for retirement.

Government handouts to companies are not the answer. They may keep companies afloat, but they don't increase the rate of return on the companies' investments. The problem is a lack of business ideas that find a previously unseen need, and create and sell something to fill it, in the process generating both a profit and a genuine return in terms of society's wealth.

Profit-driven markets work so well that the private sector seems to have exhausted itself, at least that portion of the private sector that can access the bond market, and at least for now. Clever people have been looking for these hidden needs for a long time. Perhaps so many of them have now been found that there simply aren't many left. The easy options for the private sector to make really useful new things that make us all better off, like electricity and indoor plumbing, are gone. We are left with harder cases.

To find good ideas for new investment, ideas that haven't been taken yet, ideas that will provide a positive real return on our collective investments, we may now need to turn to the less competitive, less efficient public sector. It is perhaps because government spending is so hard to get right that there are so many good opportunities left in the public sector.

Some of the government's good investment ideas, such as universal education and a national highway system, have, like so many good private sector ideas, been done already. But other opportunities remain, as we have seen in the last two chapters. Public investment may be hard to do well. But if this is the area with the best investment potential, then we need to try.

So Jen should write to her elected representatives and urge them to support spending on worthy public investments, and of course she should vote accordingly for politicians and ballot initiatives. But this doesn't solve her immediate problem. What is she going to do with the $700,000 she owns in the form of bond funds? She only wanted to put her money there temporarily, while she tries to find a better investment.

Perhaps Jen should allocate more of her money to government bonds. For example, maybe she can find new bond issues tied to a new water treatment plant, guaranteeing that her savings will be used to create physical infrastructure.

Unfortunately, most government bonds offer low interest rates.[32] And despite the low interest rates, lending to municipal governments is not risk-free. Some municipal governments, most famously Detroit, have declared bankruptcy in recent years. Detroit is not alone, but joined Stockton California, Harrisburg Pennsylvania, and Jefferson County Alabama. Many more municipal governments will soon join their ranks as they find that they cannot afford to pay the pensions they have promised their former employees. Jen could lose her money by lending to these governments, in exchange for interest rates not much higher than she would get from FDIC-insured bank deposits.

And will buying government bonds even help make investment happen? Public investment seems to be driven by other political considerations. Anti-tax, anti-government ideologies are pitted against vote-winning, patronage-based government spending. I'm not convinced that low interest rates on government bonds work well in the current political climate as an incentive to get governments to invest more.

When a company does things badly, it goes out of business completely; if there is a market need, then a new company will appear to take its place. When a government does things badly, it won't just disappear and be replaced by a fresh new government that has been created from scratch. The best we can do is vote for different politicians, who try to reform

---

32   This may be offset in part by the tax advantages of many municipal bonds.

government agencies from the inside. Some people on the right feel that this is not enough, that more complete purges are essential from time to time. Since this is not possible for governments, we might as well give up, accept that our inability to purge government bureaucracies means that they will never be any good, and make governments as small as possible so that they do the least amount of harm.

Unfortunately, this would mean giving up on the most promising possible investments in the future that we have found so far. Given the importance of public infrastructure, of fighting climate change, and of research to learn how to improve health care while lowering costs, we need government to work. It's hard, but I believe we need to try.

Let's leave government aside for now. In the rest of this book, we'll talk less about opportunities for public investments, because there isn't much Jen can do to make them happen. Jen, a private lender, is looking for one or more private borrowers to put her money to good use. These will likely be borrowers who, for one reason or another, have no access to bond markets. Jen also wants to invest in something she understands. Having reached a point of frustration with the conventional options, Jen is open to unconventional ones, and she is willing to take some risks and do some work. Let's see what she can find.

# CHAPTER 16

# PRECISION VERSUS ACCURACY

Jen wants to invest in something she understands. This means understanding how she can allocate her money so that somebody, by spending her money today, will create wealth to make society better off, and so pass the "glasses test". Taking off the glasses again, it also means understanding how a future stream of money will be created that can and will be used to pay her back.

Jen wants to know how much money she will get back later, whether it comes in the form of interest, dividends, capital gains, or as some other kind of return. She also wants to know how much risk is involved. Jen obviously wants a high return with low risk, but this can't be done. So instead she has bought a low-risk cushion of low-interest TIPS, and wants to invest the remainder of her money to get a moderately high return in exchange for a moderately high risk. To choose investments wisely, she wants information about the risk and return of each of the options.

Jen therefore wants to estimate her long-term return, and the risk on that return, as accurately as possible. Jen's estimates should be accurate, but they don't need to be precise. Precision and accuracy are not the same thing, as this chapter explains.

When you measure something multiple times, and your measurements are precise, you will get much the same answer each time (Figure 4, left). That answer may be wrong, but it is consistent. In contrast, when you measure something accurately, there may be less consistency (Figure 4, right).

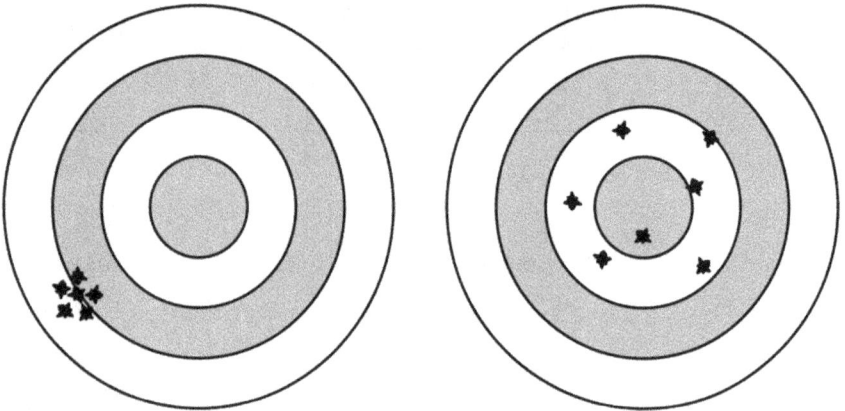

Precise but not accurate                    Accurate but not precise

Figure 4: The stock market values the long-term returns from stock ownership in a way that is precise but not accurate (left). In estimating the merits of different investments, Jen prefers to be accurate, even if that means being imprecise (right).

Obviously, if your measurements are not the same every time, they can't all be correct. Sometimes you will get too high a value, sometimes too low, but on average, an accurate measurement will be close to correct. However, when you only get one shot at measuring something, you might be unlucky and get it wrong that one time. This is still better than being precise without being accurate: in this case you will get something consistently wrong, every time.

Sometimes we have a choice in how we estimate things. We can either be precise, or we can be accurate, but we cannot always be both. This trade-off is well known to engineers who work on measurement systems.

Jen also encounters this trade-off in her job. Jen is a college professor. Imagine she wants to know how well her students write. She can assign them an essay. Essay grades are not consistent. A student may produce a good essay one week and a bad one the next. Jen may get grumpier or more lenient as she moves through the big pile of essays, so it makes a difference where a student's essay appears within the pile. A different professor might have a different opinion than Jen about how good or bad a particular essay is. All of these things mean that grading essays is not precise, because if you repeat the exercise multiple times, you don't always get the same answer. We don't even try to give essays precise scores like 84%, but stick to broad categories of grades like A, B, C and D.

Alternatively, Jen could give her students a multiple-choice exam, with vocabulary and grammar questions. While a student might randomly do well or badly on any one individual question, there are so many questions that a lot of this randomness disappears in the average. With 100 questions, Jen really can say that a student got 84% correct. In other words, multiple-choice exams are precise. Unfortunately, they are not accurate for Jen's purpose; Jen would like to know how well her students write. There are students who are consistently good at multiple-choice exams, but are terrible writers. And there might be talented writers who put a small vocabulary to excellent use, and so do consistently badly on vocabulary tests.

Precision is dangerous, because precise measurements look better than they really are. Imagine that I don't tell you what the exams are. All I tell you is that one exam is precise down to within about 5 percentage points. In other words, if a student takes the exam twice, he will get a very similar score each time. Compare this to a second exam that sorts students into only five categories, where if I give that exam twice to the same student, he might easily end up in a higher or lower category, occasionally even two categories away from where he was last time. If this is all you know about the two options, then of course you will choose the precise, reproducible exam. Precision looks good. And all other things being equal, precision is good. But all other things are generally not equal. And while the multiple-choice exam is precise, it doesn't measure what we want to know. By choosing precision, you will do a worse job finding out how well students write.

To understand how the difference between precision and accuracy affects investing, consider the stock of some company. Its long-term value to Jen's retirement portfolio depends on the future profits of the company, compared to the returns that one could get buying a different financial asset instead. We can't know this true value. Only with hindsight, many years later, could an analyst look back and say that a good price would have been $105.67. This is its real, but unknowable value. Stuck in the present with no time machine, the best the analyst can do is to estimate that the stock is worth about $100, plus or minus $10 or so. He can't be more precise than that, but he is in fact quite accurate, only about 5% off. On the market, the stock is trading for $122.39. This is very precise, down to the cent, but it is less accurate: it is 22% off. Our analyst's estimate is more accurate, while the market is more precise.

When Jen deals with stock markets, she wants to know how much profit a company will make, projected far into the future. In bond markets, she wants to know how likely it is that the borrower will pay the money back with the promised interest. Financial markets put numbers on these, down to the cent. This degree of precision should not be taken seriously. A serious assessment of the prospects of a company or borrower cannot be so exact.

Many traders are nevertheless extremely interested in small price differences. This is because they, unlike Jen, are not interested in buying an asset and holding onto it for decades while dividends and interest payments slowly come in. Instead, they want to make money faster by buying low and selling high. Imagine that there is no important news for a week, and so the value of the stock doesn't change. Its price, however, bounces around some average. If you magically knew that average, you could buy when the price was lower than average, sell when it was higher than average, and make a bit of money, week after week. Or maybe the trader is predicting the average for a day, or for a minute. Today, with high-frequency trading, the trader might be interested in price movements that occur within a fraction of a second. If you can predict the average, then by making a lot of trades, your small profit on each trade will add up to a lot of money.

To make all this money, you need a really good method for estimating the average, a method that is a little better than whatever the other traders use. Each trader tries to be cleverer than the next guy. Unfortunately, it's a zero-sum game. For everybody who beats the average, there is somebody who loses. All the activity surrounding this relative competition doesn't create any absolute wealth.

What the traders compete so hard to estimate is not the long-term value of the stock, based on its long-term profit outlook. It is the short-term price, based on what they believe they can sell the stock for next week, tomorrow, or in two seconds' time (Figure 5). When traders spend money to buy a stock, they expect to get money back mostly when they sell the stock again, rather than through receiving dividend payments over the years.

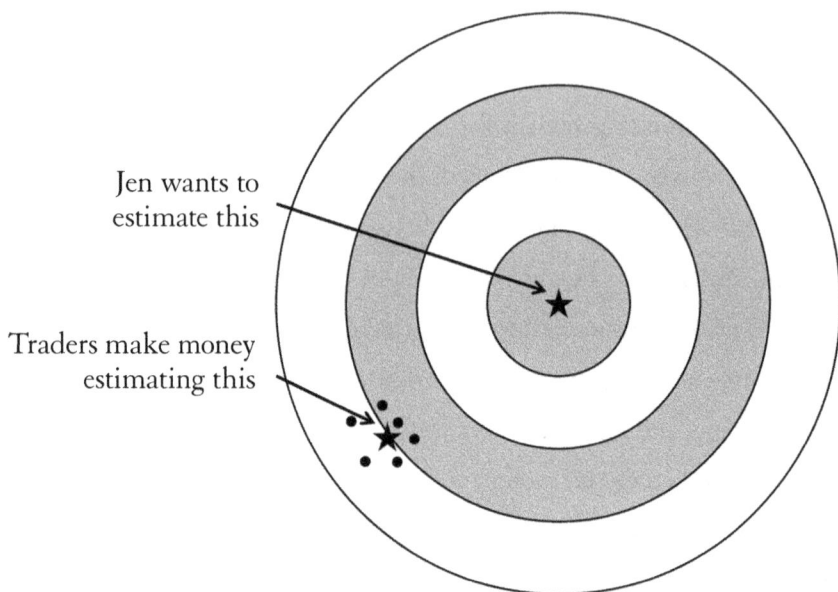

Jen wants to
estimate this

Traders make money
estimating this

Figure 5

The difference between short-term stock price and long-term dividend value is the same distinction between relative money and absolute
wealth that we learned about in Chapters 11 and 12. Relative contests,
with their focus on who is "winning" and by how much, tend to be
temptingly precise. In order to focus on wealth, trying to get more pie
in an absolute sense, an investor needs to focus on accuracy. If instead
they get sidetracked by the lure of precise stock price quotations, this
will draw them into emphasizing the points system of dollars, trying to
get more pie-shares relative to others, even if this means that the total
economic pie will be smaller.

In 1936, John Maynard Keynes described the stock market as like a
"beauty contest". Imagine that many people vote about which faces are

the most beautiful. To win the contest, you need to pick the faces that get the most votes. Keynes wrote:

> *"It is not a case of choosing those that, to the best of one's judgment, are really the prettiest, nor even those that average opinion genuinely thinks the prettiest. We have reached the third degree where we devote our intelligences to anticipating what average opinion expects the average opinion to be. And there are some, I believe, who practice the fourth, fifth and higher degrees."*

So the exquisite precision of our financial markets is not devoted to its ostensible job of allocating capital from savers towards those who can make best use of it, spending the money to create wealth. Like Jen's multiple-choice exam, financial markets are measuring, very precisely, the wrong thing. They know the price of everything, but the value of nothing. Their precision is a lure that Jen should ignore.

To invest more successfully in the future, we need accuracy instead. We need accuracy that is targeted toward what we care about (i.e., long-term returns), rather than precision that is targeted towards whatever best lends itself to precise measurement. Jen should buy stock market index funds when she thinks the stock market as a whole is undervalued, and sell when she thinks it is overvalued. Jen now has a way of working this out, using price-earnings ratios, earnings-GDP ratios, and the outlook for economic growth. Jen's method is not precise, but hopefully it is accurate over the long term.

Right now, Jen thinks stocks are overvalued, and so she sold them. Imagine that tomorrow, or perhaps in ten years' time, the stock market crashes. Imagine the stock market keeps falling, until its ratio to GDP first comes back in line with the historical norm, and then falls below it. Until then, Jen keeps her money in bonds, which don't pay a lot of interest, but nor do they lose value so dramatically. After a big crash, Jen estimates that stocks are finally undervalued, and she buys. This situation would retroactively justify Jen's earlier decision to sell. In other words, she is better off having sold and waited with her cash than she would be had she had held on to her stocks over the entire period.

It may take many years for events to prove Jen right, and it would take even longer to prove that she got things wrong. Even if the stock market stays high or rises further for many years, this wouldn't prove that Jen was wrong; the big crash could be just around the corner. Financial bubbles always last for longer than people expect. This is almost the definition of a bubble. Jen is "wrong" only if she can't wait long enough. No matter what, Jen needs to sell her shares after about 15-20 years, when she retires. If stock prices stay high until then, we can say that Jen was wrong to sell early, because at that point we finally know for sure that she would have been better off holding on to her stocks.

If Jen buys and sells based on whether she thinks the bond market or the stock market is a good deal overall, she won't be trading often. And if both stocks and bonds look like a bad deal, Jen is stuck with cash. Unfortunately, aiming for long-term accuracy means that it takes the long term before you learn whether you got things right.

In contrast, a short-term trader quickly learns whether he is doing a good job being precise. He either succeeds in making money, year after year, by buying low and selling high, or he doesn't. His incentive is to succeed in his short-term task. He gets plenty of feedback as to whether he is doing a good job.

This frequency of feedback is a major reason why humans make the mistake of favoring precision over accuracy. But to successfully invest in our long-term interest as a society, we need to become more accurate. In the fight for accuracy, precision is a false god and our enemy. In her search for good investments, Jen therefore resolves to ignore the allure of precision.

Jen made the decision not to invest in anything she didn't understand. But what does it mean to understand something? First, it means to understand how the purchasing power she hands over today will be returned to her as purchasing power during her retirement. Then, we expanded the notion of "understanding" an investment with the glasses test; now Jen wants to see not just how she will benefit personally, but also how society will benefit through the creation of new wealth. In other words, where is Jen's money going? Who will spend it, and on what? And how will that create future wealth that will allow Jen to be paid back with interest?

In this chapter, we refined yet again what it means to understand something. Understanding still involves answering these same questions. Unlike professional traders, Jen's answers to these questions do not need to be precise. But they do need to be accurate. In the light of this distinction, understanding Jen's retirement investments has not necessarily become easier or harder, just different. Next, we will see how the precision vs. accuracy distinction changes Jen's understanding of liquidity, and eventually leads Jen to consider less conventional options for her retirement savings.

# CHAPTER 17

# LIQUIDITY

Despite its lack of long-term accuracy, the stock market provides astonishing precision to inform short-term trades. At any moment, Jen can log in to her trading account and find out the current price of a stock. Except during unusually tumultuous times, if she places an order to buy or sell the stock, the price won't change much in the meantime, and so that trade will be completed at approximately the price she looked up. This convenience of nearly instant buying and selling at predictable prices is called "liquidity". Short-term, precision-driven investors need liquidity. The stock market provides it.

In a liquid market, you can always find somebody to buy from or sell to. At first, such liquidity is surprising; why is it that at exactly the moment when Jen wants to buy, there is somebody else out there who wants to sell? This matching process works smoothly because of the activities of professional traders known as "market makers". If Jen is willing to sell for a slightly lower price than the short-term average, a trader will buy from her. That trader will hang on to the asset until the next "real" buyer (i.e. somebody who intends to keep the asset) comes along, and then the trader sells the asset along to this eventual buyer, at a small profit to the trader. Similarly, if Jen is willing to buy for a higher price, that same trader, or "market maker", will sell her some of its recently acquired stock. This system means that no matter which side of a transaction Jen is on, she gets, on average, a slightly worse price than professional traders do. The longer the professional trader expects to wait for the next real buyer or seller, the bigger the "spread" between the buying price and the selling price offered by a market maker. In exchange for paying this spread, Jen gets the ability to buy and sell easily, whenever she likes.

In the absence of professional market makers, unless prices are artificially fixed, each transaction between buyers and sellers happens at a slightly different price from the average. In each transaction, one party gets a better price than the short-term average, and the other party gets a worse price. If all trades took place between two people like Jen, Jen would be on the good side of half her trades, and on the bad side of the other half. Sometimes she would win, sometimes she would lose, but taking the average across all the trades Jen ever makes, she would do business at short-term average prices. But with so many professional traders out there, acting both officially and unofficially as market makers, Jen can assume that she is on the losing side of each trade. Because those traders are so precise, prices stay close to the short-term average, and so Jen's typical loss to a professional, relative to the "true" short-term average price, will be smaller than a typical loss to another amateur in some hypothetical market that didn't have professional traders. But with professionals in the game, Jen is unlikely to make any random gains to cancel out these random losses.

In effect, Jen pays a small percentage fee on each transaction, which shows up as profit in the financial industry. She has no choice about paying this fee, and the fee is not transparent. What Jen gets in return is liquidity. Advocates for the financial industry argue that liquidity is a "financial service" that they provide to savers like Jen. If it weren't for them, trading would be slower and prices less predictable.

The financial sector now makes up over 8 percent of the US economy. That's a lot of financial services. The size of the financial sector has grown much faster than the economy as a whole. After World War II, the financial sector made up only 2% of the economy, and has been rising steadily ever since.[33] Are we getting value for all that money?

One reason that Jen is getting a bad deal is that long-term investors like her don't need liquidity, and so aren't willing to pay much for it. Before retirement, Jen won't consume a cent of her capital. She certainly doesn't need a minute-by-minute ticker over the course of every hour that the markets are open, telling her how much current purchasing power her portfolio could be exchanged for in that instant. Even after retirement, Jen won't sell stocks on a daily basis. For that kind of access to funds, she has a bank account. When her bank balance runs low, she will sell some stocks or bonds to replenish it, but the sale doesn't have to take place instantly. So long as she keeps an eye on her cash flow, it should be fine to sell any time over the course of several months, not over the course of a single second.

Sure, it would be convenient for Jen, after her retirement, to place an order and find out immediately what price she will get for her sale,

33    Philippon, Thomas. Has the US finance industry become less efficient? On the theory and measurement of financial intermediation. No. w18077. National Bureau of Economic Research, 2012 www.nber.org/papers/w18077.pdf.

with the money arriving several days later. This is more convenient than placing an order and waiting, perhaps for a month or two, for a somewhat less predictable amount of cash. Jen would happily pay $20 for this convenience. She would pay even $50, but probably not more. Paying a bigger fee seems like an avoidable waste caused by Jen's bad planning. If Jen sells around $25,000 of her long-term assets at a time, placing the proceeds in her bank account to pay for her living expenses over the coming months, this means that she is willing to pay a fee of only 0.2% for liquidity after she retires. Her implicit costs of liquidity, part of the 8% of the economy that go to financial services, are almost certainly much higher than that.[34] In stock markets and bond markets, Jen will overpay for more liquidity than she wants to buy. And right now, when she hasn't retired yet and doesn't need the money, Jen needs even less liquidity. So long as she can sell at least some of her assets in 15 years' time, that is enough liquidity for Jen right now.

Liquidity is most useful when something unexpected upsets our plans. But in those cases, there are other, more transparent ways that Jen could buy liquidity as she needs it, rather than pay for it upfront whether she needs it or not. For example, as a backup for the worst possible case of an emergency, Jen could pay unexpected bills with her credit card, and try to sell some assets by the end of the month when her credit card bill is due. Or if she needs more money than her credit card's limit, she could talk to a bank about a larger loan to spot her until the sale of an asset goes through. A financial sector that makes up 8% of the economy gives her a

---

34  Hibbert, John, et al. "Liquidity premium: literature review of theoretical and empirical evidence." Barrie & Hibbert Research Report (2009) http://www.barrhibb.com/research_and_insights/article/liquidity_premium_-_literature_review_of_theoretical_and_empirical_evidence

lot of options. A careful planner like Jen probably won't need those options, but it is nice to know that they are there – if and only if she needs them.

Not all markets are as liquid as the stock market. For example, if you want to buy or sell a house in a very small town, it could take a long while until you find somebody to deal with. Then negotiations can be difficult. Both of you know that if the deal falls through, there will be another long wait until the next opportunity to buy or sell. To avoid that wait, you might accept a deal somewhat worse than what you think is fair. Or, if the other person is in more of a hurry than you are, you might force him to settle for less, while you come out ahead. Prices are in any case less precise when there aren't many similar sales available for comparison, so there is plenty to haggle over. This makes transactions more time-consuming and stressful. Jen is willing to do a few transactions of this sort, but not too many.

With $700,000 to invest, Jen could buy a $200,000 rental property. Since she will hold it for 15 years or more, illiquidity will not be a problem for a while. But if in Jen's retirement she needs to spend down her capital rather than just live off the interest, then she will need to sell the property. Selling doesn't need to happen overnight, but she would like to be able to find a buyer willing to pay a reasonable price within about six months. That's compatible with one or two "real" potential buyers taking an interest in the property per month, enough to give Jen the confidence to turn down offers she thinks are too low, and instead hold out for the next opportunity.

Jen would rather buy a rental property in a larger town than in a smaller one, to make sure that its liquidity meets her six month salability criterion. But the high liquidity provided by the stock market is massive overkill. So long as she can complete a sale of a retirement asset within a couple of months, Jen has all the liquidity she needs. Before retirement, Jen needs even less liquidity than that. Trades completed in a small fraction of a second provide ridiculously more liquidity than Jen could possibly need, at a price she doesn't want to pay. Jen resents being forced to pay extra for liquidity that she does not value.

A certain minimum level of liquidity is genuinely useful for the economy. Imagine you started up a company, and you still own most of it. You have already proved that your company's business plan has a lot of promise, and now it is time to grow fast. Doing that means spending a lot of money now, in exchange for profits that will only come later. You can raise capital in several different ways, but let's focus on the stock market, and imagine that you decide to raise money via an initial public offering (IPO) of shares. There are many savers out there who believe in your company, and who are eager to buy the newly issued stocks at high prices. This injection of cash is good for you, good for your company, and good for the economy. But these investors don't necessarily want to keep owning part of your company forever. For example, maybe at some point they will need the money back to buy a house, pay a child's college fees, or spend on living expenses after they retire. Or maybe they will simply change their mind, and prefer to own something else. These savers want to invest in your company by buying shares, but they will only do so if they know that there is a way of selling them again later, (i.e., if their investment comes with some liquidity). This is what the stock market is for. It reassures savers like Jen that it is OK to buy stocks, she can always sell them again when she needs to. And she won't need to wait years to find a buyer, like she might for a house in a very small town.

Some amount of liquidity in stock and bond markets is useful because, by offering a secondary market, it makes the primary market of new stock issues more attractive to savers. New issues are the really important part of the capitalist economy. This is when capital gets distributed from savers towards those with a good plan for investing it. Secondary markets don't lead to new investment; they are just a mechanism that makes it easier for existing financial assets to change hands. Savers won't buy newly issued stock unless they know that they can resell it later, so it's important to have some kind of market where reselling takes place. But it's not clear why a genuine investor needs to be able to sell at less than a second's notice. The ability to sell within several months should be enough for most long-term investors.

Timescales matter. As a society, we would like companies to create as much value as possible over the long term. Long-term owners of a company, including investors like Jen, want the same thing. But short-term owners of company stock simply want the precise short-term stock price to be as high as possible. Company managers are given incentives, such as stock options, to make them want the same thing as stockholders. So companies are run with an obsessive short-term focus on how things will look in the next quarterly statement.[35] This is bad for companies, and bad for the long-term future of our economy.

To see this, let's think about how a company is run in a simple world with no stock market. Bill is a retired, successful businessman with plenty of money available to invest. He and his nephew Jack come up with a great

---

35    Rappaport, Alfred. "The economics of short-term performance obsession." Financial Analysts Journal (2005) 61:65-79. http://cmsu2.ucmo.edu/public/classes/young/Guidance%20Research/The%20Economics%20of%20Short-Term%20Performance%20Obsession.pdf

idea for a company. Jack has no money, so Bill pays all the costs needed to start the company up, including Jack's salary while he is getting going. Jack agrees to a very modest salary in the beginning in exchange for partial ownership of the company. Later, when the company has plenty of money flowing in, Jack and five other employees are paid good, competitive salaries out of company revenues. After paying salaries and other costs, there are profits left over. Jack now owns 20% of the company in exchange for his low pay in the beginning, so the company's profits are paid out as dividends, split 20:80 between Jack and Bill. Bill provided the capital at the beginning, and now that the company is successful, he is getting his money back with interest. Jack and Bill jointly own the company, and Jack runs it as the CEO.

Jack and Bill might occasionally disagree about how best to run the company and share the proceeds. For example, if Jack gets a pay raise, that means less profit for Bill, so they might disagree about what a "fair competitive salary" for Jack is. But as shareholders in the company, they both want the company to stay healthy and profitable over the long term.

Now let's add some liquidity, by allowing Jack and Bill to sell their shares on a public stock market. The true value of their company depends on its stream of profits far into the future. But it's hard to predict future profits. In practice, most market analysts and traders focus on current quarterly profits, not distant future revenue streams, as part of their preference for measuring something precisely rather than measuring the long-term right thing accurately. In other words, quarterly profits are easier to predict, to understand, and they appear quickly enough to provide feedback about which analysts are getting things right. So the stock market now ties Jack and Bill's personal wealth closely to quarterly profits, whereas it used to be tied, less precisely, to the long-term outlook.

So why doesn't the stock market care more about long-term outlook? When most market analysts follow the same easy path, it would seem like a good strategy to look just a little further ahead than the others. Imagine one trader who puts in extra work to investigate a company more deeply, and predicts earnings one year ahead, instead of one quarter. If this trader is willing to buy and hold undervalued stocks for an entire year, he will make money when his earnings predictions come true, prices go up before the end of the year, and he sells at the higher price.

Holding stocks for a year counts as a long-term strategy in today's financial world. The average holding time for stocks, including long-term individual savers in addition to professional traders, has fallen to only 8 months.[36] People are not buying stocks for the long term.

Now imagine a trader who goes even further, and is interested in the truly long-term total return on investment over decades. This is, after all, what a stock's value is supposed to be based on, and what investors like Jen care about. This trader is picking the stock that he finds genuinely the prettiest. By not picking the most popular stock, he may lose Keynes' beauty contest, and be unable to resell the stock at a profit. To be sure of making money, such a trader would need to hold the stock over the truly long term. If he did that, his profession would no longer be "trader". A fund manager who pursues such a long-term strategy at the expense of short-term success will be seen as a failure, and savers will withdraw money from his fund before his strategy has had time to pay off. As

---

36  "Average Stock Holding Periods on Select Global Exchanges" (2012) http://topforeignstocks. com/2012/11/03/average-stock-holding-periods-on-select-global-exchanges/

Keynes reportedly said, following some of his own investment attempts, *"I have reluctantly reached the conclusion that nothing is more suicidal than a rational investment policy in an irrational world"*.[37] Or, as another version of this saying goes, *"Markets can remain irrational longer than you can remain solvent"*.[38]

So long as Jack and Bill cannot easily sell their shares in their company, they care about its long-term health and profits. But once they have the option to sell, their incentives change. As insiders, they know a lot about the company's prospects, much more than analysts will ever know, whatever information is in the quarterly statements. If Jack and Bill could do something to push the stock price up above its long-term value, even for a short while, then they can sell the company while prices are inflated. They would walk away richer than if they had held on to company ownership. Their incentive is to do whatever makes the company look good to market analysts today. This may involve something as "benign" as creative accountancy, changing nothing of substance but making the numbers look good. Or it may involve spending too little money on investments in the company's long-term future, improving current cash flow at the expense of long-term profits.

Liquidity is what makes a short-term perspective possible. Liquidity shifts incentives away from investment in the long-term future, and towards making the precise numbers in the latest quarterly statement look as good as possible. As a society, we would like companies to invest accurately in the long-term future, and so liquidity is having a bad effect.

At the other extreme, zero liquidity would also be a bad thing. For example, Jack might want to take the company in a direction that Bill

---

37   Quote Investigator http://quoteinvestigator.com/2011/08/08/rational-investment/
38   Quote Investigator http://quoteinvestigator.com/2011/08/09/remain-solvent/

doesn't like; when Bill refuses, Jack might quit his job and want to cut off connections by selling his shares. Or maybe Bill loves the startup process and wants to invest in a second one, and needs his money back to do that. Or maybe Bill doesn't have enough money to fund the company's growth, and so the company needs to find new investors who do. Liquid company ownership is a good thing in all these situations. But there is a wide middle ground between "stuck with the shares forever" and "can sell with less than a second's notice". For most regular investors like Jen and Bill, being able to sell within a couple of months is liquid enough.

Indeed, many people think that when it comes to retirement savings, the ability to sell within months is too much liquidity. This is why governments set up tax incentives to encourage workers to pay into "locked" retirement accounts. "Early" withdrawal is subject to a 10% penalty. Even though most retirement accounts contain highly liquid stocks and bonds (liquidity which the account owners implicitly pay for), the early withdrawal penalty ensures that these accounts provide almost no liquidity to regular folk like Jen. The lack of liquidity is seen as a good thing, protecting the common man from his own fecklessness.

Some financial players do need a lot of liquidity. For example, in exchange for government guarantees, regulators require banks to hold "reserves" in order to pay back their depositors when asked. These reserves must be extremely liquid. The same applies to mutual funds, who must be able to sell assets quickly enough if too many savers like Jen reallocate their cash away from a fund at the same time, albeit not at a guaranteed price. And it isn't just retail institutions like banks that need liquidity to prevent a "run" on their institution by clients. Professional traders often trade with borrowed money, or borrowed shares, as well as with their own assets. Managing such "leveraged" positions also requires higher liquidity, in case lenders want their money back. There is plenty of demand for liquidity, in our financial system, but it generally comes from professional financial middlemen, not from pension savings like Jen's. Leverage increases demand for liquidity, and also makes a financial system less stable, as we'll see in Chapters 20 and 22.

As we discussed using the example of Bill and Jack's company, one effect of high liquidity is to distort incentives away from long-term investment. Another is to lower the barriers to buying shares in a company. People will not work as hard to understand a company when they hold stocks for less than a week, or when the stocks are part of an index fund across the entire stock market. The most diligent analyst, with so many strategies available to him, will never work to understand the long-term prospects of the company in anything like the way that Bill, as a major, non-liquid owner, understands his investment.

Jen has decided not to invest in anything she doesn't understand. If everybody followed suit, then each company would have only a small number of owners, and each owner would take an active interest in the company or companies they own. Large companies would have extremely rich owners, while people like Jen could own part or all of a small business. This is already the case for many businesses, not all of them small, which are owned and run by individuals or families. Investment decisions for all other businesses are currently made by managers of other people's money. Other people's money creates a lot of bad incentives. The only alternative to the perverse incentives generated by spending other people's money is for owners to be actively involved in important decisions made by the businesses they own.

Jen isn't rich enough to own a significant portion of a large company, but there is still a way for her savings to help even the largest companies invest in the future. Companies can borrow capital by issuing bonds rather than new stock. Jen is more comfortable buying bonds from a company than she is buying that same company's stock. To "understand" a company at that level means verifying that the company is basically sound, and that the interest rate is fair. This is much easier than predicting the same company's long-term profit outlook into the distant future, or predicting what irrational stock markets will do to the stock price in the shorter term.

Stock prices are based on future profits, which are very hard to predict, especially if a company is growing rapidly. The value of these future profits is so hard to predict that most savers and money managers don't even try, and instead speculate about the future predictions of others, giving rise to Keynes' beauty contest. Bond prices are based on much simpler promises to pay specified sums of money on particular dates. To decide what price Jen is willing to pay for a bond, she just needs to decide what interest rate she is willing to accept, given competing interest rates from other borrowers. Since it is much easier to calculate a fair price for a bond than for a stock, bond market analyses focus more on true beauty and behave less like Keynes' beauty/popularity contest.

Bond prices fluctuate too. The market price for bonds goes up when traders expect interest rates to fall, and down when interest rates rise. When interest rates change, the bond will still pay out the same sums of money on the same dates as originally promised, but as alternative uses of money look worse or better, people will exchange those future promises for more or less money in hand today. Bond prices also shift in response to new information about how likely a borrower is to default. But while bond prices can fluctuate, they maintain a clear link to their fundamental value. They are less of a beauty contest, and so they don't move so rapidly and crazily out of line with fundamentals as stock prices do. Liquidity in bond markets provides the same benefits to society as liquidity in stock markets. Because bond markets focus more on fundamentals and less on Keynesian beauty contests, these benefits of liquidity come with a much less serious downside.

Unmet expectations of high liquidity can make financial systems unstable, for example vulnerable to sudden stock market "crashes" when too many people want to sell and nobody wants to buy. The liquid nature of bank deposits can also create problems. Banks borrow money in the form of liquid demand deposits, and lend it out as illiquid loans. This mismatched liquidity is the dangerous part. Even the best-managed bank will collapse if there is a "run" on the bank when depositors all demand their money back at the same time. A bank is not allowed to ask you to pay your mortgage back ten years early so they can repay their depositors. The reason the bank doesn't have cash on hand to repay the depositors is that it has lent its money out, for example for your mortgage.

Bank runs used to be a serious problem. To make our financial system more stable, the government now offers insurance programs to make sure that bank depositors get their money back. We don't want people to be afraid that bank accounts aren't liquid enough, and so hoard cash instead. The liquid nature of bank deposits makes banks riskier than we would like them to be. This problem has been removed by government guarantees. Governments never have a liquidity problem so long as they control their own currency. After all, in the worst case of an emergency, governments can just print money.

Banks act as a middleman in our financial system; Jen lends her money to the bank, and the bank lends money to people and to companies. Bonds allow large organizations, including companies, governments, and government agencies, to bypass banks. By selling Jen a bond, a company can cut out the middleman and get Jen's money directly from her today, and pay her back later with interest according to some fixed schedule of payments.

By selling bonds, companies get an illiquid loan, just like they would from a bank. Without a bond market, lenders like Jen would be stuck holding an equally illiquid bond until it matures and all the money is paid back. This gets around the liquidity mismatch problem that leads to bank runs, and so it can be a good thing, but it can go too far if Jen ends up with no liquidity at all. Bond markets restore some liquidity for lenders. If Jen needs money earlier, she can sell the bond, with all of its promised future payments, to another saver. Owning a bond is less liquid than money in a bank account, but well-functioning bond markets make bonds much more liquid than they would otherwise be.

There could still be a "run" on bonds if everybody wants to sell and nobody wants to buy. Bond prices would then fall until eventually, with a high enough and easy-to-understand interest rate, somebody will take advantage of the bargain prices and start buying bonds. Booms and busts in bond markets don't stray as far from fundamentals as booms and busts in stocks, because it is easier to calculate a fair price for a bond. Bond prices are more stable than stock prices, but less stable than bank deposits. A saver who has $1,135.21 in her bank account expects to be able to withdraw precisely $1,135.21, no more and no less. In terms of predictability of price, bank accounts are the most liquid, then bonds, and then stocks.

Remember, liquidity is defined as the ability to buy or sell rapidly at a predictable price.[39] This means that by definition, whenever a market is liquid, it is also precise. And the only way for the monetary value of an asset to be known precisely is by referring to the price for which it could be sold, a price that can only be known in a liquid market. In other words, liquidity implies precision, and traders' demand for precision requires liquidity. In practice, the liquidity of financial markets and the precision of the asset valuations they provide are two ways of describing the same thing.

Last chapter, we saw how there can often be a trade-off between precision and accuracy. Jen's interests as a long-term investor, as well as the interests of society at large, are best served by accuracy. We also saw how precise measurements tend to look great, even when they are not. We should beware precision as a false god. Liquidity is convenient when an individual wants to trade, but we want a financial system in which assets are traded less often, by savers who take a longer-term perspective. Liquid precision leads to short-term thinking, whereas illiquid accuracy demands a focus on the long-term value of an investment. The idolization of precision is our enemy, and the liquidity of our financial markets can be harmful. Indeed, there is evidence that less liquid financial assets provide higher returns.[40] Jen doesn't want to sacrifice good returns in exchange for lots of liquidity. Unlike professional traders, Jen has no need for liquidity; she won't want any of her money back for at least 15 years.

---

39   Some definitions of liquidity are narrower than the one I give here; rather than require that the price be predictable, they require only that the act of buying or selling does not itself change the price. The impact of the current transaction is one of many factors that can make prices unpredictable between deciding to buy or sell, and executing the order.
40   Ibbotson, Roger G., et al. "Liquidity as an Investment Style." Financial Analysts Journal (2013) 69:30-44. http://www.cfapubs.org/doi/pdf/10.2469/faj.v69.n3.4

The value of most public investments, like building better levees to protect against storms, cannot be made precise. These public investments are not traded between owners in an open market, and so are not so liquid. This lack of liquidity and precision may be one of the reasons we have not been investing enough in these areas. When we require investments to be precise, we risk neglecting the many good ones that aren't.

In Chapter 13, we mentioned social impact bonds as one way around the problem of underinvestment in illiquid, imprecise public investments. For example, the government could sell bonds to pay for preschool programs for at-risk children, track what later becomes of them, and pay the bonds back years or decades later depending on how many of the children are kept out of expensive special education programs, and out of prison. If the preschool program is successful, the government saves money on prisons, and shares these savings with bondholders. If the preschool program is not successful, bondholders lose their money. Bondholders could trade these bonds in a liquid market, instead of holding on to them for decades. If trading becomes too much of a wild casino speculation about crime rates, the market pricing of social impact bonds won't necessarily make government investment decisions more accurate. But it will satisfy investors' appetite for precision.

Social impact bonds would make it possible for Jen to direct her private savings towards public investments, voluntarily taking on additional risks and rewards beyond those she shares with other taxpayers. These social impact bonds don't exist (yet), so Jen can't buy them. After paying the usual Social Security, Medicare, and other taxes, and having already bought a goodly amount of TIPS, Jen is therefore looking to direct the remainder of her savings to investments in the private sector. She has money to lend, and is looking for a borrower. She wants to assess her risk and return accurately, and is willing to sacrifice both precision and liquidity. Pursuing the twin evils of precision and liquidity corrupts financial markets, and with them the investment decisions on which the "real" economy is based. Jen will turn her back on this pursuit.

# CHAPTER 18

# MORTGAGE LENDING

Jen wants to invest in something she understands. She doesn't need her savings to be liquid, and she doesn't need to know their precise dollar value. While she doesn't care about precision, she does want an accurate knowledge of what it is that she has invested her money into, and how it will generate a stream of revenue into the future. Ideally, she wants an investment that she understands more accurately than other people do, to give her an edge.

Last chapter, Bill invested in the business run by his nephew Jack. Jen would like to have a nephew like Jack, whose business she could take a look at and perhaps invest in if she believed in it, and him. But she has no children, and no nieces or nephews. Understanding big public companies well enough to buy their stocks is also out of the question; even if she understood the company, she will never understand the irrational stock market.

Another option is for Jen to buy a second house and rent it out. Jen already hates dealing with maintenance issues in her own house, so she shudders as she thinks of double the maintenance trouble. Still, this seems like her best option so far, despite the hard work and stress. So Jen starts investigating prices to buy and rent properties in her town. Her timing isn't bad; the housing market has not completely recovered from the collapse that began in 2006, so there are bargains left to buy, and plenty of families still stuck with renting after losing their home during difficult times. A $200,000 house might rent for about $1,000/month. Jen figures that taxes, insurance, maintenance, and other costs will come to about $4,000 per year. This means a return of 4%. That's a real return, since after many years of renting it out, Jen will still own the house. Over the long term, Jen figures that the resale price of the house will approximately track inflation. If the house ends up vacant two months a year, or if annual costs are $2,000 higher than Jen's simplistic calculation, she still gets a 3% real return.[41] This is a better return than other investments she has considered. And this estimated return is a fairly conservative summary of her casual perusal of houses on the market right now. If she shops around carefully, she can probably find a bargain, paying less to buy a house that rents for more. Financially, being a landlady makes sense to Jen. Her big concern is how much work it will be.

Investments fall into two broad categories: equity, where Jen owns something and is more responsible for its ups and downs and perhaps

---

41    On top of this, Jen also benefits from tax deferral. Jen's rental is 3% in the red in cash terms, but Jen can also claim depreciation of the rental house as a tax-deductible expense, deducting it from her taxable income. This depreciation is generally far higher than repair expenses paid in cash. Should Jen eventually sell the rental house, she would pay tax on these amounts then, because the claimed depreciation would lower the cost basis of the house and show up as a large capital gain. But this may never happen during her lifetime. And when and if Jen's need for money in her retirement becomes great enough to sell, the capital gains tax is likely to be at a lower rate than her marginal tax rate today. Jen could avoid even these taxes by taking out a reverse mortgage instead.

management, and loans, where some other owner takes the primary risks and responsibility, with Jen carrying less. Stocks are an equity investment in companies, corporate bonds are loans. Renting out properties is a form of equity investment. If Jen prefers to avoid the headache of ownership, perhaps she could lend somebody money to buy a house?

One way to do this is by buying mortgage-backed securities. After a bank makes a mortgage loan to help somebody buy a house, the bank sells that loan to another institution, which bundles it up with other loans. Those bundles get cut up into shares and sold as bonds. Jen could buy these bonds instead of buying corporate bonds or government bonds. In fact, she already owns some mortgage-backed securities as part of her bond mutual funds.

Mortgage loans are a little safer than some other kinds of loans, because if the borrower doesn't pay, the lender can foreclose on their house, sell it, and get money back that way. Some mortgage-backed securities even come with guarantees from government agencies. Despite this government guarantee, they pay higher rates of interest than regular government bonds.

Mortgage-backed securities have a terrible reputation today, because of their role in the financial crisis of 2008. During the housing bubble, even the most uncreditworthy borrowers could get mortgages even in the absence of government guarantees, and then financiers performed some wild alchemy to turn these bad loans into AAA-rated bonds. Somehow, credit rating agencies were persuaded that having priority rights to receive the first payments from a group of bad loans was a safe bet, even if all the loans in the group were terrible. The number of defaults was much higher than the most pessimistic projections, and with collapsing house prices, only limited sums of money could be recovered by foreclosure. Some of the mortgages even turned out to be fraudulent. These bonds, needless to say, were a bad buy.

Luckily, mortgage-backed securities also come in "vanilla". Jen's own mortgage was sold by her bank to some final owners of vanilla bonds, who recently got some cash back when Jen paid off her mortgage early. Buying vanilla or "pass-through" bonds is straightforward enough for Jen to understand and accept the risks.

Mortgages provide something genuinely valuable for the borrower. Without access to a mortgage, young people would need to save for decades until finally, perhaps late in life, they have enough money to pay the entire price of a house in cash. Meantime they would need to rent from some landlady like Jen. Jen would rather lend them the money so that they can buy the house early. Decisions about when to paint the house and what color are better made by whoever lives there. And Jen would rather receive a steady stream of interest payments than a steady stream of rent payments plus a lot more hassle. The owners of a mortgaged house may not mind that hassle as much as Jen does, since it concerns decisions that directly affect their daily lives.

So Jen would like to lend her money out in the form of mortgages. In broad terms, Jen can understand them, in the same way that she can understand corporate bonds. In other words, it is clear how money lent out now will generate a stream of payments in the future, repaying the principal plus interest.

But if Jen is going to lend her money out to homeowners, she would also like to understand who she is lending to. What house does he want to buy and where? Is this more house than he can afford? What is his income, and his other assets and debts?

Banks used to ask all these sorts of questions before they made mortgage loans. Local bank managers would learn about and understand all kinds of details about the financial position of a mortgage borrower before agreeing to invest in him.

Today, banks have no incentive to put in this kind of work. This is because banks sell on the mortgages almost immediately, passing the risk to whoever buys the eventual mortgage-backed securities. That buyer will own a share in many mortgages, with limited information about each of them. This is an example of the poisonous effects of liquidity. A liquid market for mortgage lending creates short-term incentives. The bank has an incentive to process loans quickly and with a minimum of fuss, because it earns a fixed fee for each one. So the bank does only enough research into the borrower as it needs to in order to be able to sell the mortgage on. Banks no longer have any incentive to make judgment calls about the long-term repayment prospects for individual borrowers. Banks have no skin in the long-term game. The new Dodd-Frank regulations were supposed to change this, but so far, nothing has changed.[42]

As the long-term owner of a mortgage-backed security, Jen would like to understand each of the mortgages she invests in, in the same way as a local bank manager used to understand the loans he made in his community. She wants to understand the mortgage accurately, but she doesn't need precision. A borrower's situation can be summarized precisely by his credit score, current income, committed expenses such as debt and alimony payments, and current assets. These are the numbers that the bank cares about, and needs to collect information about in order to be

---

42 "Banks Again Avoid Having Any Skin in the Game" New York Times October 24, 2014 http://www.nytimes.com/2014/10/24/business/banks-again-avoid-having-any-skin-in-the-game.html

able to sell the mortgage on. Unfortunately, these numbers do not accurately capture all the relevant information. Each mortgage borrower has a unique situation. What are their future income prospects? What other assets might they inherit, leading them to pay off their house early like Jen? How likely are they to stay in the house over the long term? How easy would it be to resell the house? Jen has no way of knowing this kind of information when she buys a mortgage-backed security. But all this information is relevant, and it all increases the accuracy of the decision to lend to one individual rather than another.

And here we start to see a solution. We have already seen companies bypass banks (the middlemen) when they raise capital via stocks and bonds sold to individuals. What if an individual homeowner did the same thing, and sold a "bond" directly to one or more individual buyers?

Could Jen lend directly to help somebody buy a house, without going through a middleman? Middlemen charge a lot of fees, helping bring financial services up to 8% of the economy. Adding insult to these injurious fees, a middleman's incentives is only to make loans good enough to be sold on, which is a short-term perspective. The middleman has no incentive to assess the long-term creditworthiness of the long-term mortgage loans that he issues.

If Jen were to lend money directly to a homebuyer, her investment would not be liquid. This is fine by Jen. She doesn't need the money at all for at least 15 years, and even after that, she needs a stream of income (such as mortgage payments) rather than needing her capital back. If she really, really needed cash, maybe she could find some other retiree to sell the mortgage to, or she could offer to pay any refinancing fees so that the borrower could belatedly borrow from a bank.

There is a premium on liquidity. When Jen buys bonds, including mortgage-backed securities, on the open market, she pays for more liquidity than she needs, sacrificing returns in exchange for something she doesn't value. To get the best returns, Jen should actively look for illiquid, imprecise investments, not avoid them.

Jen goes online and starts to browse the websites of peer-to-peer lending companies. She wants to lend to a particular mortgagor, to learn a lot about who she is lending to, and not to pay a lot of fees to the middleman who puts them in touch and who handles the paperwork. She doesn't find exactly what she is looking for; each of the websites she finds will tell her only very limited information about the borrowers, and none of them do mortgages secured by threat of property foreclosure. So Jen keeps looking.

# CHAPTER 19

# JEN'S STUDENT SHOWS A BETTER WAY

As a science professor, Jen does research as well as teaching. Jen's university focuses on undergraduates, and doesn't enroll many of the PhD students who normally do the bulk of scientific research. So at her university, it is the undergraduates who conduct small research projects, as an important part of their science majors. At any given time, Jen is typically supervising the research of about six undergraduates.

This is great for the students' education. Classrooms are no place to learn what science is really like. Problem sets always have a right answer out there waiting to be found, and to find that answer, students know they need to use whatever they have just been taught. Traditional science "labs" are scripted, and feel artificial. It's hardly a process of scientific discovery when students repeat exactly the same procedures for decades, and to get things "right" means to get the same result as others, rather than to discover something new.

But in Jen's research lab, just as in real life, you never know what tool to use to solve a problem. Real science, like real life, is messy. There are many ways to approach any problem, and nobody knows ahead of time which one is "right". Perhaps no answer is possible at all, or perhaps you don't yet have the right tools. Jen loves the process of science with all its messy creativity, and loves sharing that passion with students. She loves watching her students grow up as they encounter roadblocks, even when they don't "succeed" in solving the scientific problems.

Jen has especially enjoyed interacting with her student Luke this year. A lot went wrong with his research project. Several times, he got what looked like an exciting result, only for it to disappear when he probed further and repeated things more carefully. As a result, he had to change the focus of his research project many times. Despite all these problems, Luke always stayed cheerful. Most students bring their problems to Jen and simply say "I'm stuck; what should I do next?" Luke would come to meetings always prepared with an idea for what to try next, and sometimes his ideas were better than Jen's.

Luke graduated, but since his project had finally generated a really exciting result, Jen offered him a temporary job over the summer, to tie up a few loose ends and write a scientific paper about his findings. He was accepted into his first choice of PhD program, and is making plans to move there in the fall.

Looking around for somewhere to live in his new city, Luke discovered that it might be cheaper to buy an apartment than to rent one. The housing market collapse had a silver lining for him. Foreclosures, short sales, distressed sales … all of this means real bargains for somebody looking to buy for the first time. Rental prices haven't gone down nearly so much; the steady flow of students and other short-term employees at the university are still willing to pay much the same as ever for the rental units on offer. So buying now looks like a bargain compared to renting.

Luke flew into town on a scouting mission, and found a one-bedroom condo, biking distance from the university. He put in a bid for $80,000, which seemed like a fair price given other recent sales. Paying the mortgage on this condo would not only be cheaper than renting, it would also help Luke build up equity and a more substantial credit history.

Luke has $5,000 for a down payment. This is partly because he had won a full scholarship that covered his undergraduate tuition. His parents had set aside some education bonds, and given the full scholarship, Luke didn't use them completely. Luke worked through college too, including working for Jen, and saved some of his own money along the way. After setting aside some money for the move and for living costs until his first paycheck, Luke still has $5,000 available towards a place to live.

Luke's was the best bid on offer, and the owner was happy to sell. But this was a short sale, meaning that the current owner's mortgage was more than $80,000. Unfortunately, the bank wasn't happy about that, vetoed the deal, and the sale fell through. With fall semester rapidly approaching, Luke became nervous: where would he live?

Then another, essentially identical apartment in the same complex came up for sale, this time for an asking price of only $63,000. This is exactly the amount that the current owner still owes on her mortgage. She has a new job in a new city, and just wants to cut her losses and escape. She has priced the apartment so low in order to be rid of it and get on with her life. Sight unseen, Luke quickly jumped at the chance to buy it. On closing day, when Jen wanders down to the lab, she expects Luke to be in a great mood, the drama finally over.

Instead, he looks distressed. "What's wrong?" asked Jen.

"My mortgage broker didn't get the paperwork done. The sale is falling through, and the seller is going to put the apartment back on the market. I can sack my broker and get a new one, but I probably won't get funding in time, before someone else buys it. Plus there are only two weeks left now until I move, and I don't know where I'm going to live."

"What do you mean, he didn't get the paperwork done? That's his job. You were approved, right?" Jen is flabbergasted. Financial services make up 8% of the economy. They should be doing something for all that money. Surely this isn't so complicated.

"Yes, I was approved. I guess my mortgage is so small, I am low priority for him. He just didn't get around to it." explained Luke.

Jen has been looking for a way to lend out mortgages to trustworthy borrowers. She didn't find one online, but now she has found a perfect candidate in person, in need of a mortgage loan. She would be happy to lend to Luke. She knows his character in a way no mortgage broker ever could. Jen has seen how well he deals with setbacks. She knows he makes a great employee, and will have no trouble holding down a job. As a PhD student, his small stipend will be enough to make his mortgage payments. Indeed, with this apartment being so cheap, he is financially better off owning than renting. Assuming no crazy unforeseeable events, he should be financially OK, and geographically stable, for his next five or more years as a student. His PhD program has a great placement record, and after that, Luke will almost certainly earn more than Jen. The long-term prospects for repayment are excellent.

Financially, this is what Jen has been looking for. An investment she understands accurately, and more accurately than others do, even if her understanding is not precise. A loan that is not, and does not need to be, liquid.

And on a human level, it also seems the right thing to do. Luke wants this condo, and unless she steps in, he may lose it. He is getting a bargain price from a frustrated and distressed buyer in a hurry; next time he might not be so lucky.

"It would be a real shame if this fell through. I guess you have so little time to make things work. Um, what would you think if I lend you the money instead? Not as a favor, but because it's a good thing for me too", ventured Jen.

"That would be kind of weird," replied Luke. "I mean, you're my boss."

"Only for the next two weeks. After that, I'm your ex-boss. Somebody you might occasionally call in on if you're in town, but that's it."

"I guess so," said Luke. "But what about all the legal stuff? I don't have much of a credit history yet, and I'd like to build one up. And also have everything official and in writing."

"Of course," replied Jen. "We would need to work all that out. You'll want to make sure you can deduct your mortgage interest from your taxes, too. We need a formal contract, for both of us. Look, how long will the seller wait? Do you want to have a think about it, see if your mortgage broker pulls off a miracle today, and if not, make a decision tomorrow?"

The mortgage broker produced more excuses and promises, but no miracle. Luke slept on it, and then early in the morning, he phoned Jen to ask if she still wanted to do it. When Jen said yes, Luke quickly phoned the seller, who agreed to give Luke a couple more days to come up with the money.

Meantime, Jen found the website of a company that handles within-family loans. The company handles the essential paperwork. It files a lien, meaning that if Luke did not make his payments, Jen would then be able, as a last resort, to claim the property through foreclosure. It also processes the mortgage payments, keeps track of the balance, and prints tax statements. It leaves out some of the other usual steps in a mortgage because they are not necessary when the parties already trust one another. As a result, this company only charges $725, much less than normal closing costs, so Luke needs $59,000 to close the deal, on top of his own $5,000. Jen spent a while on the phone trying to persuade them to take her as a client even though she is not a close blood relative of Luke. In the end, the company agreed. Papers were signed, Jen wired the money, and Luke had a place to live.

Jen gave Luke the same interest rate that he would have got if the mortgage broker had come through on time: 4.3%. Luke will make regular payments of $292 each month, calculated as though he were paying the loan off over 30 years; at the beginning, $215 of this is interest, dropping slowly over time in favor of repayment of the principal. Luke will likely sell the apartment after he graduates from his PhD after 5-7 years, and pay the balance back then. For Jen, this is a great deal. Luke is perhaps a bigger risk than US Treasury bonds or a certificate of deposit at the bank, but she would only get 2% interest at the bank, or maybe less, over this kind of time period. To get an interest rate of 4.3% within the options that she can browse within her retirement account, Jen would need to choose a borrower who looks much riskier than Luke. And this arrangement is much less work than finding, buying, and renting out an apartment like the one Luke found and wants to buy for himself.

Jen believes Luke will do well in his PhD, which pays a guaranteed stipend. But even if Luke doesn't finish his PhD, Jen knows that Luke is a great employee and could find a good job without it. The mortgage broker doesn't know any of these things about Luke. Jen has finally found a way to invest in something she understands.

# CHAPTER 20

# HEDGING ONE'S BETS

As I was writing this book, I told many people about Jen's investment decision. Some were enthusiastic. A few had even done something similar themselves already. Others asked for advice about how to tactfully find a partner to borrow from or lend to, and how to figure out what interest rate was both fair and better than what either of them could get elsewhere.

Other people, however, were skeptical. The skeptics' objections came in two flavors. One concerned the inevitable messiness of human relationships; we'll talk about this in the next chapter. The other was that Jen would not be diversified enough. In other words, she would have too much of her money invested in just a single individual, Luke.

We already talked about diversification back in Chapter 1, when we mentioned how dangerous it would be for Jen to invest all her money in the stock of a single company. Something terrible, like an asbestos lawsuit, might wipe out the entire value of that one company. Jen's money is safer if she spreads it between many investments, since this kind of disaster probably won't happen to all of them at the same time. This is why Jen originally invested in a passively managed S&P 500 index fund, which spread her money across 500 companies. Then she sold that fund because she decided that shares were overpriced, and bought bond mutual funds instead. These bond funds also spread her money between many different borrowers.

How many different investments does Jen need to make before she is diversified enough? Jen's current strategy is to divide her money among a number of different assets: equity in her own home, a rental house, inflation-protected government bonds, and loans to a handful of individuals like Luke. Is this enough different assets? Would she be safer if she avoided large individual investments like a rental house and personal loans, and instead placed that money in index funds that spread that portion of her wealth across 500 stocks or 500 borrowers?

To figure out how much diversification is enough, let's start by going back to basics and reminding ourselves why Jen is better off splitting her money between two companies or individuals, rather than just one. To make this discussion simple, imagine that all the companies whose stock or bonds Jen might buy are generally safe, but on rare occasions, one of them goes bankrupt, for example because of unpayable damages from an asbestos lawsuit. Similarly, let's assume that borrowers like Luke either pay the money back exactly as agreed, or they run away with her money and Jen never sees them again. Real risks are more complicated than this dichotomy between total safety and complete loss, but making risk an either-or question keeps our discussion simpler for now.

So what does Jen gain by splitting her money across two investments rather than just one? If we track any single dollar of hers, that dollar is equally likely to be lost, whether she invests in one place or in two. This is because no matter how she splits her money, any one particular dollar or cent ends up invested in a single place. One dollar doesn't know how her other dollars are invested, and the chance that that dollar is lost is based on whether the company or individual it is invested in defaults. Each dollar ends up going to an equally risky place.

But Jen is not interested in the fate of any one of her dollars; she cares about what happens to her $700,000 as a whole. Invested in just one place, she might lose all her money at once. With two, she will lose at most half of her money. This is the big improvement brought by diversification.

Now imagine investing in three companies or people rather than two. Now instead of losing half her money, Jen shouldn't lose more than a third. This is also an improvement, but it is a much smaller improvement than losing half her money instead of all of it. The improvement is even smaller when investing in four companies rather than three, or five rather than four.

The benefits of investing in ever more companies get smaller and smaller, but they are still benefits, so why not split her money between thousands of assets for the largest possible diversification benefit? Passively managed index funds offer Jen the opportunity for a mind-bogglingly high level of diversification. But the problem is that such high levels of diversification are in conflict with Jen's one big investment principle: don't invest in anything you don't understand. It is impossible to truly understand thousands of different investments. Jen wants to split her money between multiple things, but she also wants to understand each of them.

The common wisdom that diversification is good says that you should not "put all your eggs in one basket". Mark Twain perhaps saw things better and gave the alternative advice to *"put all your eggs in the one basket, and – WATCH THAT BASKET!"* [43] Diversification does not come for free. When Jen's money is scattered, so is her knowledge about what is being done with it.

The Bible gives sensible investment advice about diversification, recommending a middle ground. It says *"Cast your bread on the surface of the waters, for you will find it after many days. Divide your portion to seven, or even to eight, for you do not know what misfortune may occur on the earth".* [44] Seven or eight different investments seems to Jen like a reasonable place to stop. Investing in Luke took surprisingly little work, but maybe that was just beginner's luck. Buying a second house to rent out will be more work than lending to Luke. Finding, understanding, tracking and troubleshooting seven or eight investments at a time is certainly doable, but it will not be trivial. Maybe, if the investments are safe enough, Jen could stop at five or six. She certainly doesn't want to go above eight. Adding more investments after eight doesn't bring a lot of extra diversification benefits to compensate for the extra work. Meantime, an index fund of thousands of asset types is diversification overkill, and makes it impossible for Jen to understand her investments.

Life was rather different in Ecclesiastes' time, so perhaps the Bible is not the right place to go for financial advice. But while the economy has changed profoundly, human psychology has not. Seven or eight things corresponds to the maximum that humans are good at keeping track of. In other words, the Bible advises us to diversify as much as possible, up to the maximum that we are able to understand. This limit of seven or eight things applies just as much to Jen as it did in Biblical times.

---

43   Twain, Mark, and Charles Dudley Warner. Pudd'nhead Wilson. Vol. 21. Harper, 1899.
44   Ecclesiastes 11:1-11:2.

In the interests of diversification, and following the advice of the Bible, Jen would ideally like to split her $700,000 into as many as seven different assets. And then investment number eight is her own house, worth about $350,000. We won't count Jen's $10,000 investment in solar cells on her roof as one of the seven; after installation, she can forget about it and enjoy the ~8% return in lower energy bills, and consider it a supplemental investment into the value of her home. A second house worth $200,000 would be one of the larger of the seven. Then she will keep $200,000 in long-term TIPS, and $50,000 of short-term money in a money market fund or perhaps an even safer, FDIC-insured bank deposit. A $50,000 cash buffer should be plenty to cover unexpected expenses, including a dry spell if she is having trouble renting out her second house, perhaps even coming at the same time as she does repairs or renovations. A good cash buffer takes away the need for her other investments to be liquid.

That leaves Jen $240,000 to invest in up to four different places, places where she is willing to take a little more risk in order to get a better interest rate than from her TIPS. Her $59,000 loan to Luke is about the right size then, as one of those four. After buying a good rental house for $200,000, she needs to look for three more investments that add up to about $181,000. There is some flexibility in this sum. If it takes her a while to find suitable investments, the money can stay parked in her money market account. If she finds more great investment opportunities than she was looking for, she can sell some of her TIPS in order to make those investments while she has the chance. These won't be the last three investments Jen makes; Luke will eventually pay her back, and she will also keep saving money as she keeps working. Sometimes good opportunities will come along earlier than the ideal time, sometimes later, so she needs to be flexible.

Jen is definitely not investing too much of her money in a single individual, Luke. With $700,000 split among seven investments, her loan to Luke is in fact smaller than her target; assuming he could make his payments, she would happily have lent him more. Even somebody with only half as much money as Jen would have been able to lend to Luke while still easily passing the Ecclesiastes-diversification test. If Jen continues to invest according to this strategy, she will be diversified enough.

If Jen had just one amazing investment option with no risk at all, then she would not have to diversify. But there is no such thing as a 100% risk-free investment. Once we accept that risk is inevitable, we see that Luke is a pretty good bet. Consider a worst-case (and unlikely) scenario. Imagine Jen lent somebody like Luke more, perhaps $140,000, and then lost a quarter of her money ($35,000) in a financial hiatus and/or short sale. This is still only 5% of Jen's $700,000.

To put this in perspective, compare this to a "normal" investment portfolio. Most retirement accounts are split between stocks and bonds, with most of the money in stocks. The stocks are diversified in the sense that they are split across many different companies. But despite this supposed diversification, it is not unusual for the supposedly diversified S&P 500 stock index to drop by 7%. If Jen had her $700,000 in a conventional 70% stock: 30% bond split, and stocks fell by 7%, then Jen's portfolio would lose 5% of its value, the same as her worst-case scenario of personal mortgage lending. A 5% drop, if disaster struck Luke, is still nothing like as bad as a worst-case scenario for a conventional retirement account. Luke is low-risk compared to a diversified stock portfolio.

Now let's compare lending to Luke to buying conventional bonds. Bond mutual funds don't often drop suddenly in price like the stock market does, but they can still lose substantial value over longer periods of time. Bond prices fall when interest rates rise. Jen's loan to Luke is equivalent in some ways to a mortgage-backed bond, so she hasn't avoided this interest rate risk. Luke is currently paying 4.3%, an interest rate that Jen is happy with, compared to what she can get elsewhere. But if interest rates were to rise steeply, Jen's money would be locked up and unable to take advantage of those better opportunities. Luke will still repay at 4.3%; however if Jen had her money back early, she would be able to do better than that. To spread out this interest rate risk, Jen will try to find investments that pay her back at a variety of different times.

Rising real interest rates aren't a serious risk. That would actually be good news for Jen the capitalist in the long term, creating new and better investment opportunities for whenever Jen gets her money back, most likely when Luke graduates and sells the condo.

The serious danger in making any form of fixed-interest loan is that inflation might go up. Jen's portfolio is partly protected against this danger by having some equity investments, namely her own house that she lives in, as well as the one she plans to buy and rent out. Jen is also protected by owning TIPS, so that the government promises to compensate her for whatever harm inflation does to that portion of her investment. Inflation is one of the many misfortunes that could hit Jen's investment, but on her current investment plan, quite a lot of her capital is already well protected against it. If she wanted even more protection, she could negotiate a different deal with Luke, with a variable interest rate linked to the consumer price index or to the interest rate on some benchmark bond. It's too late to do this for Luke's mortgage contract, but this is something to think about for the next loan.

It may seem surprising that Jen can diversify so effectively with only eight investments. Jen's diversification strategy works because each of her investments is subject primarily to what is known as "idiosyncratic" risk. In other words, there is no connection between Jen's own house needing major repairs, Jen having trouble finding a new renter for her second house, or Luke having problems paying his mortgage. There's no reason for these things to happen at the same time. They are loosely linked to the state of the economy at large, but the main reasons for trouble are unique things specific to one investment at a time.

Modern financial markets make it easy to use a mutual fund to diversify across a mind-boggling array of stocks. In theory, this should average out all idiosyncratic risks down to the level where they aren't really risks at all, in contrast to Jen's strategy, where diversification makes these risks smaller but still big enough to worry about it. The reason that massive diversification doesn't make stock market index funds safe is that a lot of stock market risks are not idiosyncratic. Instead, the prices of different stocks tend to rise and fall in synchrony. When the same factors affect each of thousands of investments at the same time, the mutual fund owner doesn't get the promised benefits of diversification. This is a serious problem, and there is evidence that it is getting worse.

Non-idiosyncratic or correlated risks are not just a problem with the stock market. Correlations between different conventional asset classes are also large – and rising.[45] In other words, when stocks go down, so do

---

45   Global Financial Stability Report: A Report by the Monetary and Capital Markets Department on Market Developments and Issues, International Monetary Fund, April, 2015 https://www. imf.org/External/Pubs/FT/GFSR/2015/01/pdf/text.pdf

bonds, meaning that in practice, investors who split their money between stocks and bonds are not diversified after all. Making matters significantly worse, these correlations can be largest just at the moment when terrible things happen and diversification is most needed.[46]

The most important reason for Jen to diversify is so that no single event can destroy a large portion of her wealth in one hit. Spreading her wealth across any number of stocks will not achieve this goal; a stock market crash will take them all down at the same time. The 2008 financial crisis was mainly about the banking system and bonds, especially mortgage-backed securities, but it brought the stock market down with it. Similar events in the future are likely to also hit bonds and stocks at the same time. But those events won't necessarily mean that Jen can't rent out her second house, or that Luke will stop paying his mortgage. Jen's new investment strategy doesn't just have the superficial appearance of diversification; even with only eight investments, it's the real thing.

How can Jen successfully diversify where all these professional mutual fund managers fail? The answer is that Jen does not share the stock and bond markets' insatiable desire for liquidity. The reason that stocks crashed when the bond market froze up is that both markets depend on the liquidity of professional traders. These traders routinely hold "leveraged" positions, which means that they are trading with borrowed money. When there is trouble in the financial system, whoever lent out that money may ask for it back. Traders therefore need a lot of liquidity, so they are able to give the money back when asked. So when things

---

46   Preis, Tobias, et al. "Quantifying the behavior of stock correlations under market stress." Scientific Reports 2:752 (2012) http://www.nature.com/srep/2012/121018/srep00752/full/srep00752.html

go bad, traders all want to sell at the same time, across many different financial markets. The more leverage there is in a financial system, the more that each trader cares about his assets being liquid enough to sell in order to satisfy other people's demands of liquidity from him. Leverage can therefore prompt an arms race in the demand for liquidity. We'll come back to the issue of leverage in Chapter 22, when we talk about only investing money that is yours, rather than being both a borrower and a lender at the same time.

Leverage and liquidity are not important to Jen in the way they are for professional traders. Jen trades with her own money, not borrowed money, so nobody is going to beat down her door asking for their money back. She has all the liquidity she needs in her bank account and money market fund. Her other investments do not need to be, and are not liquid. Liquid assets traded on open exchanges all move together in response to short-term crises; illiquid ones are less affected by the crisis, and continue to obey the same long-term logic as they always did. Jen's loan to Luke is not very liquid. In desperation, if she really needed her money back for some emergency, she could try to sell it on to somebody else. But this is certainly not part of the plan, and even if Jen did have such an emergency, it would probably be an emergency that was idiosyncratic to Jen's private life, rather than being in sync with a financial crisis.

There is great irony in investors' rush to massive diversification through mutual funds and other tools. Diversification does give any one investor protection against idiosyncratic risks. But if everybody diversifies in exactly the same way, by buying small shares in the same indexed collections of assets, a lot of risk is unfortunately transferred from individual investors to the system as a whole.[47] At the same moment when one investor is in deep trouble and needs to sell, then everybody else is in trouble at the same time. Everybody trying to sell at the same time, when nobody is buying, leads to instability and collapse. To reduce the systemic risk of the financial system as a whole, different investors need to do different things. So by selling index funds and lending directly to Luke, it turns out that Jen is not only doing what is right for her; she is also, in her own small way, contributing to the stability of our financial system.

Jen doesn't benefit much from diversifying across more than seven or eight genuinely different investments. Seven or eight is enough to cancel out the vast majority of idiosyncratic risk. But stocks and bonds today have become so linked to one another that holding thousands of different ones isn't enough to diversify away all the risk. Idiosyncratic risks are simply replaced by systematic ones. Pursuing diversification through index funds is not only futile for Jen, but damaging to the global financial system. Jen can relax about diversification. She is doing enough.

47    Battiston, Stefano, et al. "Liaisons dangereuses: Increasing connectivity, risk sharing, and systemic risk." Journal of Economic Dynamics and Control (2012) 36:1121-1141 http://www.sciencedirect.com/science/article/pii/S0165188912000899; Stiglitz, Joseph E. "Contagion, liberalization, and the optimal structure of globalization." Journal of Globalization and Development (2010) http://www.degruyter.com/view/j/jgd.2010.1.2/jgd.2010.1.2.1149/jgd.2010.1.2.1149.xml; Haldane, Andrew G., and Robert M. May. "Systemic risk in banking ecosystems." Nature (2011) 469:351-355 http://www.er.ethz.ch/Systemic_risk_in_banking_ecosystem_Nature_Jan11.pdf

# CHAPTER 21

# LENDING TO PEOPLE IS MESSY

We all know friends and family who no longer speak to each other after quarrels about money. Jen's strategy of lending to people she knows seems like an invitation for trouble. If things go wrong, she risks losing not just her money, but relationships too.

So far, Jen hasn't lent to family, to personal friends, or to employees or coworkers, but only to a former student. This doesn't seem so bad. As far as relationships go, the best she can hope for is that a former student who happens to be back in town after graduation will knock on her office door to say hello. However close a mentorship relationship Jen has with one of her students, after graduation it always turns into a happy memory rather than an ongoing human contact. Jen doesn't have much to lose.

On the other hand, there are huge advantages to the messiness inherent in lending to people she knows. In particular, Jen knows Luke's character. She also knows his skills and so perhaps his job prospects. Jen doesn't have to lend to just anyone amongst her students. She can pick out only those who she thinks have good job prospects and a reliable character.

The financial system uses credit scores and other precise metrics to judge who is a good person to lend to. These blunt instruments do not measure the things that really count, especially when they are applied to young people with short credit histories. Jen can do better than the precision of a credit score; she can be accurate instead. Based on her personal knowledge from her messy human relationships with her students, she can do a much better job at picking out the talented and trustworthy ones than the financial system can. Local bank managers used to do this job, talking to prospective borrowers, and perhaps even knowing them as members of the local community. Those days are long gone. But Jen, by knowing young prospective borrowers so well, can probably do better not just than today's faceless credit-score-based financial system, but also better than the local bank managers of the past.

As a professor, Jen has an easier time than most of us in finding the best young people to lend to. Young people often need to borrow soon after graduation, just when Jen knows them best, and also just when she has the least to lose on a personal level, should something go wrong.

In this book, I recommend that more people try to follow Jen's example. You may feel that this is fine for Jen, but that it wouldn't work for you. You don't know suitable people to lend to, and anyway, you are worried that the human messiness will all end badly. Spouses quarrel about money all the time. Siblings often fight about their inheritance. Why do I have so much faith that we can all work it out if things go wrong?

I do not recommend lending to siblings. (Lending to children is better, as we will discuss in Chapter 23, and is in fact already common and uncontroversial.) While siblings sometimes cooperate beautifully, often they are competitive rivals instead. Children benefit from their parents' attention, and parents' attention is finite; this creates an intrinsic conflict of interest between siblings. This biologically rooted conflict colors their relationships, often making them hypersensitive about money and other advantages that parents can bestow. In other words, there are deep biological reasons why siblings might be the messiest possible people to lend to. Sibling relationships are also too important on a personal level to risk over retirement savings. For this reason, you should also avoid lending to friends or relatives who you regard "like a brother" or "like a sister" in your life. That still leaves a lot of acquaintances in your life, some fraction of whom you regard as highly reliable, and some of whom you would never trust enough to lend money to. Your ability to judge which is which provides accuracy in investing.

One big barrier to making loans to people you know is not knowing, out of those acquaintances you think are reliable, which have a good reason to borrow money. I recently visited a friend, let's call him James, who can no longer work due to a disability. James inherited a significant amount of money and would like to earn a steady return with which to pay his living expenses. He recognizes that at today's low interest rates, he will eat into his capital, but wishes to do this as little as possible. James's position is therefore quite similar to that of a retiree. With time on his hands, he was interested in the ideas in my book, but did not believe he knew anyone suitable to lend to. The next day, I met a mutual friend of ours, let's call him Thomas. Thomas, an extraordinarily trustworthy person with a stable income, told me he was house-hunting. James could easily lend a portion of Thomas's mortgage, if only the two had discussed it. Thomas could get an interest rate quote from the bank, and James could look at the quoted yields on bonds with somewhat comparable risks. By choosing an interest rate half-way between the two rates of return, both James and Thomas would come out ahead.

Like James, you may know more trustworthy potential borrowers than you think. Try bringing up this topic indirectly in conversation with people who you don't think need to borrow money, but who you would happily lend to if they did. Talk about what you learned from this book, how it was interesting and that you would love to try it. Complain that the one problem with the ideas in this book is finding the right borrower. You may find that one of the people you talk to has a student loan or mortgage that they would happily refinance with you, were you to offer them a lower interest rate. I have had many such conversations after people ask me what the book I am writing is about, even though I am not currently looking to lend.

In those conversations, I have also discovered that a number of my friends already lend money to people they know; not one of those friends had a negative story to tell. We usually hear about direct loans only when they go wrong. When everything goes smoothly, we have no reason to know that one of our friends is lending to another. This selective filter in hearing about the disasters but not the successes makes the business of lending to friends look riskier than it really is.

There are still some complications. James does not have enough money to cover Thomas's entire mortgage while staying diversified, including diversification between liquid and illiquid investments. Some retirees could fix this problem by pooling their savings and making a joint loan. Otherwise, it would be nice if the financial industry offered a "shared mortgage" product, where the professional agrees to lend the remainder and to administer the accounting. An equal arrangement would give both lenders equal returns, and would spell out a decision-making procedure to be followed should the mortgage go bad. In exchange for handling the administration, the professional financial partner would benefit from access to lower-risk borrowers who come pre-vetted by somebody who knows them and still trusts them well enough to risk their own money.

Loans to friends should not be sealed with a handshake. A proper legal contract should be drawn up and notarized. An interest rate should be negotiated that is mutually beneficial while reflecting the riskiness of the loan. Creative terms of the contract are fine, but they should be carefully thought through in advance, and be legally binding. Both lender and borrower need to understand that this is a mutually beneficial commercial arrangement, not a charitable "helping hand".

Picking low-risk borrowers is one advantage of lending directly to people you know. Better interest rates in the absence of a middleman is a second. Reasonable flexibility about contracts is a third. If Luke goes through a temporary crisis such as unexpected medical bills, Jen has the legal right to demand payment on the terms agreed in the contract. But she also has the option to offer to renegotiate the contract on mutually acceptable terms. An impersonal, highly automated financial system can't tell the difference between a genuine emergency and a flaky borrower who overspent on a shopping spree. But Jen can; she will actually talk to Luke, and have a pretty good idea whether he is lying. If Luke's troubles are clearly temporary, Jen may choose to lend him more, at higher interest. While compassion may affect Jen's decision, this is not charity alone, but also helps secure Jen's original investment, as well as create a second higher-yielding one. Alternatively, if Luke fails to pay and Jen is unsatisfied that he is on track to catch up, she has the same punitive options available as the regular banking system. Foreclosure is a terrible option, but it is always there as a last resort.

During the recent housing crisis, some foreclosures were described as "strategic defaults" rather than a last resort in a desperate situation. In the newspaper, Jen read about a family who bought a house for $400,000, then found after the crash that it was only worth $300,000, even though they still owed $380,000 on their mortgage. The family was doing fine and could make the mortgage payments if they chose to. But by walking away without paying another cent, they came out $80,000 ahead. They sent their house keys to the bank as "jingle mail" and were done with their debt.

Luke probably wouldn't do this to Jen. While primarily a business arrangement and not a matter for charity and a handshake, the arrangement between Luke and Jen ultimately has a moral dimension as well as a legal one. But Luke might still point out how he could, were he a different person, play the jingle mail game. On the basis of this guarded threat, Luke and Jen can negotiate. If Jen had lent to the jingle mail family in the newspaper story, she would have agreed to write off part of the mortgage, and reduce the balance to $320,000. The family who was willing to move out of their house and destroy their credit history for $80,000 probably wouldn't do it for only $20,000. This arrangement would also be better for Jen. Jen doesn't want the hassle of going through the foreclosure process and then renting or selling the distressed real estate. What is more, if the family had sent her jingle mail, she would have only got back $300,000 from the sale, minus the significant costs of foreclosing on and selling the house. This was the unfortunate fate of whoever owned mortgage-backed securities backed by the jingle mail family's mortgage.

A variety of different creative solutions can often be found when one human being negotiates directly with another, rather than the mortgage borrower dealing with "the system". For example, maybe the family could lose ownership of the house, but stay there as renters. Jen could then keep the house as their landlady. Even if she didn't want to keep it, she could sell it for a better price rented out in good condition than she could if it were empty following foreclosure.

Today's financial system cannot find these sensible, mutually beneficial solutions. During the housing collapse, "underwater" homeowners could not find a human being to negotiate with. Mortgages are issued by banks or brokers, often sold within a day or two, packaged with many other mortgages into pooled securities and sold perhaps to pension funds. The eventual owners of the mortgage-backed security don't know what they own, let alone understand its complexities. As a result, pension funds received less money back from foreclosures than they would have if they had been able to negotiate. This is because foreclosure was the only option that the system, rather than individuals in it, knew how to do.

The messiness of real human relationships allows for flexible negotiations to find creative and mutually beneficial solutions. Without a human being, there is nobody to negotiate with.

So how does all this apply to one particular human being, Luke? Right now, he seems like a pretty safe person to lend to. So long as he is in good standing with his PhD, his stipend is guaranteed for five years. If he decided that the PhD isn't for him, he would almost certainly stay enrolled and keep drawing a stipend until he found a job. And when he did get a job, he would earn more, probably much more, than his PhD stipend.

Luke might of course get into financial trouble some other way; for example, a medical emergency seems like a bigger worry. Luke will have health insurance through his new university, with out-of-pocket costs capped at $5,000 per year. Graduate students like Luke, scraping by on a small stipend, rarely have $5,000 in their bank account ready to pay a sudden hospital bill. Under normal circumstances, students (and other people who live paycheck to paycheck) charge such emergency expenses to their credit card if they can, and then skimp and save as best they can to pay the debt off before the interest piles up too high. But since Jen trusts Luke, they should be able to reach a much better arrangement than that. Jen could make Luke's mortgage payments interest-only for a while, and in the meantime offer Luke a second, unsecured, shorter-term loan to cover the hospital bill. For this second loan, Jen would offer a much lower interest rate than a credit card, but higher than his mortgage.

She would happily extend a similar kind of deal if Luke didn't want to take the first job he found after graduation, but instead wanted to wait a little and try for a better one, perhaps even doing an unpaid internship to persuade his ideal employer to take him on. Or if he simply needed help with moving expenses to a city with better job prospects. As Luke's boss for over a year, Jen knows he is resourceful and employable, so she is sure he will land on his feet in the end. Lending him more money in a way that helps his career is a good deal for Jen, especially if it is at an interest rate even higher than the 4.3% mortgage.

The biggest risk of all would be if Luke died or become disabled and hence unable to work. After thinking this unpleasant possibility through, Jen asks Luke if he would be willing to take out life and disability insurance. For a young and healthy nonsmoker like Luke, this turns out to be fairly cheap. In retrospect, Jen should have made this part of the mortgage contract, but Luke nicely agrees to take out the insurance anyway. So if Luke were hit by a bus and killed, Jen could not only reclaim and sell his apartment, but they now have a contract that also gives her a claim on his life insurance policy should the proceeds of the sale fall short of the debt.

The bigger risk is that of Luke becoming disabled, and needing all the disability money he can get. This is the sort of misfortune the Bible talks about, and this is why diversification is really needed. But even then, Jen is unlikely to lose all her financial investment. Luke would still need a place to live. If his existing apartment is suitable, then his mortgage payments are probably more affordable than almost any other option, so he could keep making payments out of his Social Security disability payments plus his private disability insurance. If he needed to move into residential care, then the apartment would be sold, and Jen should get her money back from the sale; apartment prices are unlikely to fall much further than $63,000. Of course, there could be a short-term financial hiatus and Jen could lose some of her money during that. But even in the worst scenario she can dream up, she probably wouldn't lose all of it. Importantly, Jen is diversified enough so that she wouldn't lose more than she can afford to. Indeed, as we saw last chapter, the risk of a loss of this magnitude is lower with Jen's current investing strategy than it is with a conventional one of stock and bond index funds.

The messiness of actually knowing Luke, rather than buying mortgage-backed securities on an exchange, provides many financial benefits to both Luke and Jen. One human being can talk to another and make arrangements that leave them both better off. What is more, an accurate assessment of risks cannot be obtained without the messiness of real human relationships. Yes, lending to people is messy, but it is inevitable. The current financial system doesn't avoid the messiness, but merely hides it from us, by hiding what is being done with our money. There is no avoiding the messiness of being human. In order to generate a return, money must be spent by real people on real things. Our choice is to deal personally with the messiness and even profit from it, or else to pay high fees to a financial industry to reimburse them for the service of hiding the messiness from our view.

# CHAPTER 22

# EITHER A BORROWER OR A LENDER BE

Jen has $450,000 inheritance money on hand to lend, and another $250,000 in her retirement account. Her loan to Luke came out of her inheritance money. Jen had no choice about which pot of money to use; the rules of her retirement account don't let her lend those savings to Luke. When she logs in to her retirement account, she has a certain range of options available. Nothing else is allowed. For example, she can invest $200,000 of her retirement account in TIPS, but her $200,000 rental property, like her loan to Luke, needs to come out of her inheritance.

This is annoying and inconvenient. And Jen can't simply withdraw her money from her retirement account and invest it however she likes. Even though she would still be investing for her retirement, this would count as early withdrawal, and be subject to a 10% penalty.

However annoying it is now, Jen had good reasons to lock up her savings in the retirement fund. Each paycheck, the money was deducted from her pre-tax salary. She will eventually have to pay tax when she withdraws the money to pay for living expenses during retirement, but in the meantime she has been earning compound interest on pre-tax dollars. And in retirement she will probably pay the taxes at a lower marginal rate than she would if she paid taxes on those savings at the time she earned the money. Even more importantly, her employer matches her savings dollar for dollar, instantly doubling her money. On those terms it would have been crazy for Jen not to pay in the maximum possible.

Jen was only able to lend to Luke because her inheritance gave her $450,000 of investable money outside of her retirement account. Most people, even those who are financially well-off, don't have that kind of flexibility. I myself am a good example of this; indeed, Luke's story is based closely on real events concerning a student of mine. The numbers I used may seem unrealistically low and the mortgage broker's behavior extraordinary, but all those details were taken directly from real life. Only the names were changed, and the date; this incident occurred in the summer of 2012, and in the three years since then, there has been a modest improvement in the housing market, with fewer distressed sales leading to such obviously good bargains. I would happily have lent money on Jen's terms to the real Luke, who would have accepted the loan. I would do the same today for a somewhat more expensive condo. But I couldn't do it then, and still can't. All my savings were and are in my retirement plan, or locked up as equity in our own home.

When the mortgage broker fell through for the real Luke, I had more than enough money in my retirement account to lend $59,000 while remaining diversified; I just wasn't allowed to use it. In fact, if I were able to withdraw the money, without penalty, from both my retirement account and that of my husband, we would have not only made a loan to the real Luke, but we would also have paid off the entire balance on our own mortgage, with change left over.

By paying off our mortgage, we would be investing our retirement savings into equity in our house. As soon as she inherited money in Chapter 1, Jen invested $100,000 in this way because it was simple, and because it was a good deal. No longer needing to make mortgage payments is an extraordinarily low-risk investment; other investments that are almost as safe all come with even lower interest rates than 3%. It is true that Jen lost the tax-deduction on her mortgage; but if she had invested that $100,000 elsewhere, she would also have seen a tax hike, via paying tax on the additional income she would be receiving in the form of interest on that new investment. So unless her alternative investment came with some tax incentive, Jen wouldn't have gained any tax benefit by keeping her mortgage debt. Many people are unduly swayed by the benefits of the mortgage interest tax deduction. All it does is level the playing field between paying off debt and buying a new income-producing asset. If the mortgage interest tax deduction were abolished, then Jen would have an even stronger reason to pay off her mortgage first, before looking elsewhere for investment opportunities.

Shakespeare's Polonius advised his son to *"neither a borrower nor a lender be; for loan oft loses both itself and friend, and borrowing dulls the edge of husbandry."* Indeed, a lot of borrowing is driven by desire for instant gratification, and could be avoided if we were more patient and willing to save. For example, it's usually better to save in advance for a new car than it is to take out a car loan and pay it back later with interest. But for really major, once in a lifetime purchases, Polonius's advice is unrealistic. Most of us have no choice about borrowing if we want to go to college or buy a house. By the time we have saved enough money for these major purchases, it may be too late in our lives to benefit much from them.

We also all need to be lenders at some point; if we wish to save money for retirement, some of that money will be lent to others. Yes, our retirement savings may well be lost, but if we want a comfortable retirement, we need to try. When we are too old and sick to work at the end of lives, we are counting on the next generation to owe us something, and take care of us. Unless we intend to work until we drop dead, we all need to be lenders.

Given our different needs at different ages, it is fine to borrow money, and it is also fine to lend. This, however, does not justify the current financial system, which encourages us to be *both* a lender and a borrower at any point in time. Many people are lending money via their retirement accounts at the same time as they are borrowing money for their mortgage and student loan. I would like to propose an amendment to Shakespeare's advice: instead of "*neither* a borrower nor a lender be", I suggest "*either* a borrower or a lender be". If everybody followed this advice, there would be less borrowing and lending in the economy than there is today. Over the course of our lives, there is a time to borrow, and a time to lend, but they do not occur at the same time.

In our current crazy system, I both make mortgage payments on the house I live in, and also receive mortgage payments from others, via ownership of mortgage-backed securities within my retirement account. For all I know, one of those securities might even include my very own mortgage within the bundle. In other words, by being a borrower and a lender at the same time, I might literally be lending money to myself. Each month, some of my mortgage payment would then make its way back to me via securities in my retirement account. Unfortunately, a considerable cut from each mortgage payment is diverted en route, in order to pay the many brokers who put the financial architecture together. Obviously, I would be better off using my savings to pay my mortgage down directly, rather than using it to buy loans that include the one to myself.

If I invested only in things I understood, I would never lend to myself in this way, where as the borrower I pay 3% and as the lender I am paid 2.5%. I don't even know whether I am, in fact, lending money to myself or not; I know that I own mortgage-backed securities, but I know almost nothing about which properties are involved. The fact that I can't decisively answer the question as to whether I am currently lending money to myself proves that I do not understand my investments. And even if my portfolio of mortgage-backed securities does not include my own mortgage, I am still not happy about borrowing at 3% while buying securities that pay only 2.5%. I have the option of a zero-risk 3% return by paying off my own mortgage, and I would like to take this option. My ownership of the asset that is my house is subject to the leverage of my mortgage loan. I would like to get rid of this leverage, and own my house outright, before I lend to anyone else. Unfortunately, our system of locked retirement savings accounts does not allow me to invest my money in this clearly sensible way.

Let's consider for a moment how finances could work in a different system, one without locked retirement accounts, one in which people try not to borrow and lend money at the same time. Let's follow the financial path of Kate and Craig, a typical middle-class couple in this different system. When they are young, they take out student loans to go to college. Within a few years after graduation, they settle down in steady jobs. They haven't finished paying off their student loans yet, but they nonetheless want to put down roots, so they borrow again to buy a modest house. Then, while they earn well (at least relative to their student days), they avoid changing their lifestyle too much; while their spending goes up, they nevertheless spend less than they earn, and use the difference to pay down their student loan and mortgage at a rapid rate. Instead of paying money into a retirement account, they save the same amount of money and more, and use it to pay off their debts more quickly. Kate and Craig's rate of saving goes down for a while with the expenses of having children, and goes up again later as their careers progress. Despite the slowdowns, their student loan and mortgage debts are paid off completely some time before the children graduate high school. Only then, with their debts paid off, so that they are no longer borrowers, do they look to become lenders. They start accumulating savings, and looking to place them somewhere that will generate an income in retirement.

Next, their daughter Rebecca wants to go to college. Kate and Craig don't want Rebecca to be too crippled by inflexible student debt. Instead of making Rebecca take out a regular student loan, Kate and Craig use their retirement savings to lend her the money instead, on more flexible terms. These flexible terms turn out to be useful. After Rebecca graduates college, she finds a great internship, but it is unpaid. Kate and Craig keep lending Rebecca money for living expenses rather than demanding repayment; they haven't retired yet, and are in no hurry to get the money back. Six months later, Rebecca's internship is converted into a good job. Only then does she start paying her parents back the money she borrowed during her student and intern days.

When Rebecca started college, Kate and Craig's mortgage was completely paid off. This is faster than most people pay off their mortgages today. But remember, unlike most middle-class workers today, Kate and Craig's paychecks didn't have a retirement account deduction; instead, they were sending that portion of their paychecks directly to prepay their mortgage.

Once their mortgage was completely paid off, Kate and Craig continued deducting the same amount automatically from each paycheck, but diverted it into a special savings account rather than to their mortgage. At first, that money sat in a money market account earning relatively little interest. There wasn't enough money yet to find a good investment, so Kate and Craig let the cash accumulate for a while until it amounted to a large enough sum to do something significant with. Meantime, it was a good cash buffer against the unexpected.

By the time this sum was getting large, an obvious use for this money came along: paying for Rebecca's college fees and living expenses. Kate and Craig didn't yet have enough cash savings to see Rebecca all the way through four years of college. When they ran out of saved cash, they calculated how much more Rebecca needed, and remortgaged their house by that amount. Then they lent that money to Rebecca to get her the rest of the way through college. The interest rate they got on this new mortgage was lower than the interest rate that Rebecca would have got on a regular student loan. As Kate and Craig continue to spend less than they earn, they can split those savings between paying down the mortgage, and lending Rebecca whatever additional money she needs, in particular her living expenses during her internship.

For the first time in their lives, Kate and Craig are borrowing and lending at the same time.[48] They wouldn't do this to lend to just anyone. They did it to help Rebecca, their own daughter, because they want to help

---

48    Technically, Kate and Craig's modest cash buffer in their joint bank account was a form of lending that they had even before their first mortgage was paid off. In other words, they did not completely empty their bank account each month in order to pay down their debts as fast as possible. This was not because they wanted to pursue a high return via lending money in the form of an interest-earning account, but was instead a simple precaution to maintain an appropriate amount of liquidity in the face of unpredictable expenses.

her, and they can borrow more cheaply than she can. In a sense, Rebecca is getting an advance on her inheritance. Indeed, Kate and Craig rewrote their wills to make it clear that if they died tomorrow, Rebecca's student debt would disappear, and their son, who did not go to college, would get a larger sum of cash than their daughter.

Conveniently, taking out a mortgage for the second time in their lives gives Kate and Craig a simple way to invest their savings again: paying down this mortgage. When Rebecca's internship turns into a real job, she begins paying her parents back. At first, this helps Kate and Craig pay off that mortgage. After that is done, they will have to find other uses for the money accumulating in their savings account, just like Jen does. If Rebecca stays in debt to her parents until after they retire, perhaps via a mortgage loan rather than a student loan, then Rebecca's loan payments will go directly towards her parents' daily living expenses in their retirement.

There are some times in our lives when it is really useful to spend more than we earn. There are other times when we earn more than we need to get by, and spending our entire paycheck is a luxury. When we are earning well, we can either save for a future retirement in which we no longer earn anything, or we can save to pay back student and mortgage loans from the past. In other words, lending and borrowing allow us to smooth out our spending over the course of our lives, rather than spending some parts of our lives in luxury and other parts in poverty. But to do this smoothing, we should borrow or be repaid for what we once lent when our income is low, and lend or pay back what we once borrowed when our income is high. Either a lender or a borrower be, depending on our stage of life.

When we invest with borrowed money rather than our own money, this is called "leverage", and it lets us make larger investments. As we saw in Chapter 20, leverage is dangerous for the financial system. If your investment goes bad and you lose your own money, things are grim for you. But when your investment goes bad and you lose *other people's money,* then their investments in you go bad too. And if they have also borrowed heavily, then somebody else's investments are also in trouble, continuing on in a chain reaction. With so many investors in trouble at the same time, many of them need to sell something in order to service their loans. When so many people need to sell at the same time, market prices collapse catastrophically, because there are too few people who are able to buy.

This might explain why the real Luke was in the end able to buy a condo at a distressed bargain price of only $63,000, making buying so much cheaper than renting. The real Luke's parents stepped in with a loan, and so Luke now pays $800/month including HOA fees, mortgage, and insurance, compared to ~$1,100/month for comparable rentals. What is more, now that the housing crash is over, condos in Luke's building now sell for $120,000.

During the housing crash, too many professional investors in the supposedly efficient real estate market were having trouble paying back their loans, and so unlike Jen and Luke, they were not in a position to snap up bargains. A highly leveraged financial system is a fragile financial system that is prone to catastrophic collapses. When we lend and borrow at the same time, we create leverage. Professional investors tend to be highly leveraged, while ordinary folk are hopefully less leveraged. Indeed, if they follow my advice and pay off all their debts, they will not be leveraged at all. People like Jen who actively invest their own money are in a better position to step in when the bottom falls out of a market, restoring sanity to prices at a time when leveraged players have no room to maneuver.

Leverage can be a good thing when we borrow to invest in a real life-long asset like a college education or a house to live in. But such loans should be paid back, removing the leverage. And unless you are a professional investor, borrowing in order to buy financial assets such as stocks and bonds, rather than to invest directly in a tangible asset you understand and that directly benefits your life, is crazy. Every time we lend or borrow, somebody in the financial industry makes money from the transaction. By persuading us to lend and borrow at the same time, our current system leads to more transactions, and more opportunities for the financial industry to earn fees on them. We can pay fewer fees by making sure that at any time, we are either a lender or a borrower. When we are currently a borrower, the best way to save, with no extra fees, is to reduce our leverage by paying back our debt, rather than lend to someone else. Leverage is bad for us as individuals by increasing the fees we pay, and it is also bad for our system as a whole, by making our financial system less stable and more prone to catastrophic financial crises.

Being a lender like Jen is more complicated than being a borrower; she needs to search carefully for people like Luke that she wants to lend to. As we get closer to retirement age, we should all be transitioning from the simple life as a borrower to the somewhat more complicated life as a lender and investor. It may be difficult to understand our investments, but outsourcing that understanding to the financial industry does not solve our problems, either as individuals or as a society.

# CHAPTER 23

# HOW TO MAKE MORE JENS

There are many forces encouraging us to save money through retirement accounts. When we do so, we hand over our savings to just a few companies, such as Fidelity, Vanguard, and T. Rowe Price. These companies organize the purchase of stocks and bonds, or of mutual funds of stocks and bonds, mutual funds that are often managed by the same set of companies. Our money is then locked up for decades.

We can reallocate our savings between the options that we are given, but if we are unhappy with all of the options on offer, most of us have no way to break out and find a genuine alternative. Jen's retirement fund has a long list of options to choose between, giving the impression of choice. In Chapter 20, Jen learned that the prices of all these conventional stocks and bonds and mutual funds tend to go up and down at the same time. They are so tightly linked that diversifying among them will not protect her against some of the risks that matter the most to her retirement.

When Jen decided that the stock market as a whole was overvalued and incomprehensible and that she wanted to stay away altogether, the only real alternative offered by her retirement plan was bonds. For most of the bonds available through her plan, Jen doesn't even know the name of the individuals, companies or governments that she would be lending money to. Jen has access to precise information about projected yield, but no accurate information about the borrowers' prospects of default. Except for TIPS, none of the options on offer through Jen's plan are options that Jen wants.

Jen educated herself and figured out how she wants to invest for retirement, including becoming a landlady and lending to Luke. Perversely, these eminently sensible options for retirement investment are not allowed within the rules of Jen's employer-provided retirement plan. These rules are supposed to help Jen make good choices, but in practice the rules prevent her from carrying out the perfectly reasonable and well-educated choices that she has made.

Luckily, not all of Jen's money is locked inside her retirement account, giving her some flexibility to invest outside these straightjacket rules. Many people, including me, are not so lucky; we have all of our investable assets inside retirement plans, limiting our options. Let's make more Jens by unlocking the money in retirement accounts. Let's allow more people to invest however they like, just like Jen can invest her inheritance money in retirement options that make sense for her. Many people may continue to choose conventional assets such as shares in a passively managed index fund. That's fine, but let them make that decision in an open rather than a closed market. Let's allow disruptive innovations to come along and give investors radically new choices. If the retirement plan offered by an employer does not offer satisfactory options, savers need the freedom to reject it, and like Jen, to discover or invent their own ways of investing.

It seems extraordinary that ordinary people agree to hand over their life savings, one pay check deduction at a time, and lock them up with only limited choices as to how to invest them. Many people feel that retirement accounts offer a good deal because of tax incentives. To get those tax incentives, retirement accounts must comply with intricate rules. Employers contract out the business of tending to retirement savings to a financial oligopoly who are protected by those intricate rules from disruptive competition from novel alternatives; employees have only the choices offered within the oligopoly, not the full range of choices open to Jen. But using tax law to explain why people are happy to lock their money away in retirement accounts over which they have limited control merely shifts the question. How did we as a society agree to use tax incentives to create a system that would take our life savings and hand them over to a small and protected number of private companies within an extraordinarily profitable financial sector?

Company retirement accounts were originally invented as a loophole to help top managers avoid taxes on their high incomes. Later, ordinary wage-earners at the same companies were allowed to have retirement accounts too. As this became more common, retirement accounts were promoted not just as a tax-avoidance mechanism for those with a lot of money, but also as a mechanism to promote responsibility in saving. The discipline of having money deducted from your paycheck before you even see it can make you forget you ever earned that money, so that you learn to live with less. It's a nice idea. This incentivized transfer from ordinary savers to the financial industry might even have been well meant, and not merely a cynical ploy by vested interests in the financial industry to increase and stabilize the amount of savings under their control and hence their own profits.

Unfortunately, in the real world, retirement accounts may do little to help the poor save for retirement. Saving money for a rainy day or a long retirement is a good idea. But many poor people can't manage it; they struggle just to make it from month to month, week to week, or even day to day. For the poor, savings means a simple cash buffer of a few hundred or hopefully thousand dollars as protection against unexpected expenses or unexpected disruption of income.

When people this poor are given retirement accounts, they get little tax benefit from the scheme, because they pay little or nothing in income taxes anyway. Worse, when life throws them a curveball, their least bad option in a time of trouble is often to raid their retirement savings, despite the punitive 10% penalty for early withdrawal. Saving for retirement is important because of the loss of income after you stop working. But why should protection against retirement loss of income trump protection against job loss in a bad economy, perhaps combined with ill health? Savings are savings, and rainy days take a variety of equally valid forms.

The poor need to save too, but locked retirement accounts offer too little liquidity, and do not serve their need for a stable buffer against the variety of hardships ahead. As things stand today, many would be better off placing their small savings into a regular savings account, where interest rates do not even keep up with inflation, rather than a retirement scheme subject to a punitive 10% early withdrawal penalty, often combined with high hidden fees and excessive investment risks relative to the likely shorter time horizon of the savings. The US Treasury myRA scheme does a better job serving the savings needs of the poor, providing higher interest than a bank account, principal protection, and no fees. The myRA scheme has been criticized for failing to prevent withdrawals for non-retirement purposes, but this is in fact one of the strengths of the myRA scheme in serving the poor.

Tax-sheltered individual retirement accounts are not an effective way to protect the poor in the face of the many other demands on their limited savings. Instead, the Social Security system does a good job providing a retirement safety net. Living on Social Security alone means living in poverty or close to it. But "poor but making do" is a reasonable standard for people who were already too poor to save throughout their working lives. Social Security payments don't have to be generous (and they aren't). The Social Security retirement plan covers only the minimum necessities of life. This seems right. In a civilized society, nobody should go without that minimum and be left to freeze or starve. But if you want a comfortable retirement, then it is reasonable to hold you responsible for planning that yourself, by saving. In other words, a certain minimum standard of life should be universal, provided for via compulsory savings and/or redistributed taxes. But the rest can be left to personal choice. People can of course disagree about how much is the necessary "minimum" on which one can live, but however one defines it, few people are callous enough to inflict less than that on the poor in their old age. Few wish to see old people going without food, adequate heating, or some humane minimum amount of nursing and medicine.

The Social Security system mixes several elements in meeting these goals. First, it is a compulsory, government-run retirement savings plan, guaranteeing a minimum income in retirement in exchange for payments throughout your working life. Second, it is an insurance plan, where those who die young subsidize those who live long past the time they retire or become disabled. Finally, it is also a progressive tax; during each month of retirement, the poor get back a higher percentage of their lifetime contributions than do the middle class or the rich.[49]

Social Security takes compulsory savings/tax payments out of each paycheck, and sends them to the Federal government. It also sends checks from the Federal government out to people who have already retired (or who are disabled). Right now, the checks going out are all paid for by the payroll tax coming in, as well as the interest on the accumulated surplus. After more of the baby boomers have retired, likely around 2020,[50] the incoming money will no longer be enough. For this reason, Social Security has for many years collected more money than it paid out, and invested the difference in a Trust Fund. This is saving for retirement at the national level. This act of saving the surplus at the national level helps to partially cushion the impact of the change in the dependency ratio.

The money that was saved up by the Social Security program was used to buy US Treasury bonds; in other words, it was lent to the US government. We want our government to invest this money wisely for our future benefit. As we have seen in this book, there are many good ways for the government to do this, by spending money improving physical infrastructure like roads and power grids, and by funding comparative effectiveness research to find out how to provide better health care at lower cost. These sorts of government spending meet the definition of real investment. When we wear the magic glasses, we can see how they make society as a whole better off.

Employer-provided, tax-protected retirement savings accounts provide discipline in savings, but so do Social Security payments. Jen now feels

49  Social Security Administration "Your Retirement Benefit: How It's Figured" (2015) www.ssa.gov/pubs/EN-05-10070.pdf
50  Social Security Administration "Summary of the 2014 Annual Reports" http://www.ssa.gov/oact/trsum/

comfortable investing for retirement on her own, and would prefer to do that. But if forced to hand her savings over to someone else to invest for her, Jen would rather be forced to make payments to the government than be forced to make payments to a private investment oligopoly. In other words, Jen would be willing to pay more Social Security tax in exchange for higher Social Security benefits, while abolishing her compulsory payments to her 401(a) private retirement account. The government will unfortunately have trouble paying Jen back as much as she put in, because of the change in the dependency ratio. But as we saw in Chapter 10, this is also true of Wall Street; there is no magic solution to the dependency ratio problem, just different ways of disguising the problem.

Jen doesn't entirely trust the government, but she trusts Wall Street even less. At least the government is in a position to do really great things, like infrastructure investments and cost-saving medical research, that no group of private individuals could ever coordinate on their own. Jen thinks that she can now make investment decisions on her own, but she understands that there are other people out there who would make terrible decisions, and need to be protected from their own folly. But if we don't trust ordinary citizens to make wise choices about investing their own money for retirement, why should we trust Wall Street to do better with other people's money? The financial oligopoly is subject to various laws that are supposed to protect consumers. In other words, government regulation is supposed to tame the financial industry's shark-like tendencies and protect the common saver. Government regulations are there to protect investors from their mistakes. But if we trust the government to regulate the intrinsically untrustworthy financial sector and its unsophisticated customers, then why not simply trust the government to invest directly? At the end of the day, somebody has to make investment decisions, whether it is individuals like Jen, the government, or the financial industry. Each decision-making option has its flaws, and there is no perfect alternative. Among the options, Jen rates herself and the government above the financial sector.

Jen supports the Social Security system, and thinks the government should use tax money to invest more in infrastructure and medical knowledge. But there is only so much she can do to make that happen. Much as she would like to, Jen cannot solve all the problems of the world. Her immediate responsibility is what to do with the private portion of her savings, outside of the current Social Security system. She wants to make her own choices about how to invest this money, unconstrained by the options within her retirement account plan.

Before she received her inheritance, Jen, like most middle-class Americans, could have channeled savings into extra payments on her mortgage. If it weren't for the tax incentives and employer-matched payments, this would be a better option than either a locked retirement account or a savings account. Making extra mortgage payments before buying any bonds means waiting until you are no longer a borrower before becoming a lender. Home equity is saved primarily for retirement, but can be accessed earlier if needed. As we discussed last chapter, home equity makes a great piggy bank. If windfall cash arrives, for example an inheritance or the sale of a business, you can lock the money away as savings by making an extra one-off mortgage prepayment, on top of your regular monthly transfer. Getting money out of the piggy bank by taking out a home equity loan is, appropriately, harder than putting it in, making people pause before lifting the hammer. But breaking open the home equity piggy bank is a better deal than early withdrawal from a retirement account. The home equity piggy bank provides a valuable safety net against unexpected loss of income or unforeseen and potentially catastrophic extra expenses. Breaking it open generally beats paying a 10% penalty for early withdrawal from a locked retirement account.

For many people earning modest incomes, home equity is the only asset they will ever save enough money to own, perhaps paying off their mortgage just as they retire. Then in retirement, they have three choices. First, they can live off Social Security payments, but with the added cushion of no longer needing to pay rent or mortgage, making the Social Security payments go further towards their living expenses. Second, they can sell their home, either renting or buying a cheaper home, and use the money from the sale to supplement Social Security in their retirement. Finally, they can take out a "reverse mortgage", where they receive a check every month in exchange for gradually giving up equity in their house, re-accumulating mortgage debt until they die or sell. These reverse mortgage checks supplement their Social Security payments, and hopefully, they won't run out of home equity before they die.

So the poorest in society end up with no private savings, living on Social Security alone. Meantime, people who are financially stable enough to pay off a mortgage can live on Social Security plus a return on their saved home equity, paid out as free rent and/or a cash supplement in their retirement. Still more affluent people like Jen may, over the course of their lives, save or inherit more money than their home is worth. Once the mortgage is paid off, figuring out how to keep investing for retirement is harder. Jen has found lending money for the first time, instead of paying loans off, is a big transition. It's hard to find someone trustworthy to lend to.

To avoid this hurdle, one obvious option is to buy a more expensive house, thus building up even more home equity through a new or bigger set of mortgage payments. I have argued that buying a house to live in can be a good investment, and a good way to save by making mortgage payments instead of rent. But this doesn't mean that buying a more expensive house is the best investment for those who can afford it. Just like the primary long-term value of stocks comes from dividends, not the final sale price, the primary value of owning a home comes from living in it, not from selling it later. And larger, more expensive houses come with higher taxes, higher maintenance costs, and higher energy bills, which can easily make people "house poor". Most people see renting a mansion as an extravagant expense. Buying a mansion is an equally extravagant expense, not a prudent investment strategy. Whether you pay mortgage or rent, a fancier home means spending more each month on living expenses. The best investment strategy is to buy the sort of home for which you would be prepared to pay rent; nothing flashier than that. Then the value of owning the home comes from not having to pay rent.

It doesn't always make sense to buy a home. It all depends on the cost of buying vs. renting. The *New York Times* published a good online calculator to help work out whether buying or renting a home is the better deal.[51] The aftermath of the housing crash made buying a good deal compared to renting in most parts of the US. For this reason, this book has been positive on buying homes, both to live in and as investment properties to rent out. But the housing market in many areas is now improving, and this may not always be the case. People looking for a home should look

---

51   Bostok, M, Carter, S, and Tse A, New York Times The Upshot "Is It Better to Rent or Buy?" interactive calculator http://www.nytimes.com/interactive/2014/upshot/buy-rent-calculator.html

at both rental and buying options, and choose whichever offers the best deal, while living within their means.

Kate and Craig had the right strategy. Instead of buying a house that was the maximum they could afford, they bought a house for which, through aggressive saving, they were able to pay off the mortgage well before they retired. Then after the mortgage was paid off, they kept saving. People like Jen, Kate and Craig, who wish to continue their comfortable lifestyles into retirement, need to own additional investments by the time they retire, beyond having paid off their home mortgages. This is because they cannot support those comfortable lifestyles on Social Security and reverse mortgage payments alone.

Buying vs. renting is not just a question of relative pricing, but also personal circumstances. Owning a home doesn't make sense for everyone. For example, some people may earn enough, but they never stay in the same place for long enough, so shorter-term rental leases make more sense. This unfortunately means no access to the easy savings option of paying down a mortgage. These people are forced much earlier in their lives into Jen's situation of creatively looking for investments, before getting used to the discipline of mortgage payments. For these people, saving may be harder to manage, but not impossible. The myRA program is a good start, as a safe and simple investment with a modest interest rate, no fees, and the ability to withdraw the money later. If life becomes more stable later, those savings go into a down payment on a mortgage. Otherwise, a good savings starter account will still help build up a pot of money large enough to kickstart some other carefully chosen investment.

So let's go back to Jen and her investment options beyond her own home. The savings in her 401(a) retirement account can only be invested in standard financial products like stocks and bonds. Jen is forced to go through a giant financial company, like Fidelity Investments, that has been chosen by her employer from a small handful of options. Jen is relatively lucky. Her 401(a) includes a "brokerage account" that gives her a broader range of options than many retirement accounts. She can choose from an apparently wide selection of mutual funds and exchange-traded funds, and she can pick individual stocks. Jen wanted to buy individual long-term inflation-protected Treasury bonds, but this wasn't one of the options. Luckily, she was still able to achieve approximately the same strategy via an exchange-traded fund. But despite all these options, there is no way that Jen can use her retirement account to buy a second house to rent out. Nor can she use it to make a mortgage loan to Luke, only to buy funds of mortgage-backed securities.

Jen would like to eliminate this system, and have direct access to invest her private savings however she sees fit. When Jen lent directly to Luke, she cut out a lot of middlemen and the fees and commissions they charge to do the matchmaking and paperwork. Even if Jen wants the option of not using them, we can still ask whether those middlemen provide good service for the money. In other words, if Luke took out a standard mortgage from a bank, and Jen bought mortgage-backed securities, would the charges for these services be reasonable or unreasonable, compared to bypassing these services by doing business directly? In Chapter 17, we saw that the financial sector has steadily grown from 2% of the US economy after World War II to over 8% of the economy today. This makes Jen suspicious that someone in the financial sector must be overcharging her. The fees and commissions between taking out a mortgage and buying a fund of mortgage-backed securities are opaque; Jen has no idea how much she is paying. Suspecting the worst, she wants no part in transactions she cannot understand, and so takes matters into her own hands.

My suggestion in this book is that rather than stick to bank accounts, stocks and bonds, people with investable funds should consider buying a second property to rent out, and also making loans directly to people they know, people who would both benefit from the money, and be able to pay it back. For Kate and Craig, this means making student loans and mortgage loans to their own children. For childless Jen, it means lending money to former students, who are in some sense her surrogate children. Some younger people might lend reverse mortgages to the elderly; this is a great way to enforce the discipline of regular saving, because the borrower is counting on those monthly payments to live. The problem is that most people have all their investable savings locked into retirement accounts that offer only stocks and bonds as options, denying them the alternatives advocated in this book. What can we do to make more Jens, who are free to follow the suggestions I have made, or perhaps to find other imaginative ways to reinvent the financial sector?

The obvious way forward is to liberate retirement account savings. If the government wants to offer incentives for saving, it should find a way to encourage the act of saving, not the act of depositing money in particular kinds of institutionalized assets. If it wants to be a nanny state, overseeing how people's savings are invested, then it should do so directly through the Social Security system and investing in public infrastructure and medical knowledge, not by outsourcing its job of taxing and investing in the future to a private financial oligopoly.

A good start would be to give everybody the option to exit their company 401(k), 401(a), 403(b) or similar defined contribution retirement plan, and place their contributions in a self-directed IRA instead. This would help Jen (and me). Self-directed IRAs, unlike regular retirement accounts, can be used to buy rental property, or to make private party mortgage loans to people like Luke.

While this would be a great start, it wouldn't be enough to empower Kate and Craig. Self-directed IRAs allow most kinds of investments, but they prohibit "self-dealing". This means that Kate and Craig can't use their retirement savings to pay down their mortgage early, for example by having their retirement account lend them the money to make extra payments. Nor are they allowed to lend to their daughter Rebecca.

These rules are presumably there in order to make sure that tax-deferred money in a self-directed IRA is really flagged for retirement, and not for current spending. But Kate and Craig *are* using the money to save for retirement. Prepaying a mortgage is an excellent way of saving, as much for retirement as for anything else. After their mortgages are paid off and money has accumulated in a self-directed IRA, then the only difference between Kate's situation and Jen's is that Rebecca is Kate's daughter, while Luke is not related to Jen. The line between their two situations is thin; Kate can legally lend from her self-directed IRA to a niece or sister, but not a daughter.

A more radical possibility is to abolish tax-deferred retirement accounts altogether. If the aim of employer-provided retirement accounts is to help employees with the discipline of long-term saving, why don't they offer mortgage prepayments as one of the options? The short answer is that the retirement account rules don't allow it, making this savings option ineligible for tax benefits. But why do we have such stupid rules?

The home mortgage tax deduction is meant to encourage people to buy their own homes. But it also discourages current homeowners from paying off their existing mortgage debt, one of the simplest, safest, and most effective ways for ordinary people to save money every month, at an interest rate that is more than competitive given its near-zero risk. Meantime, we give preferential tax treatment to buying stocks and bonds within a retirement account. In other words, the tax rules actively encourage us to be a borrower and a lender at the same time. This benefits the financial industry, not the ordinary folk who are its retail customers.

There are currently three reasons to use retirement accounts: matching employer funds, the tax advantage, and the way that automatic payroll deductions help provide discipline in saving. If transfers are set up to run automatically each payday, mortgage prepayments can provide the same kind of discipline as automatic deductions to a retirement account. Employers who wish to encourage saving amongst their employees could offer a range of savings options, with retirement accounts being one (currently tax-preferred) option, and a direct link from paycheck to mortgage prepayments being an alternative.

With Jen's mortgage paid off, she may find the discipline of savings harder now, without a mortgage bill due each month. To keep the discipline of saving, Jen sets up an automatic deduction from her checking account to a special savings account, and she makes that deduction the same size as her mortgage payment used to be. This helps remind Jen not to spend that money on daily living, by placing it somewhere that Jen has mentally dedicated to investing for retirement. In the short term, the savings accumulate in a bank account. From time to time, once the balance has grown, Jen invests those savings elsewhere, looking for a place that will generate a higher return than the bank account. People who don't buy a house need to do something similar, saving and investing accumulated savings in the same ways as Jen. Jen is a disciplined and organized person and can do this on her own. Employers can help out by nudging employees to act like Jen, but by providing a broader range of options for where the payroll deductions can be sent, rather than stocks and bonds alone.

Individuals and employers can do their part here, but perhaps most importantly, tax rules need to be changed. The current rules encourage people to do as much business as possible with a financial oligopoly, including both borrowing and lending at the same time. A level playing field that took away these incentives would be an improvement on the status quo. What if we abolished the mortgage interest tax deduction, and also abolished the preferential tax treatment of locked retirement accounts? With these tax deductions gone, we could either lower regular tax rates, or increase government investing in infrastructure and comparative effectiveness research. Another advantage is that people could channel savings to the best use of the money, rather than in the way that is most tax-smart. Our current system does not give an incentive to save per se, but rather an (expensive) incentive to save in particular ways that are in the best interest of the financial oligopoly. Let's unlock those savings, and let people like Jen find new ways to invest and invigorate our economy, outside of the current oligopoly.

# CHAPTER 24

# THE SERVICE INDUSTRY JEN NEEDS

Last chapter discussed how to make more Jens through large changes to the tax code. In this chapter we look at more modest ways of making Jen's decisions easier within the system that we have. In particular, Jen is happy to pay fees to service companies that make it easier for her to lend to people she knows. We therefore ask what sort of financial services these would be, for Jen to want to buy them.

In any financial contract, there are many things to discuss upfront, and amateurs like Jen and Luke might not think of everything. A service industry can help. The cheapest, no-frills option is simply to provide prototype contracts, checklists, and directions for how to file the appropriate paperwork. DIY legal "kits" are already common for some other legal services like wills. They are increasingly available for simple private loans too. For example, LoanBack is one company that charges $15-$30 for help with a basic contract. There is plenty of competition in this market, with companies competing to offer extra conveniences for an additional charge.

These services, as they exist today, are ideal for simple, unsecured loans. Jen doesn't have a borrower in mind right now for this kind of loan, but perhaps one will come along. For example, some people get into financial trouble due to one-off disasters, e.g. surrounding a divorce or a medical emergency, ending up deep in credit card debt at crushingly high interest rates. If they are smart, they can consolidate that debt at somewhat lower interest rates such as 9%. Jen can imagine giving an unsecured loan at the still lower rate of 7%, in a win-win arrangement for them both. When Jen knows a borrower personally, she may know why that borrower got into financial trouble, and whether these troubles are now over, or likely to escalate until the borrower files for bankruptcy. Once Jen finds suitable borrowers that she trusts, companies like LoanBack help make this kind of lending easy to do.

For a larger, more complex loan, it might be worth paying for more expensive consultations to help navigate the contractual options, and manage the accounting. National Family Mortgage provides a more extensive service for mortgage loans,[52] charging $725-$2,100 for the initial paperwork (depending on the size of the loan, and amounting to much less than closing costs for a commercial mortgage) and with optional charges starting at $15/month for handling monthly payments. Proper paperwork includes a lien on the property, and the correct documentation to help Luke deduct mortgage interest from his taxes.

---

52    National Family Mortgage markets itself for loans between family members. I do not know whether National Family Mortgage would agree to handle the fictional loan between Luke and Jen. Interfamily loans have some special characteristics. In particular, wealthy parents may lend money to their children on deliberately generous terms. If these terms are too generous, the IRS deems such a loan a "gift" that is subject to the same gift taxes as a simple transfer of dollars. National Family Mortgage, through scrupulous paperwork, helps ensure that the interest rate is not so low as to incur gift taxes; this is part of the current appeal of the service.

At a basic level, help from service companies ensures that no documents are lost, and avoids misunderstanding about the legal status of what was agreed. Every loan should have clear legal obligations on the borrower, with agreed penalties for lateness / missed payments etc. We have talked about how a lender like Jen might under some circumstances agree to be flexible about repayment, for example if Luke had an expensive medical emergency. This flexibility can be one of the (mutual) advantages of direct lending, but is always the lender's prerogative, not the borrower's right. With the legal situation clear and witnessed by a third party, there should be less to argue about, posing less danger to relationships than if the deal were sealed with a handshake alone. It should be clear from the outset that the individual lender has all the same legal rights as a bank lender. While renegotiations of the loan contract are always possible by mutual agreement, they are never guaranteed.

A support industry can help manage and enforce existing contracts, as well as set them up. At the simplest level, this means handling the arithmetic of interest rates and payments. Irregular prepayments can make the math harder, making accounting help from a third party especially useful. More sensitively, automatic late fees, as specified by the agreed contract, can be imposed by an impersonal and professional third party rather than directly by the lender. And in the worst case, collection agencies are a service industry available as a last resort for a loan gone horribly wrong. Even when they are not used, their existence looms as a credible threat to use during renegotiation.

Luke's condo was unusually cheap, keeping his mortgage small enough to fall within Jen's investment budget. Most good borrowers buy more expensive homes. Jen would happily lend to them, but she can't afford the whole house price herself while remaining diversified. I glossed over this problem in Chapter 21; in real life, James's diversity and possible liquidity needs were not compatible with a full mortgage to Thomas, only a partial one.

Some of Jen's friends have money to invest too, and would happily pool resources so that several of them could jointly make a mortgage loan. A service industry that manages mortgages of this type, providing a similar sort of service to National Family Mortgage, would be useful. Clearly this requires a somewhat more complicated contract, but it should be doable. To the best of my knowledge, this service is not yet available, inhibiting peer-to-peer mortgage lending.

The technical term for what Jen is doing is "affinity lending", i.e. lending to people she already knows. But when Jen browses "peer-to-peer" lending on the internet, most of the "buzz" is about companies that help match investors with borrowers that they do not already know. Jen still has money left to invest, and hasn't found another good prospect like Luke to lend it to yet. Seeking new borrowers, she next takes a look at LendingClub and Prosper, two of the leading companies in the online peer-to-peer area.

LendingClub and Prosper specialize in unsecured loans, mostly credit card consolidation. Borrowers fill in their details, and the company checks their credit record, verifies other claims about their finances, and assigns them a score and interest rate. Lenders browse the listings, and typically spread their money out across many loans. For a traditional loan, banks act as middlemen, borrowing from depositors in order to lend. These new companies are an innovative alternative middleman, charging fees for matching borrowers with lenders. Compared to bank lending, this means more risk and hopefully more return for investors like Jen, and less risk for the middleman.

Jen browses borrower profiles, looking for good prospects to lend to. But what she finds does not satisfy her. Jen can access precise scores to assess each borrower, but she cannot find the kind of personalized and hopefully more accurate knowledge that she values. The information given about which borrowers are a good risk is nothing like the information that Jen has about Luke. These companies replace the traditional middleman, hopefully giving lenders and borrowers a better deal. But they do not change the nature of precise vs. accurate information in a way that allows Jen to invest in things she understands.

Jen finds upstart.com more interesting. The idea behind this company is to back a person you believe in. Returns are paid back as a function of that person's future income. Unlike the completely anonymous LendingClub and Prosper, communication and mentoring interactions between investors and "upstarts" are encouraged. Unfortunately, investing in upstarts is open only to "accredited investors".

Jen's net worth, excluding her primary residence, is less than $1 million, so she doesn't qualify. Apparently she is not sophisticated enough to understand the risks, and so is prevented by law, for her own good, from investing in this way. The same restriction applies to SoFi, another interesting peer-to-peer lending company that specializes in student loans.

Jen wants to invest directly in people she knows, doing things she understands. She doesn't need precise risk scores, but accurate and imprecise information about the borrower's character, plans and prospects. If websites can help her find such people, great. Right now, the internet is not helping her find worthy borrowers. She will have to find them on her own, in the real world rather than in cyberspace.

Across the world, many people are ill-served by our current financial system. In poor countries, group-guaranteed microfinance organizations have appeared as an alternative. In rich countries, people too poor to have a bank account find their own innovative ways of managing money outside the formal financial sector, for example the "sou-sou", where highly disciplined weekly payments are pooled and paid out to a different member each week as an occasional jackpot. These alternative microfinance systems rely heavily on the power of personal relationships and peer pressure to ensure that money gets paid back. We are all familiar with the idea that the financial sector does not do a good job serving the poor, leaving the door open for these more direct and personal alternatives. Jen is beginning to believe that the regular financial sector doesn't do such a good job serving the middle class either. Jen wants to create a kind of microfinance, suitable for the American middle class.

What Jen wants resembles the traditional "rich uncle" system of informal lending. It is up to the uncle (or aunt) to decide who to lend to, and on what terms. Old-school rich uncles lent on trust, outside the formal sector. To reinvent the rich uncle system for the American middle class, Jen wishes that there were companies offering payment services to simplify accounting, and legal contracts to formalize what is agreed. But aside from making use of simple and transparent service companies, the essence of Jen's strategy is to bypass an overly powerful financial sector that has grown to 8% of our economy, and take investing back into her own hands.

# CHAPTER 25

# LENDING STUDENTS MORE THAN MONEY

Jen's new retirement plan includes lending money to former students. This means she needs to keep finding suitable students. Luke was a good find; he was ready to take out a home mortgage straight after college. Luke's financial position was unusually strong for a new college graduate. Between his full scholarship, his parents' education bonds, and his hard work, he graduated not just debt-free, but with $5,000 in savings for a down payment. His timing was also good, graduating right after housing prices collapsed. In this time of financial upheaval, home prices had fallen so far that buying was a no-brainer compared to renting. Jen's inheritance allowed them both to take advantage of this coincidence of events.

Unfortunately for Jen, mortgage borrowers like Luke might not come along often. With rising tuition, most students now leave college with a heavy burden of student loans, and so are not yet ready to take on even more debt in the form of a mortgage. If Jen wants to lend to former students, she needs to consider other kinds of loans too.

The obvious option is student loans. Jen could offer to refinance student loans for a handpicked selection of her most trustworthy former students. If the refinanced interest rate is lower than the student's current rate, but higher than the return Jen expects elsewhere, then this is a win-win situation.

The rate that students currently pay can vary a lot. Some student loans, called "Stafford loans", are guaranteed by the federal government. Because of the government guarantee, interest rates on Stafford loans are low, currently 4.29%, although higher for loans that were dispersed some time ago.[53] Student loans are riskier for Jen than mortgage loans; if things go wrong, she can't foreclose on a property and get some of her money back that way. The greater the risk, the higher the interest rate Jen should charge. Even for the most trustworthy of her former students, Jen wouldn't want to offer a lower interest rate than Stafford loans. Jen can't compete with the government guarantee.

But there are limits to how much money each student can borrow through the Stafford loan program. With rising tuition, many students max out on the Stafford program, and need to borrow more money than it allows. This extra money comes with a higher interest rate, sometimes much higher.

This opens up great lending opportunities for Jen.[54] With her accurate knowledge of students' talents and characters, Jen can cherry-pick the best

---

53   Edvisors "Interest Rates and Fees on Federal Stafford Loans" https://www.edvisors.com/college-loans/federal/stafford/interest-rates/ accessed August 29, 2015
54   Most graduates can deduct interest payment on "qualified" student loans from their taxes. A disqualified loan would need to offer a substantially lower interest rate than a qualified one in order to stay competitive when this tax disadvantage is taken into account. Loans from family are disqualified, but because Jen is only lending to non-relatives, those borrowers can still take the tax deduction, so Jen's loans will qualify. Jen has not yet found a service company to help calculate the allowable interest deduction each year, which is inconvenient but does not disqualify the deductibility of the interest.

borrowers. She can offer her favorite students a much lower interest rate than they can currently get from the financial industry, because she knows things about prospective borrowers that the banks don't. The financial industry works off average repayment rates, giving similar interest rates to each student, modified a little by loan size and credit score. With her more accurate knowledge, Jen can choose to refinance only the lowest risk borrowers. High-risk students will continue paying higher interest rates to the traditional financial industry.

Student loan refinancing provides great opportunities for Jen's retirement savings. But not everybody can copy Jen. There are only so many high-quality borrowers overpaying on their student loans at interest rates that are high relative to their real level of risk. Jen's job puts her in a good position to find and cherry-pick the lowest-risk borrowers in the pool. If everyone else was looking for the best borrowers too, quality borrowers would be harder to find. Lots of Jens would be competing to lend to the same few low-risk students.

When Jen and a student refinance a loan, the student owes the same amount of money, but at a lower interest rate. Jen gains in interest a little less money than the financial sector loses, and the difference between the two benefits the student. Money is redistributed from the financial sector to Jen and to the student. Jen approves of this redistribution; she thinks financial sector profits are too high, and would rather have that money go to herself and to the student. But seen through our magic glasses, no new wealth is created. The same student received the same education and now has the same job prospects. No new students are getting educated because student loan interest rates are going down. All that has changed as a result of Jen's refinancing is how the benefits of the student's education are divided up. That's why not everyone can copy Jen. But if Jen had a strategy for creating new wealth, that would be something valuable to copy.

Jen would like to lend to students in a way that creates value. Luckily, this is something Jen knows something about. Jen is an educator. Her job is to help young people, and create value in their lives. Mentorship can be more important than money when investing in young people. Mentorship means spending time, giving advice, and steering students towards better choices.

A crisis is brewing in the student loan market. Students take out loans for college degrees that do not increase their income the way they expect. To get the kind of value visible through our magic glasses, students need to borrow and spend less on education, while getting more benefits from it. Young people don't necessarily need more education, attached to more student loans. They need better education that sets them up well in life, both financially and in other ways. For the "efficiency" of education to be improved, students need to get the same benefits from fewer years of education, with less time and money spent on that education. For example, better mentoring could help students achieve their goals, including but not limited to becoming more employable, even while spending fewer years studying.

Before long, Jen gets a chance to put these ideas into practice. Dylan comes to Jen's office hours in a fairly desperate state, after failing a midterm exam in Jen's class. This isn't the first time Dylan has come to her office hours for help. He completed a set of remedial math classes before enrolling in Jen's class, but somehow it wasn't enough, and he doesn't have the preparation he needs. He has been trying hard, but Jen's course is a struggle for him. With this terrible performance in the midterm exam, Dylan is now at serious risk of failing the class.

This kind of situation is pretty common for Jen. Normally, she would spend time together with Dylan going over each question in the midterm, and explaining all the science again. Today, she tries something different, and asks Dylan about his study habits. He is such an earnest student that Jen had assumed that he was working hard. But now Dylan looks embarrassed and says that actually, he hasn't had much time for studying lately. Dylan usually works about 20 hours per week as a line cook, but the sous chef just quit with no notice, and Dylan was asked to cover for him. For the last couple of weeks, Dylan has worked almost every evening, clocking in at more than 40 hours per week. He isn't sleeping enough, is exhausted during day-time classes, and is barely managing to turn in routine homework, let alone study for exams. This schedule is set to continue until Dylan's boss finds a new sous chef.

Dylan was offered the job as a promotion, but that would be full-time, and he is afraid that if he takes it, he will never finish his college degree. But why does Dylan want or need a college degree? Many students today hope that a college degree is their ticket to a good job. But Dylan already has a good job offer, without getting a college degree first.

Jen takes the mentoring a bit further, and asks Dylan more about his plans. Maybe he doesn't want to be a chef, and is only doing it to pay the bills. But it turns out that Dylan loves the restaurant business. From childhood, he loved helping his mother cook. He began working in a professional kitchen in high school. While the hours are brutal, working in a kitchen is something he loves and is good at.

So Jen takes the direct approach and asks the obvious question: why is Dylan in college? Why not quit school, take the promotion, and work full time?

Dylan doesn't have a good answer. He talks about the importance of education, about how it opens up new opportunities. His vague answers sound like platitudes, echoes of what he has heard before and thinks he is supposed to say. They do not sound like they come from the heart.

On average, people with college degrees earn more. There are many possible reasons why this could be. Maybe students learn useful skills in college, skills that help them get and keep better jobs. But maybe the people who choose to go to college are simply more talented than those who don't, and they would have earned more anyway. College might have had nothing to do with it.

A college education can also act as a "signal" to help employers find the best workers. If people who graduate college are on average more talented and hard-working than people who don't, then employers will want to hire them. This is true even if nothing they learned in college was at all relevant for the job. When employers act this way, requiring an irrelevant college degree simply as a way for potential employees to prove their talent and conscientiousness, then this forces talented and conscientious individuals to pay tuition and go to college in order to buy this expensive signal, as an entry ticket to a good job. Unfortunately, this doesn't mean that it makes sense for society as a whole. Education can become an arms race to buy ever more expensive signals. Where a high school diploma would once have been enough, today's employers ask for a college degree, even when the same individuals could have done the same work if they had been hired straight out of high school.

In any case, the fact that people with college degrees earn more on average than people without isn't relevant to Dylan's case. Dylan doesn't represent the average, he is simply himself. With or without a college degree, he has a promising career as a chef, where his employers care about his cooking and management skills, not about his diplomas. He will earn the same, with or without the degree.

As the conversation proceeds, Dylan admits as much. Right now, he wants to be a chef. Maybe in twenty years' time he will want to do something else, but if he needs a different education for that, perhaps he can go back to school then.

Deep down, the reason Dylan is at college is to prove to himself and others that he can do it. He has never been a good student, and is insecure about being seen as stupid by his friends and family. By getting a college degree, he wants to prove that he is not. Especially now that he has started, he wants to see it through. Otherwise, he'll feel that he failed because he wasn't smart enough.

People cite some other reasons for going to college. For example, the new economy is rightly said to be knowledge-based. But Dylan already has important knowledge and skills in the kitchen. He is already part of the knowledge-based economy.

Many people value college for the intellectual and personal development they experienced during their student days. Most of these people were strong students. There is no sign that Dylan's experiences are similar. College is a struggle for him. Yes, Dylan gets satisfaction when he succeeds at mastering something difficult at school. But he gets that feeling of satisfaction at work too, with less frustration and fewer feelings of inadequacy along the way. Dylan is not an intellectual by nature, and college is not awakening that kind of personal development in him.

Dylan is better off dropping out of college, taking the promotion opportunity available to him right now, and working full time. This doesn't mean he should stop learning. But a traditional college degree is expensive, and he is not getting value for all that money and debt.

Jen steers the conversation towards what sort of learning would be really useful to Dylan. What holds him back at work now? What might hold back his career over the next ten or twenty years? Dylan's struggle with math is a real issue for him. He doesn't need to know the calculus or statistics he is currently flunking out of in college. But he does need to be able to calculate the right quantities of ingredients to buy, and the right prices to assign to different dishes. And if he wants to have his own restaurant one day, he will need more advanced business skills.

So studying does make sense for Dylan. But not the studying he is doing now at an academically-oriented university. The local community college has more appropriate offerings. Dylan needs to keep going with remedial math courses, but instead of battling calculus, his courses should focus on accounting and planning for small businesses. And he doesn't need to do all his studying now as a full-time student, with the career coming later. Taking one community college course at a time is plenty, and compatible with taking the promotion and working full-time.

Dylan thinks it over, and then withdraws from Jen's course, and from the university, a week later.

Jen did a good job providing mentorship, albeit by handing out advice that goes against the grain of conventional wisdom. Dylan is better off for her advice. And society too; fewer resources will be wasted paying for an education that wasn't benefiting him.

But Jen hasn't yet solved her investment problems. She can refinance student loans to her own benefit, and to the benefit of her former students, at the expense of current student-loan-backed securities. This is a redistribution rather than a net benefit to society. And Jen can provide mentorship to people like Dylan, providing a benefit to society through spending and borrowing less for education, but without benefiting herself by lending out her retirement money at interest. In the next chapter, we will explore strategies that allow Jen both to benefit society by providing valuable mentorship, and to retain a personal financial share in those benefits, a share that can fund her retirement.

# CHAPTER 26

# REINVENTING THE APPRENTICESHIP

Jen wants to combine financial investment with mentoring. Where she invests time and mentorship, she is happy to back up those intangible commitments with money. And where she invests money and counts on a financial return, she is happy to do what she can to help put the borrower in a good position to pay the money back.

The apprenticeship model has been used since antiquity as a way to combine financial investment with training. An employer pays a small stipend in exchange for an apprentice's labor, and invests valuable time training the apprentice. Because of the training he receives, the apprentice agrees to work for little money, in the hope of a successful career to come. In modern times, apprentices may also attend technical school at least one day a week, adding to their training.

Traditional apprenticeships are rare in the US today. Indeed, the apprenticeship system is shrinking even in its traditional strongholds such as Germany. A typical apprentice today is about 18 years old when he starts work/training with an employer, although in some countries apprentices can be as young as 15, and in the Middle Ages, some children began apprenticeships when they were as young as 10. Such early starts to a practical education have disappeared from the US. Completing high school is almost mandatory, and most 18 year olds aspire to college rather than to an apprenticeship. But interestingly, mini-apprenticeships are nevertheless making a stealthy comeback for white-collar jobs, after being renamed "internships". Rather than starting an apprenticeship straight out of high school or even earlier, interns must be college students or college graduates before beginning their on-the-job, practical training.

Unlike traditional apprentices, many interns receive no stipend at all, and must rely on their parents or take out additional loans in order to live. Interns agree to work for free in the hope of receiving training and getting a good job later. Unfortunately, some employers fail to fulfill their side of the bargain by providing good training. Instead, they exploit interns as free or cheap labor.

This isn't supposed to happen. In the US, unpaid internships are expected to satisfy certain legal requirements. Interns should receive and benefit from training, and interns should not displace regular employees, but instead work under their close observation. The employer should get no immediate advantage from the interns' activities, and on occasion the employer's operations may actually be impeded.[55] In practice, many internship programs do not seem to comply with these rules.[56]

Whenever two parties have conflicting interests, the stronger party tends to win. Unfortunately, apprenticeships and internships are vulnerable to

---

55   U.S. Department of Labor Wage and Hour Division, Fact Sheet #71: Internships Under The Fair Labor Standards Act, April 2010 http://www.dol.gov/whd/regs/compliance/whdfs71.pdf
56   Perlin, Ross. Intern Nation: How to earn nothing and learn little in the brave new economy. Verso Books, 2012.

conflicts of interest between mentor and protégé, making the exploitation of interns seem almost inevitable. The mentor wants cheap labor today, while the protégé wants training that will qualify him for a well-paid job in the future. The mentor makes promises, the protégé believes them and accepts the internship, and then the mentor either delivers on the expensive promise, or exploits the vulnerable protégé. Even when an employer is keen to retain a particularly talented protégé at a regular salary at the end of the internship, the conflict of interest does not disappear altogether. It is still in the employer's interest to delay the promotion as long as possible, while the intern wants an immediate promotion.

"Good" mentors will set aside their own narrow interests in order to do the right thing by their protégés. But society works better when instead of relying on people to unselfishly do the "right" thing by others, we structure incentives to remove conflicts. And a carrot giving positive incentives for mentorship would be better than the current, largely unused stick of prosecuting illegal exploitative internship programs. In other words, rather than simply obligating the mentor to provide the training that the protégé wants and needs, how can we structure a contract to make the mentor share the intern's interest in receiving good training?

Aligning incentives is worth doing, because good mentor-protégé relationships are good for society. The mentor puts in effort today, effort that will pay off many times over for society after the protégé goes on to a successful career. Seen through our magic glasses, and so ignoring the details of who pays and who benefits, mentorship is an ideal way to invest in the future. Mentorship via apprenticeships is more personal, targeted, and probably more cost-effective than sending everybody to expensive colleges for an ever-increasing number of years. Apprenticeships benefit the apprentice, and benefit society; the trick to making them happen is to give better incentives to prospective mentor/investors.

In Chapter 13, we identified four ways to store true wealth – not just money – in investments that still make sense when seen through our magic glasses. These four categories for true investments are stockpiles, physical infrastructure, intangible improvements, and human capital. Stockpiles have limited potential. We found opportunities in physical infrastructure and intangible improvements, but unfortunately most of the best options are in the public rather than the private system, and so outside Jen's control. Jen is a private individual, not a government, and wants to invest her inheritance in the private sector.

This leaves human capital. By lending to Luke, Jen owns a piece of his future earnings. But lending, on its own, is a zero-sum game. By offering to lend money at a given interest rate, Jen bids on a share in human capital that will exist regardless. Because Jen knows Luke's character and prospects accurately, she picks up his mortgage as a bargain that yields a better return on her money for less risk. Jen poaches the best customers from banks that lack her personal knowledge.

In contrast, mentorship creates new human capital in a cost-effective way. Importantly for Jen's investment plans, mentorship, unlike major infrastructure investments, is something Jen can do herself, with her own time and money.

Of our four types of "real" glasses-proof investment, human capital seems to be the area with the most potential for true investment that exists today, dwarfing even infrastructure or medical knowledge. After all, rich countries are service economies. And the quality of services depends on the quality of the people providing them. Even manufacturing depends increasingly on human capital. Today's factories employ far fewer people than before, because so many repetitive tasks are now done by machines. The few workers left in factories must be highly skilled, in order to operate the increasingly sophisticated machines and processes. Throughout today's economy, from manufacturing to farming to services, everything depends on having a quality labor force. This means that human capital is a huge proportion of the bottom line. In other words, investing today to improve the quality of the labor force can provide enormous payoffs over the working lives of the individuals we invest in.

So how can we make successful mentorship/apprenticeships more common? I believe that we need an innovative kind of student loan contract that covers internships rather than college degrees. Many young people currently go to college motivated not to learn, but simply to get a better job by acquiring a credential. In the absence of the right motivation, most of these students learn little at college, and making matters still worse, they may not achieve their job aspirations either. Instead of expensive college degrees, can we reinvent the apprenticeship system for the modern era of white-collar work? Can we give these young adults the training that they want, and that college is not giving them?

The key is to give mentors incentives to make their apprentices/protégés into successes, overriding the intrinsic incentives to exploit interns as cheap labor. The simplest contracts will have two parties: mentor and protégé. Let's use Jen as an example for how such an innovative contract could work.

Imagine that Jen chose to live off her capital, quitting her salaried job. She still wants to spend her time teaching and, as part of that teaching, involving students in scientific research. But she now does these things independently rather than via her university job. Imagine also that Jen finds a way to recruit bright young high school graduates like Luke to apprentice with her instead of enrolling at the university.

With no other job except for recruiting and mentoring students, Jen could handle around eight apprentices at a time, and give them better training than they would get at college. Jen spends her time helping each apprentice to identify the direction he wants or needs to go next, finding the right resources to get him there, monitoring that he is on track, and giving pep talks as needed (with the threat of throwing him out of Jen's home academy if things go too badly).

Jen doesn't need to stand in the front of a classroom and teach an entire college syllabus. Her apprentices can learn college-level material by enrolling in Massive Open Online Courses (MOOCs), i.e., free online classes taught by top professors, while at the same time getting extra guidance and individual tutoring from Jen. Or they can simply read a textbook, the old-fashioned equivalent to a MOOC, typically costing around $100 and containing the same information as a much more expensive class. Either way, Jen acts as guide and tutor as students study and learn, and controls their progress so that they master one set of material before moving on to the next thing that builds on it. Jen doesn't need to be an expert on every subject in advance of her students. She simply needs an overview of what subjects are useful when, and how to approach a subject she doesn't know.

At the end of their apprenticeships, Jen wants her protégés to be at least as employable as a new graduate with a quality science degree. Many employers like to hire science majors because of their quantitative skills and problem-solving ability. The best way to acquire these skills is by solving problems, ideally real problems in real scientific research. So Jen gives each apprentice a research project.

Jen doesn't need a lab to give each student a scientific research project. This is the era of Big Data, where improved technology is generating data faster than it can be analyzed. Jen's current research already concentrates on analyzing data that has been collected elsewhere. All Jen's apprentices learn how to work with this data: how to program a computer, how to design databases, how to perform rigorous statistical analyses, and how to interpret what it all means.

Jen assigns each apprentice a scientific question, and points them to one or more datasets that can help answer that question. This task provides structure and motivation for what topics to study next. Computer programming and statistics are on everyone's curriculum in Jen's home academy, but many other "elective courses" are specific to each apprentice. As an apprentice's personal interests develop, there is room for adjustments to the scientific question he studies and/or the training needed. Many of the research questions are related to one another, providing opportunities for Jen's apprentices to work in teams. Jen makes all her apprentices write regular reports and give oral presentations to one another, and she tutors her apprentices to improve their written and oral communication skills.

Jen's apprentices typically take three years to reach the equivalent of a four-year traditional college degree. This is partly because Jen's academy has no long summer break, but also because apprentices receive so much more mentoring than college students do, with a more personalized focus on exactly which skills they most need at any point in their education. Jen's apprentices waste less time on busy-work and navigating hurdles, and spend more time learning. If graduates want a formal credential, Jen might be able to work with a college willing to offer alternative, competency-based credits, but this may come with substantial fees for the credentialing process. Otherwise, instead of a college diploma, students graduate with a recommendation letter from Jen that describes what they know and what they can do, comparing them to college graduates that Jen knew in her former job as a professor.

Some apprentices begin with more skills than others; catching up to the minimum level necessary to start research is a top priority, and apprentices need to make that leap to avoid flunking out of Jen's academy. Students who are badly prepared from their high school take about a year to catch up, for example with basic math skills, so these students "graduate" after four years instead of three.

Even with this option of extra time for the ill-prepared, a few apprenticeships don't work out. Jen can expel an apprentice from her academy at any time, relieving that apprentice of any obligation. During an initial trial period, apprentices can also choose to leave under no obligation.

With about 8 apprentices at a time, a few dropping out or being expelled early on, and the others taking 3 or occasionally 4 years to graduate, Jen will see about two apprentices "graduate" from her home academy per year. With their excellent quantitative and communication skills, critical thinking, programming abilities, and ability to see through a complex project, they have no problem getting good jobs.

So far, we have talked as though Jen were running a home academy from the goodness of her heart alone. Now let's consider how the right financial model can align Jen's interests with those of her apprentices.

Assume that the typical student recruited by Jen would, if they went to college rather than Jen's home academy, pay or take out loans for $20,000 per year in tuition, making $80,000 in total. This is about the same as out-of-state tuition at many public universities. In-state and community college students pay less than this, while many students at private universities pay considerably more.

The average college graduate today ends up owing less, more like $29,000. Students eligible for government grants such as Pell, as well as in-state students, pay less because the federal or state government pays part of the tuition cost instead.[57] Community college students pay less because community colleges really are cheaper.

However, the average college graduate with $29,000 in debt is not as well trained as Jen's apprentices. The training that goes on at Jen's home academy is best compared to the elite tutorial system of Oxford and Cambridge, rather than to the typical US college degree with large lecture-based classes. Oxford tuition (for full-fee-paying international undergraduates, excluding living expenses) is about £21,000-£28,000 (US$35,000-$47,000), with 3-4 years needed for a degree, so $105,000 to $188,000 per degree. Even after allowing for the rich extracurricular benefits of going to Oxford, this makes Jen's home academy seem like a bargain. And Jen is available to teach her students most of the year, not just for three 8-week terms per year like Oxford. However, students do get less prestige, and also fewer networking opportunities with Jen, relative to Oxbridge, even if they gain in actual education from this increased contact time. That said, we should also note that prestige and exclusive social networks are arms races where, by definition, not everybody can come out on top, and the bidding can just go up and up. Genuine learning is more like a race against the clock;

---

57    In this discussion, we ignore the market distortions created by government subsidies for college, and assume that the student or the student's family pay the tuition. For example, we could assume that Jen's apprentices all come from affluent families, who are not so rich such that price is not an issue, but who are sufficiently well-off to qualify only for loans and not for grants, and who choose not to attend a taxpayer-subsidized university or community college.

everybody can improve and be a winner. Prestige, both direct and via high-prestige social networks, is in contrast a zero-sum game.[58]

Considering the range of prices from the unsubsidized cost of community college, to a large public university, to an elite college, and the range of education provided in these places, it seems reasonable to take $80,000 as a fair market price for the training provided by Jen's home academy. Jen's apprentices/students therefore make a $80,000 financial commitment to Jen, just as they would to any other student loan source, with an important difference; if things don't work out such that they don't even graduate, they owe nothing.

$80,000 is a large debt to pay back, with Jen rather than the protégé now bearing much of the risk. Luckily, with skills in computer programming and data analysis, as well as general problem-solving, critical thinking and communication skills, Jen's graduates can find well-paid jobs in high-tech industries, including finance and the military-industrial complex. Many or most of Jen's graduates will pay off an $80,000 debt fairly easily and quickly. And as we shall see below, Jen has a plan to deal humanely with the others.

Of course, the students need to be able to afford to live during their apprenticeship, too. We'll assume that most families can cover a student's living expenses, allowing them to share a crowded apartment and get by in typical cash-strapped student style. For students from poorer families, Jen could lend them stipend money, on top of "tuition" loans. Note that one advantage of apprenticing with Jen instead of studying at college is that she can teach them in three years rather than four, saving apprentices

---

58    For those competing to gain prestige; for those assessing the talents of others, having reliable information is useful.

living expenses for the extra year and also saving them the opportunity cost of another year's forfeited income.

Jen has around 8 students at a time, and each year, 2 of the students graduate successfully and incur an $80,000 debt. So now Jen has a paper income of $160,000 per year, which she receives in the form of IOUs from her graduates. If they all pay her back, this is twice as much money as she was earning with her university job! This gives her some scope for forbearance with graduates who do less well.

Of course, we need to deduct Jen's expenses. Jen's apprentices could study at home or in a café, coming in to see Jen in her home office for regular appointments. But they would probably learn better if they all worked in the same space, forming a supportive community. Jen needs to provide that space. For example, she might build an extension to her house with eight desks, computing resources including plenty of internet bandwidth, and a separate entrance and bathroom. Or she might move to a larger house that is already suitable for the purpose. Or rent a small office somewhere else. All these options require financial investment now, and come with higher utility and maintenance bills in the future. Library access is another issue for Jen and her apprentices, and Jen may need to keep a loose association with her former university-employer in order to access the latest scientific publications. Despite the obstacles, with her revenues potentially twice as high as Jen's previous income, Jen has some scope to pay overhead costs.

Whether Jen's financial model is viable depends most of all on the terms on which her former apprentices pay back their debts. This is where the magic of aligning incentives needs to happen. Jen should be paid more when her graduates do well, and less when they do badly. Jen does not expect to get $80,000 plus interest every time. Instead, this is a ceiling on how much Jen will be paid when a former apprentice does well. A 6% interest rate seems fair, as a maximum to be repaid. But for graduates who do less well, how much can and should Jen make them pay?

The federal government has devised a formula to solve a similar problem. Federal student loans are eligible for "income-based repayment" plans, which cap total payments based on the borrower's income and family size.[59] Until July 2014, borrowers were, quite reasonably, expected to pay 15 percent of their discretionary income, defined as the difference between the Adjusted Gross Income on their tax return and 150 percent of the poverty guideline set by the Department of Health and Human Services as a function of family size and state of residence. This formula seems a good benchmark for how much Jen should ask her graduates to pay. For example, a single apprentice who finds a job earning $30,000 straight after graduating in 2012 would pay $2,000 per year. That isn't enough to cover even the $4,800 interest on $80,000 of debt. To cover the interest alone, a single graduate needs to earn $49,000 per year, and a married graduate with no children needs to earn $55,000. Jen now has an incentive to give her apprentices the skills they need to get good jobs, so that as many of her graduates as possible earn more than these thresholds, allowing them to eventually pay Jen back in full.

For the students who don't do well financially, Jen sets an end-date. The contract between Jen and her apprentices specifies that graduates must pay at least the minimum each month for up to 20 years, according to the income-based repayment formula. After that, their remaining debt

---

59    Federal Student Aid, US Department of Education, "Income-Driven Repayment Plans for Federal Student Loans" http://studentaid.ed.gov/sites/default/files/income-based-repayment.pdf

is forgiven. With a modest income of $30,000, a less successful graduate pays back only $2,000 per year. If the repayment amount keeps track with inflation, Jen still gets paid $40,000 eventually, in the form of a long-term inflation-protected bond. With two such "underperforming" graduates per year, Jen still earns almost as much as she did with her university job.

On the upside, computing jobs paying $100,000 per year will not be uncommon for Jen's graduates. Such a graduate is required to repay $12,500 per year (if single). At that rate, his debt to Jen will disappear fast, with the option of clearing his debt even faster if he chooses to make additional prepayments. Within 7 years, Jen will get back not only the full $80,000 tuition, but also interest at a respectable rate of 6%, far better than what she can find for other investments. Jen doesn't need too many high-fliers like this in order for her home academy to fund her retirement.

Financially, it makes sense for Jen to quit her job and open a home academy instead. Jen can do this because she doesn't need a paycheck straight away; she can live off her inheritance alone for the next three to four years, until income-based repayments begin to come in. After that, income-based repayments will rise each year, and her need to spend her inheritance will fall. Although Jen's inheritance may all be spent before she retires, payments from her graduates will secure a comfortable retirement income.

Even if she didn't have the financial cushion of an inheritance, Jen could still open a home academy if she had the help of a financial partner with deep enough pockets and a desire to invest in the idea. Instead of 2-way contract between Jen and her apprentices, this would require a 3-way contract in which the financial partner initially pays Jen a salary of $80,000 per year, or maybe a bit less. Then Jen and her financial partner would split the income-based repayments coming in from graduates, according to some agreed formula. Opening a home academy, like starting any small business, is simpler for people who have their own capital, but it can also be done in other ways.

Jen's biggest obstacle (other than the fear of jumping into the unknown) is not funding, but recruitment. How will Jen find suitable high school graduates and persuade them to come to her home academy rather than do the "normal" thing and go to college? This is a difficult, but not impossible problem. As college provides a worse and worse deal, alternatives start looking attractive.

Looking through our magic glasses, it is clear that apprenticeships are a great way to build human capital in society as a whole. By working through the numbers, we can see that it is also possible to embed apprenticeships in a financial structure that is both attractive to potential mentors and also competitive for students compared to college tuition.

The best thing about reinventing the apprenticeship system via income-based repayment contracts is that it aligns the interests of mentors with those of their protégés. When Jen quits her job and opens a home academy, she gains a financial incentive to study the job market and position her apprentices to do well there, in a way she never needed to do in her university job. For example, Jen could build relationships with prospective employers. Instead of giving every student a scientific research problem, Jen might give some of them a more applied data analysis problem, taken directly from a possible future employer. That employer might even pay a consulting fee if the job is done well, offsetting part of the apprentice's tuition debt, as well as building a relationship that increases the chance that the employer will offer the apprentice a job after graduation.

This highlights the potential for a broader range of people, not just ex-university professors, to act as financially incentivized mentors. Many people who run small consulting businesses could apprentice high school graduates in the same way, training them on the job to be employable at a level normally associated with a college degree. In fields where apprentices get useful work done, this would allow tuition to be much lower than what Jen charges.

Today, such on-the-job training is not a good investment for employers. It is time-consuming and thus expensive. Once training is complete, trainees can quit and take their skills to a higher-paying competitor firm, providing no return on investment for the mentor or the mentor's company.

For an apprenticeship system to work, potential mentors need to have a reason to do the hard work of training someone. Altruism alone doesn't go far enough. Family firms may give jobs to and train their own young and inexperienced relatives, but other employees are expected to earn their wages.

The economically rational thing to do with low-paid, not-yet-trained interns is to assign them low-skilled tasks, ensuring that they will be immediately useful. This jeopardizes the training value of the internship. A true apprenticeship allows the apprentice to try his hand at jobs that are a little too hard for him right now, so he can learn. To learn, one must make mistakes. Mistakes are expensive for an employer to observe, correct, and redo.

Some employers train apprentices in the hope that they will stay for long enough to make the initial training pay off. The employer loses money on an apprentice early in his training, but benefits from newly-skilled and underpaid labor later. The catch is that newly-skilled employees might leave for another employer who is happy to pay a higher salary to an employee that someone else has already trained. This danger was once prevented by a system of "indenture", from which many apprentices literally ran away across state boundaries. We don't want to go back to the indenture system. And with today's mobile labor force, counting on loyalty isn't enough; it is only natural for many newly trained employees to do the rational thing and leave for the highest bidder.

When trainees are free to leave at any time, without owing anything back to their trainer, employers have no economic incentive to take on apprentices and train them well. Income-based repayment schemes create this incentive for long-term training rather than the exploitation of short-term cheap labor. Instead of a contract prohibiting an apprentice from leaving his mentor/employer, we could write contracts that give the mentor a share in any financial incentive for the apprentice to leave. Such contracts have the potential to radically reinvent the apprenticeship system. They could vastly increase its scope, perhaps replacing a substantial fraction of today's lengthy and inefficient higher education system.

Jen's focus is on training apprentices, not on getting "the job" (or scientific project) done. Alternative apprenticeships, for example at a small business rather than at a home academy, can shift this balance, combining "real work" with training. When mentors benefit from the "real work" that trainees get done, they can charge less than $80,000 in income-based repayment of tuition. Some of these newly invented apprenticeships can be shorter than the 3-4 years with Jen, and train apprentices in more basic skills, reducing tuition still further. A truly open market may emerge with a diversity of promised benefits and prices. Novel risk-sharing arrangements can emerge on a case-by-case basis, matching the training offered by a mentor with the prior skills and career ambitions of an apprentice, with an income-based repayment "price" that varies according to how much training the mentor needs to do and the likely income that can be derived from the skills acquired.

I am not proposing disruptive change to the few remaining apprenticeship systems that currently work well. Instead, I am mapping a path to reinventing apprenticeships for jobs for which apprenticeships are not currently available. These new apprenticeships can replace both college degrees, and many of the exploitative internships available now. The biggest obstacle to substantive on-the-job training is that it is expensive. When those doing the training are paid for success, new opportunities arise. After all, why should colleges be paid for training workers, while employers are not? With that kind of favorable treatment, it should not be surprising that colleges become bloated while on-the-job training is neglected.

Income-based repayment plans for college tuition are not new. They already exist in Australia, where the federal government finances the universities upfront, and collects a graduate tax later. The Oregon state government considered a similar plan. Senator Marco Rubio has proposed a "Student Investment Plan" where private investors pay tuition in exchange for a proportion of graduates' future incomes.

My scheme is a little different from these. A core component is the direct, human connection between mentor and protégé, and the alignment of their incentives. When the protégé does well, income-based repayment goes not to a distant private or government investor, but directly to pay the retirement expenses of the mentor.

This scheme works best when the mentor owns her own small business, so that there is a simple contract between two people. Unfortunately, most of us are not in this position. For my plan to scale up and become in society at large, larger companies and their employees will also need to take on apprentices, without losing the personal touch or the alignment of incentives.

When an apprentice signs a contract with a large employer, things are more complicated. Companies usually have a shorter-term perspective on monthly and quarterly figures; individuals' focus on multi-decade returns affecting retirement plans is more in line with what is needed. The short-term corporate perspective is not ideal for investment in apprentice training. What is more, the training of apprentices is ultimately delivered not by "the company" as an abstract entity, but by individual mentors within the company. Those mentors need to be given incentives to spend their time training apprentices rather than doing other things that advance their careers more rapidly.

Despite the short-term incentives, a motivated employee, perhaps one who finds mentorship personally satisfying, should be able to strike a deal to bring on a promising apprentice. Two-way contracts between mentor and apprentice are simplest, but 3-way contracts between employer, mentor/employee, and apprentice, can also be designed. For example, income-based repayments can be split between the company and the individual employee/mentor who takes personal responsibility for a particular apprentice. Or the employer might pocket the immediate cash of an employee's retirement account contributions, using them to offset the costs of taking on an apprentice, in exchange for the employee taking a solo stake in the apprentice's income-based repayments. Contracts would be more complicated than for a small business where the owner is the mentor. But it is still possible to design contracts in a way that benefits all parties.

Some of my readers may be shocked at my focus on financial incentives. Surely the primary purpose of education is not training to make money in the workforce! I agree that education has much more to offer than preparing students for the workforce. But many students do not agree. The only reason they enroll and study in college is to get a better, higher-paying job.

As a society, we have decided that a certain amount of general, non-vocational education should be compulsory. We have set this limit somewhere between the ages of 16 and 18, or at the end of high school.[60] Students are not and should not be required to pay tuition for education that society has made compulsory. That bill for public and charter schools goes to the taxpayer. In contrast, college students are customers, paying high fees and expecting value for money. As adult paying customers, they have the right to choose an education that will maximize their income and other career goals, rather than their growth as human beings, even if you personally disapprove of the informed choices they make.

Of course, a few young people do love learning for learning's sake, and prefer lower-paying but more personally fulfilling careers. You might worry that mentors paid on an income-based repayment scheme will nudge these students towards high-paying careers rather than letting them follow their less worldly intellectual, artistic, or moral passions.

I am not worried. Many mentors are also motivated by more than money. And students who love learning are a joy to teach, making it easy for these students to find like-minded angel investor/mentors. A small

---

60   National Center for Education Statistics, Digest of Education Statisitcs, Table 165: Age range for compulsory school attendance and special education services, and policies on year-round schools and kindergarten programs, by state http://nces.ed.gov/programs/digest/d08/tables/dt08_165.asp accessed August 29, 2015

percentage of them may even earn spectacularly well, despite their initial lack of focus on money. Or they may be highly successful in a different, non-financial realm. Either way, they provide a high-risk high-return to their mentors, including non-monetary returns.

For all the other students who now go to college in order to get a better-paying job, income-based repayment simply puts mentor and protégé on the same page, striving for the same thing.

This chapter gives only a hint of the possibilities and practicalities of reinventing apprenticeships on a large scale via income-based repayments. Institutional innovations are needed to help match apprentices with mentors, and to design fair contracts for a variety of circumstances. Some professions, such as medicine, will remain within the university system. But when a potential mentor who is skilled in a field with less rigid credentials meets a high school student aspiring to a similar career, then there is nothing stopping them from setting up a mutually beneficial apprenticeship contract right now, with appropriate legal help to make that contract binding.

Because human capital is the key to a modern service economy, it is essential for our retirement investments to build human capital in the next generation. Those of us with plenty of human capital in the form of skills, knowledge and wisdom should consider becoming mentors. We must reinvest our human capital into the next generation, multiplying it to create a return. We already do this for our own children. When we do it for other people's children, it is OK to be motivated not by altruism alone, but instead to write a contract that lets us share the fruits of our investment.

# CHAPTER 27

# WHO WILL LOOK AFTER YOU IN YOUR OLD AGE?

Jen was born in 1966, so she is a little younger than the baby boomers. When Jen retires in 2031 at the age of 65, the baby boomers will be between 67 and 85 years old. Because of all the baby boomers, there will be fewer people working for each person who needs to be looked after.[61]

Unless we invent effective robotic carers or allow a massive increase in immigration, labor will be in short supply, and expensive. Inflation can increase the dollar cost of hiring carers, relative to the eroded value of any money that Jen saves in bank accounts, bonds, or under the mattress. The prices of stocks, land or other real assets that Jen bought with her savings might also collapse, relative to the future wages of her carers. What is more, inflation may underestimate the increase in the cost of living; inflation tracks only how the same things cost more dollars, and does not take into account how new inventions may expand what purchases are "necessary",

---

61    United Nations Department of Economic and Social Affairs, Population Division, Population Estimates and Projections Section, Probabilistic Projections: Total Dependency Ratio http://esa. un.org/unpd/wpp/ accessed August 29, 2015

both medically and otherwise. Saving lots of money doesn't guarantee that Jen will be able to afford care in her old age.

Once upon a time, old people lived with their children, and their children looked after them. The large investment in the work of bringing up children paid off in parents' old age. This traditional system is less sensitive to inflation, because children's debts to their parents are not counted in money. The terms of repayments are not sensitive to a change in the ratio of workers to dependents in society as a whole, but instead to the ratio within your own family. The more children you have, and the more they prosper, the better you are likely to be looked after.

Jen has no children of her own. Somebody else's children will look after her, not out of love, but for money. Jen's carers' paychecks could come from taxes collected after 2031 and redistributed in the form of Social Security and Medicare. Or the money could come from the returns on Jen's private investments. However the payments are organized, Jen is counting on the next generation as a whole, on other people's children, to owe her something. Insofar as Jen has saved "money" for her retirement, what "money" means is a points system to score how much the world owes her.

In exchange for paying taxes now, Jen receives promises from the government that Social Security, Medicare, and general government services will still be there when she needs them in retirement. In exchange for not spending all her after-tax income, Jen receives more promises in the form of a points system, where the points are called "dollars". Spending all of her income is in fact not an option; some of it is confiscated by force. Some taxes are taken from her income in order to be immediately spent or redistributed by the government. But other taxes are invested on Jen's behalf, in exchange for a promise of purchasing power later. Contributions to Jen's privately managed retirement account are, just like Social Security and Medicare, also taken out of Jen's earnings by force for the purpose of investment on her behalf.

Whether forcibly through Social Security and Medicare government programs, forcibly through compulsory private retirement accounts, or by choice, Jen exchanges some of her current purchasing power for purchasing power in the future. She hopes that the dollars and other promises can still be converted in the distant future into something real that she needs, namely care in her old age.

Relying on only one or two people to look after you would be risky; what if something bad happens to them and they can't do it? Having ten people owe you something, rather than only two people, is a good way to spread your risk, in case not all of them can repay. But having the entire next generation owe you something, via a points system, does not lower your risk even further. When the obligation is so diffuse, default can be collective. With safety in numbers, the next generation can simply change the rules of the game via the value of the points. Having "society" owe you something is risky. It is safer to have specific and trustworthy individuals owe you something.

For Jen, the individuals she is counting on are not her children, but other people's children. People like Luke who she lent money to, or who she trained in her home academy. Jen's protégés are not going to move in with her and care for her themselves. But after Jen retires, her protégés will be working and earning money. Part of that money will go back to Jen in order to pay for a carer. If there is a labor shortage when Jen retires, then her protégés will have higher incomes then too, offsetting the higher cost of employing carers.

If this problem of how to save for retirement were Jen's problem alone, then she could solve the problem simply by saving enough money. So long as Jen accumulates significantly more money than most people, she will have enough to buy what she needs in retirement, even if there is not enough to go around and prices go up.

But it is not possible for most people to do better than most people. This is the critical insight in this book, an insight that is widespread in biology, but dangerously rare in economics. Some competitions are relative, and all that matters is doing better than your neighbor. It is easy to focus on these relative competitions, but if we do this, then we as a society are making a terrible mistake.

Saving money and other financial assets can be a relative competition. Money and money-like assets indicate what percentage we own of whatever wealth society has. The bigger question is how much wealth there is in total. Wealth means stuff of real value, like food and shelter and medical care. If everybody, not just Jen, is to have a comfortable retirement, we need to create more true wealth, not just compete to buy shares in existing wealth. Otherwise, baby boomers approaching retirement will, by racing to save money, drive up the price of scarce assets, creating a long-term, slow-motion bubble. Eventually as the baby boomers get older, more of them will be trying to sell assets to pay for their retirement than are trying to buy assets to prepare for it. When this happens, the process will go into reverse, and asset prices will gradually collapse in value, relative to current wages and daily living expenses.

With fewer people taking care of more dependents, society must become more efficient in providing the basics of life to everyone. That efficiency is part of society's wealth. We need to create more wealth, rather than saving more money in an arms race to buy a larger share of existing wealth.

This means protecting stockpiles of natural resources and creating institutions like carbon taxes to reduce and adapt to climate change. It means building efficient physical infrastructure, from filling potholes to levees to smart electricity grids. It means doing research into how to provide better medical care at lower cost, for example by doing randomized trials to find out which expensive medical practices are useless or even harmful. And most of all, it means investing in human capital.

Many of these investments require collective action, generally by governments. A barrier to such public investment is political resistance to letting a "nanny state" confiscate our income by force of taxation. But a system of mandated "private" retirement accounts controlled by a financial oligopoly is also a form of nanny state. People of different political views take different positions on the extent to which we should take individual responsibility for providing for our own retirement vs. be coerced into doing the "right" thing for our own good. For example, some people want Social Security, either in its current form or in some alternative privatized form, to simply be a safety net against the direst forms of poverty. Others want it to take a greater role in ensuring secure retirements for the middle class.

While disagreeing about the ideal proportions, most people nevertheless accept that the best solution involves some coercion and some personal choice. Once we accept some role for coerced savings, we have the choice of channeling them through public taxation vs. regulated private accounts. What we have learned from our analysis of magic-glasses-proof investment opportunities is that governments have better opportunities to invest these coerced savings than Wall Street does. And while many people do not trust the government, we have no reason to trust Wall Street more.

As for that portion of our savings which remains in the private sector rather than under government control, our current system of retirement accounts prevents too many of us from investing our money in the ways recommended in this book. Instead, our money is directed to a financial oligopoly, who funnel it into stock and bond markets.

Too few of us take private investment into our own hands, and find our own ways to create true wealth. Mandated and tax-incentivized retirement accounts are only one reason for this. Even if our hands were untied, most of us would be only too happy to outsource the hard work of finding productive investments. We leave investing to "capital markets" and to the education system. We assume that if we supply capital markets with enough unspent cash, they will figure out how to create wealth for us, and pay us a healthy return for the privilege of using our money.

But what if they don't? We are teetering on the edge of a world with negative real interest rates. This is a clear sign that the system is broken and failing. The solution is not to save even more money to shovel into this broken system.

"Creative destruction" is part of the capitalist system. Progress often comes not from improving existing systems, but from the unexpected appearance of new and disruptive alternatives. Existing businesses do not drive this shift. Instead, the new steals business from the old. For example, internet-based news and classifieds stole business from and destroyed traditional print newspapers.

The financial sector has grown to 8% of the economy, without providing corresponding value. The growth of the financial sector shows no sign of slowing down, to the benefit of its own employees rather than the benefit of the economy at large. The financial sector extracts ever greater fees, most of them hidden, in exchange for liquidity that long-term investors do not need. It is a parasite on the real economy, extracting a percentage of each transaction while adding little or no value. It is ripe for creative destruction.

We continue to use this financial system, buying stocks and bonds, and taking out mortgages and student loans, partly because we do not realize how bad a deal we are getting, and partly because we feel we have no choice. In some cases, we really do have no choice; laws prevent us from investing our retirement accounts as we see fit. In other cases, we are simply not imaginative enough, brave enough, or simply involved enough to see and pursue the alternatives.

It is time to begin the next round of creative destruction, shunning bloated and corrupt financial markets in favor of new options. Instead of placing money in retirement accounts while our own mortgages and student loans sit in the retirement accounts of others, we can *"either a borrower or a lender be"*. The financial sector wants us to have a retirement account at the same time as a mortgage and student loan, allowing them to charge us percentage fees on all of them at the same time. By liquidating our retirement accounts to pay off our mortgage and student debts, we would rob the financial industry of business. They would be worse off, and we would be better off.

Being either a borrower or a lender means that we spend part of our lives paying off *all* our debts, not just credit card debt but also mortgage debt, car loans and student loans. Paying off debts, starting with those with the highest interest rates and working down, offers a healthy return on investment at essentially zero risk. The return, relative to the extraordinarily low risk, is hard for an active investor to beat, and impossible for a passive investor. Rapidly repaying debts is an easy choice. Only once we are debt-free do we need to start the harder work of investing elsewhere.

To take investing into our own hands, we can again cut out the inefficient financial sector middleman and his high fees. Instead of taking out a mortgage from a bank, or buying mortgage-backed securities within a bond fund, we can arrange contracts among ourselves.

Instead of taking out student loans to go to college, with high tuition going to bloated administrations and fancy gyms, we can search for an individual mentor who can teach us or our children on mutually beneficial terms. Instead of borrowing from and lending to faceless corporations, we can invest human-capital-equity in people we know, formalized by income-based repayments. Instead of adding years upon years of competitive college and internships in a struggle to "get ahead" of the competition in a relative arms race, we can focus on learning something of absolute worth from an instructor incentivized to care.

Jen set out to invest money for her retirement following just one simple rule: *"Don't invest in anything you don't understand"*. But Jen doesn't want her retirement comfort to come at anybody else's expense. Relative competitions to "get ahead" are different from absolute competitions to create something of absolute value. A bigger share of an existing pie is not the same as making a larger pie. Money is not the same as wealth. Jen wants to invest in something that still makes sense when she puts on magic glasses that obscure who owns what. On moral grounds as well as financial ones, she wants to understand how her investments create wealth that would not otherwise exist.

"Understanding" an investment means having an accurate but not necessarily precise idea of its long-term value, both for Jen and for society.

Stocks and bonds sold on open markets give the illusion of understanding through the precise short-term dollar prices quoted at any point in time. But accurate knowledge looks quite different. What are the long-term prospects of the person or business who you are investing money in? How much will they earn over the next few decades? Putting a precise number on this is ridiculous.

Most of us don't know enough to judge the prospects of a large business accurately. But we can judge people, and the likelihood that a particular person will pay money back. We certainly won't do this job perfectly, but we can nevertheless do a better job assessing individual risks than the current impersonal financial system can. To make accurate judgments, the messiness of real human relationships is inevitable. And this can be a good thing; contracts between two human beings can be tailored to circumstances, and renegotiated whenever doing so is mutually beneficial. This flexibility would have been extremely useful in avoiding expensive foreclosures during the housing crisis. Of course it is more comfortable to invest our money anonymously in an impersonal stock or bond market. But we pay a high price for that comfort, which eats into our ability to provide for our retirement.

The future is always uncertain. Betting on "typical" or "expected" returns is not a good enough way to handle this uncertainty. Having enough on average means that there is only a fifty-fifty chance that you will have enough. To be 95% sure of having enough, we all need to count on having a lower return than "expected" and living longer than "expected". To maximize the amount that we can be 95% sure of having, it makes sense to accept lower returns in exchange for less risk. This is yet another reason to stick to safe returns by paying off debt first.

To mitigate the "risk" of living past 100, we should buy annuities and/ or support the expansion of Social Security, which acts as a government annuity program. To mitigate the risk of particularly expensive end-of-life care, we should buy long-term care insurance or support similar government programs – and realize that these are expensive for a reason, and that the cost of living in retirement may not be lower than the cost of living before.

Variation in life expectancy, end of life care, and in historical returns on stocks and bonds are the known unknowns. There are also unknown unknowns. The first half of the twentieth century didn't work out the way people thought back in 1900. War and Depression destroyed wealth and upended people's lives, financially as well as in other ways. Since World War II, life has been much more stable. But who knows what is coming? Maybe there will be more wars. Maybe environmental catastrophes, whether they hit locally in the form of floods or fires, or more globally in the form of shortages of food and water.

Knowing the people who owe you something provides more security against unknown unknowns. When your children look after you, then however disrupted their lives may be, they will hopefully share with you whatever little they have, when your needs are at least as great as theirs. Their debt is a bond that goes deeper than money. The same, albeit to a much lesser degree, applies to Jen's protégés. The messiness of lending to and investing in people you know has its problems, but it also has an upside. Even in a world where the value of money has catastrophically disintegrated, or where a breakdown in law and order means that monetary debts can no longer be enforced, the people Jen mentors and invests would still owe her a favor, which some might choose to honor. Debt means that one person helps another today, on the understanding that they will receive help back in the future. Often the help is monetary, but it can take other forms too, either when the debt is incurred, or when it is paid back.

So what message should you take away from this book? Hopefully you have learned something about how the economy does or could work. But how can you apply this to your own life? Some recommendations in this book are clearly outside your control. You may want the government to collect more tax and invest it in building and maintaining physical infrastructure, in creating and refining certain kinds of institutions, and in doing certain kinds of medical research. Unless you want to become a politician yourself, all you can do to make these things happen is write to your representatives, and vote.

As for the money that you do not give up in taxes, it would be nice to have complete control of it. Too many of us have part of our paycheck confiscated "for our own good" and directed into a compulsory retirement account. Others are bribed to contribute to such accounts by matching funds from our employer, and by tax incentives. Here again, the best you can do is complain to your employer that you would rather get the money directly, or at least have the option of a self-directed IRA. Similarly, you can complain to your political representative that retirement accounts should not come with special tax breaks.

But if you do have control of your own money, what then? First, remember that being OK "on average" is a dangerous bet, so you need to save more than you think. With few people working and more people in need of care, the future could be tough. Avoid conspicuous consumption to keep up with the Joneses and instead live modestly and save. Buy a home if it offers a good financial deal relative to renting. But don't buy more home than you can afford.

Second, pay off your debts, starting with the highest interest rate and continuing, the faster the better, until all debt is gone. Refinance to lower your interest rate if you can, perhaps borrowing from somebody who knows you and trusts you. Long before you retire, you should be rid of all student loans, car loans, and mortgages. After that, keep saving to invest elsewhere.

Third, don't invest in anything you don't understand. Invest in properties, businesses, and people that you know and trust. Understand who will pay you back and how.

Finally, as well as making ordinary loans to people you know, consider making equity investments in them too, investing in their human capital and sharing the risk. Take on an apprentice if you can, as a way of truly investing in the next generation. Young people are our future wealth; let's invest in them.

# ACKNOWLEDGMENTS

I thank Jack Fajgenbaum for first suggesting that I write a book of this sort. Without the support of the Wissenschaftskolleg zu Berlin, this suggestion would never have left the realm of fantasy to become a reality. My year in residence there was as close to a perfect removal from the external pressures of everyday academic life as is possible in the modern era. Unconventional choices such as the one to write this book are nearly impossible without such a break. I also thank Olivia Judson for mentoring me throughout the process; without her encouragement, I doubt I would have been brave enough to make the leap. Without the support and encouragement of Oliver Monti-Masel, and his tolerance of so many lost weekends after our time in Berlin was over, this book would never have been completed.

I thank Henry Braun, Andrew Conway, Alex Field, Olivia Judson, David Liberles, Sandra Masel, Oliver Monti-Masel, Rob Neivert, Marcus Perry, and Mark Sage for helpful comments on the manuscript, as well as comments by Georges Borchardt, Druin Burch, Anna Dornhaus, Susan

Grantham, Dave Quin, Rob Neivert, Alan Renwick, and Damien Ryan on earlier materials that only distantly resemble the current book. I also thank Pete Goss, Sarah Goss, Ryan Gutenkunst, Lucas Mix, Henry Smith, and many others for substantive discussions that helped shape my views.

# AUTHOR BIO

Joanna Masel is an Associate Professor in Ecology & Evolutionary Biology at the University of Arizona, following undergraduate work at the University of Melbourne, a D. Phil. at Oxford and postdoctoral work at Stanford. She has been a Rhodes Scholar, a Pew Scholar, and an Alfred P. Sloan Fellow. She has published academic work in behavioral economics in addition to her primary research program in evolutionary theory, and she teaches Evidence-Based Medicine.

www.ingramcontent.com/pod-product-compliance
Lightning Source LLC
Chambersburg PA
CBHW021030210326
41598CB00016B/964